# AN INTERNATIONAL HISTORY OF THE VIETNAM WAR

Revolution versus Containment, 1955–61

# AN INTERNATIONAL HISTORY OF THE VIETNAM WAR

## Revolution versus Containment, 1955–61

R. B. SMITH

St. Martin's Press      New York

St. Martin's Press, Inc., 175 Fifth Avenue, New York, NY 10010
Printed in Hong Kong
First published in the United States of America in 1983

ISBN 0–312–42205–9
ISBN 0–312–42209–1 (pbk.)


Library of Congress Cataloging-in-Publication Data
Smith, R. B. (Ralph Bernard), 1939–
An international history of the Vietnam War.
Bibliography: v. I, p. 289
Contents: v. I. Revolution versus containment,
1955–61.
1. Vietnamese Conflict, 1961–1975.   2. Vietnam—
History—1945–1975.   I. Title.
DS557.7.S64   1983        959.704′3        83–3248
ISBN 0–312–42205–9 (hc.)
ISBN 0–312–42209–1 (pbk.)

*For my students*

# Contents

# List of Tables

# Acknowledgements

My first and principal debt of gratitude is to Judith Stowe, both for her helpful comments on the chapters of this book at various stages of its evolution and also for her general encouragement of the project, without which the work might not have been completed. I am also grateful to many of my colleagues at the University of London with whom I have had the opportunity to exchange ideas over several years, both in seminars and in conversation. Without wishing to associate them in any way with my own conclusions, I should like to mention in particular Professor D. C. Lau, Dr B. N. Pandey, Dr M. Yahuda, Dr M. Leifer, Dr R. A. Boyd, Professor E. H. S. Simmonds, Mr P. J. Honey, and also the late Malcolm Caldwell. Like most writers on any subject, I am indebted to many scholars for their previous writing in the same field. The list is long, as will be evident from the Bibliography at the end of the book, but my special indebtedness to the researches of Carl Thayer on the origins of the National Liberation Front for South Vietnam will be apparent from the notes. Although I have not at any stage relied on oral interviews for specific factual information, I have from time to time had the good fortune to talk with several people who played an active part in the events of this or later periods. Without embarrassing them by claiming their acquaintance in association with interpretations on which they have had no chance to comment, I feel an obligation to express gratitude for the insight into world affairs which I have gained from such encounters. Finally, in common with many writers on near-contemporary affairs, I owe a special debt to the translators of the FBIS and BBC monitoring services, whose inevitable anonymity does not reduce the value of their product as a contribution to the historical record. For their help in preparing the final typescript for the publisher, I am grateful to Janet Marks and Dewi Anwar; and for his work on the index, to Bryen McManus.

R.B.S.

*December 1981*

# List of Abbreviations

For additional abbreviations, used in note references, see Bibliography.

*United States and anti-Communist side*

| | |
|---|---|
| ARVN | Army of the Republic of Vietnam |
| CIA | Central Intelligence Agency |
| CINCPAC | Commander-in-Chief Pacific Forces (Honolulu) |
| JCS | Joint Chiefs of Staff |
| KMT | National People's Party (*Kuo Min Tang*, now *Guomindang*) |
| MAAG | Military Assistance Advisory Group |
| MACV | Military Assistance Command, Vietnam |
| NATO | North Atlantic Treaty Organisation |
| NSAM | National Security Action Memorandum |
| NSC | National Security Council |
| RVN | Republic of Vietnam |
| SEATO | South-East Asia Treaty Organisation (Manila Pact) |
| TERM | Temporary Equipment Recovery Mission |
| TRIM | Training Relations and Instruction Mission |

*Communist side (including North Vietnam)*

| | |
|---|---|
| CCP | Chinese Communist Party |
| CPSU | Communist Party of the Soviet Union |
| DRVN | Democratic Republic of Vietnam |
| ICP | Indochinese Communist Party |
| KGB | Committee on State Security (*Komitet Gosudarstvennoi Bezopasnosti*) |
| NLFSVN | National Liberation Front of South Vietnam |
| PAVN | People's Army of Vietnam (North Vietnamese) |
| PKI | Indonesian Communist Party (*Partai Komunis Indonesia*) |
| PLA | People's Liberation Army (Chinese) |

| | |
|---|---|
| PLAFSVN | People's Liberation Armed Forces of South Vietnam |
| TASS | Soviet Telegraph Agency (*Telegrafichnaya Agentsiya Sovietskogo Soyuza*) |
| VNFF | Vietnam Fatherland Front |
| VNWP | Vietnam Workers' Party |

# A Note on Chinese and Vietnamese Names

Chinese names are given in the 'standard' Peking form of Romanisation (*pin-yin*), which has been generally adopted by Western news media since January 1979. Vietnamese now has a Romanised script (*quoc-ngu*) which became 'standard' long before 1945 and requires no transliteration; diacritical marks, however, have been omitted. In the use of 'surnames' the Chinese usage is invariably to take the first (family) name, as in 'Chairman Mao', 'Premier Zhou'. The Vietnamese normally use the last (personal) name, as in 'President Diem', or 'Premier Dong', but in very special cases they may use the first (family) name, as in 'President Ho'.

Vietnamese terminology is used for the three regions of Vietnam, as follows:

| | |
|---|---|
| North (Tongking): | Bac-Bo |
| Centre (Annam): | Trung-Bo |
| South (Cochinchina): | Nam-Bo. |

Before 1954, non-Communist usage referred to the same divisions as Bac-Ky, Trung-Ky and Nam-Ky.

# A Note on Chinese and Vietnamese Names

# Part I
## 1955–6

# 1 Introduction

> Our people stand in the vanguard of the world's peoples fighting against imperialism, headed by American imperialism. As a member of the socialist camp, the Democratic Republic of Vietnam is also its forward post in South East Asia.
>
> Vo Nguyen Giap, December 1969

> Marxism-Leninism has shown that national movements, so long as they are truly aimed against imperialism, objectively promote the general revolutionary struggle; and that national demands and national movements should be judged not by their local, narrow political or social nature but by the role they play in opposition to the international imperialist forces.
>
> Ho Chi Minh

## I

One of the most remarkable features of the Vietnam War is that no one can say precisely when it began. There was no formal declaration of war by either side, no dramatic event comparable with the attack on Pearl Harbor in 1941 or the North Korean advance across the 38th parallel in June 1950. On their side, the Vietnamese Communists commemorate two anniversaries marking the start of their conflict with France: the beginning of resistance in the South on 23 September 1945, and the general uprising of 19 December 1946 in the North. But they have no equivalent anniversary for the resumption of armed struggle against Ngo Dinh Diem, which occurred long before the founding of the National Front for the Liberation of South Vietnam on 20 December 1960. The political struggle against Diem, which had begun immediately after the Geneva partition, developed imperceptibly into armed struggle as a result of decisions taken over a period of years. On the American side, efforts to record the sequence of decision-making in Washington have also failed to produce agreement on precisely when the commitment to support Ngo Dinh Diem became an actual military conflict. Guerrilla warfare had already begun by the time Kennedy assumed the presidency, and whilst his decisions of 1961 affected the degree of United States participation they did not initiate the conflict. Most Western writing has in fact tended to emphasise continuity between the French and American periods of a single war, from 1945 to 1975, and to trace the origins of United States 'involvement' to Truman's decision to aid the French in the spring of 1950.

The *Pentagon Papers*, the publication of which in 1971 exerted a profound influence on subsequent interpretations of the war, reinforced this notion of underlying continuity in United States policy towards Vietnam. Compiled in 1967–8, at the period when 'escalation' reached its peak, they may even have been partly intended to demonstrate that Lyndon Johnson's administration had done no more than follow Eisenhower and Kennedy in pursuing the course originally set by Truman in 1950. In the circumstances of American politics during the eighteen months before the 1968 election, it was especially important to show that Kennedy had been at least as responsible for the Vietnam commitment as Johnson himself. But in the process of tracing the roots of involvement all the way back to 1950 (or even 1945) the *Pentagon Papers* played down the significance of both American and Communist decision-making in the interval between the Geneva Agreements and Kennedy's inauguration. The Agreements and Declarations of July 1954 thus appeared as no more than an unsuccessful attempt to resolve a continuing conflict, relatively little attention being paid to the origins of the second war as a distinct historical problem. Indeed almost all studies have treated the years from 1955 to 1959 perfunctorily or not at all – a desert to be traversed as rapidly as possible.[1]

Any attempt to produce a new and more satisfactory interpretation of the origins of the second war requires a re-examination of the Geneva settlement and its aftermath. During the 1960s, when denunciation of the war became an intellectual industry in Europe and North America, the precise meaning of the Agreements and Declarations of July 1954 became the subject of acute controversy. By then, however, both sides in the debate were focusing attention on issues which had not necessarily been central to the deliberations of the Geneva Conference itself: in particular, the attitude of the American and South Vietnamese governments towards the

Vietnamese elections envisaged for July 1956. For the historian it is more important to relate the Geneva documents to the international realities of 1954–6. The essential purpose of the ceasefire Agreements – the only documents actually signed by the French and the Viet-Minh – was to bring an end to the war; which in practice required both the partition of Vietnam and an agreement on the separate political development of Cambodia and Laos. This was accepted by all the 'great powers'. The North Vietnamese might cling tenaciously to the promise of eventual political reunification, outlined in somewhat nebulous terms by the (unsigned) Final Declaration of the Conference; but for several years they were unable to secure more than token support for that idea, even among their Communist allies. In practice, the partition was expected to last indefinitely. But if that interpretation can be substantiated, it becomes necessary to ask why the situation changed between then and 1959–60 when armed conflict resumed. At what point in time, and for what reasons, did the Communist side take the fateful step of returning to armed struggle in South Vietnam? This is essentially a factual rather than an ethical question: for the historian the problem is not whether the partition was (or was not) justifiable, but when and how the Geneva ceasefire broke down. The present volume is largely an attempt to answer that question, by relating developments in Vietnam to the wider international perspective.

A serious limitation of the *Pentagon Papers*, inevitable in the circumstances of their compilation, was that they concentrated on bilateral relations between the United States and Vietnam. In documentary terms that in itself is an enormous subject and historians should not underestimate the value of the resulting contribution to our knowledge of American decisions. Nevertheless it is a fallacy to suppose that the origins – or for that matter the subsequent escalation – of the second war can be fully understood in terms of Vietnam alone. It was not merely the right of one individual member of the 'free world' to Western military protection that called forth the deployment of over half a million troops and the loss of over 50,000 American lives during the years 1961–72. The conflict is intelligible only in the broader context of events in the whole of Asia and beyond. A second limitation of most existing studies of the war is that they have focused almost exclusively on the decision-making of only one side – usually that of the Americans – rather than attempting to relate the two sides to one another. Even the 'hawks' – more willing than others to lay blame for the war squarely on the shoulders of Hanoi, Moscow and Peking – have never attempted to show in detail how specific American moves were made in direct response to Communist actions.[2] Many aspects of the war, especially its initial phase, become intelligible only when it is seen as a struggle for international power, not just an 'involvement' for which the United States was unilaterally responsible.

To examine the Vietnam conflict in its global perspective, and at the same time to pay attention to the decision-making of both sides, may seem over-ambitious. But it is a case of necessity being the better part of valour – for *only* the global perspective is enough. Studies of the Second World War have already come to terms with the need to relate particular campaigns, and their political consequences, to a broader context of 'grand strategy'. That approach is even more necessary in the period of the Cold War and its aftermath. It is absurd to try to write the history of any period after 1945 as if statesmen in the White House, the Kremlin or the Zhongnanhai could afford to devise a separate foreign policy towards every individual country across the world, taking only bilateral considerations into account. The assumptions and calculations of both American and Communist decision-making in the 1950s and 1960s could not be anything but global; nor is international decision-making ever unilateral. In Washington, Moscow and Peking – the three major capitals whose decisions will figure most prominently in the present study – it is impossible to ignore the continuous interaction between conflicting political opinions, different government agencies, and sometimes rival personalities; and the key to the debate within any one of those capitals is often the study of day-to-day decisions and intentions – and above all changes of mind – on the part of the *other* major powers. Whatever the limitations and failings of individual leaders, there can be no understanding the actions of any one global power without reference to the debates and uncertainties of its adversaries. One would not, after all, try to write the history of a game of chess, move by move, recording and analysing only the moves of 'black'.

These then are the principles on which the present study is based: the need to look more carefully at the years from 1955 to 1960; the need to examine the decisions of both sides simultaneously; and the need to relate Vietnam to the regional and global perspective at every stage in the evolution of the conflict. First and foremost it is an attempt to study the period in question as history. The 1950s have in general attracted relatively little attention from international historians – as opposed to political scientists, serious journalists or writers of political memoirs. There is still a tendency to regard that decade as part of a continuing 'present' which began after 1945 and which has not so far been interrupted by any dramatic upheaval comparable with the First and Second World Wars. But despite many elements of continuity, the world of the 1950s was very different from that of the 1980s and an effort of disciplined historical imagination is required in order to understand it in its own terms.

Some may argue that genuinely historical study of so recent a period will remain impossible until unrestricted access to government archives is permitted under the 'thirty-year rule', or its equivalent in other Western countries. It is true that diplomatic historians, free to wander through all the major archives of Europe and North America for the eighteenth and nineteenth centuries, have set a standard of scholarship in international history which cannot be attained without such access. More recently, when the Second World War ended in the capture of many German and Japanese records by Western governments, writers on that period too have secured access to a vast body of archives from the opposing sides. With such material to work on, historians have often succeeded in producing a clearer understanding of the global situation at a chosen period than politicians and diplomats can possibly have enjoyed at the time. Ideally, perhaps, that should be the historian's aim – although he would be wise not to imagine that he thereby becomes more intelligent than the men he is studying, who made their decisions in circumstances of actual conflict.

But the historical method does not in itself depend on that type of documentation. For much of the twentieth century the method must be applied to the limited sources that happen to be available on a given subject, so that a measure of incompleteness is inevitable. In the case of the Vietnam War the limitations will not necessarily be resolved by the passage of time. In the United States, it is true, a significant body of official papers from the 1950s and 1960s has been declassified or made available through the *Pentagon Papers*, and in time a great many more will be opened for research or will be used in the writing of official military histories. It will no doubt be possible, too, for historians eventually to make full use of the mass of documents captured from the Communist side in the course of the fighting. However, there will never be a time when Western historians can expect to examine the internal archives of the Hanoi Politburo or the People's Army of Vietnam, in the way they can now study at leisure the Japanese imperial conferences or Hitler's war directives. The same problem arises indeed for all Communist history since 1917: the chances of Western scholars ever being admitted to the secret government and Party records of the Soviet Union or the People's Republic of China are virtually non-existent. This easier availability of United States sources may reinforce the temptation to concentrate on decision-making in Washington and Saigon, or perhaps on the writing of military history from the American side. But for precisely that reason historians have an obligation not to confine themselves solely to archival study. The Western evidence must always be related to whatever can be gleaned from available sources on the Communist side; and the sooner a start is made in that direction the better. A vast body of material published by the various Communist media already exists, some of it originally in English; a substantial portion has been monitored and reprinted in translation by Western news organs – particularly the Federal Broadcasting Information Service and the British Broadcasting Corporation.[3] When American official documents and Western news reporting are related directly to these Communist sources, it immediately becomes possible to achieve a clearer understanding of the sequence of events on both sides.

In making the attempt, historians certainly have a duty to avoid the simplistic notions which too often figured in the rhetoric and propaganda of the time: their concern must be with the consequential study of actual decisions and events. Moreover, the adoption of the global perspective may also bring them into apparent conflict with the standard assumptions of other academic disciplines. The tendency of specialists in international relations and political science has been to treat global and national situations as separable, distinct planes of analysis, and even to cast doubt on the validity of attempts to explain national politics in terms of global conflict. But the global approach need not mean ignoring the complexity of Vietnam itself, which is by no means a small country. Historians must beware the temptation to rely on the global perspective as an excuse to simplifying the analysis of 'internal' politics. Indeed, Vietnam is a case where it is especially important to relate movements at the political grass-roots to decision-making in the corridors of international power. Events on both the global and Vietnamese plane can be fully understood only in terms of a developing situation in which every move, on any level, might have significant consequences. A specialist who aims to know only about Vietnam may end up by not understanding even Vietnam.

## II

The global perspective raises special problems when it comes to analysing the Communist side of the Vietnam conflict. One interpretation of the war, essentially sympathetic to the National Front for the Liberation of South Vietnam, sees it as a case of United States intervention to oppose a national revolution, which by the 1950s happened to be led by Communists. At the other extreme is the notion that Communist actions everywhere in the world, are always determined in Moscow. Neither of these interpretations offers an adequate representation of the inherent complexity of decision-making in the international Communist movement, to which the Vietnamese Communist Party and its predecessors have self-consciously belonged since 1930.

Another strand in much Western writing on Vietnam since 1945 has been its concentration on the analogy between Vietnam and China. It is true that traditionally, and in their experience of Communism, the histories of the two countries exhibit a number of common themes whose importance should not be underestimated. But structurally their revolutions have been very different; so too has their attitude to the 'world revolution'. In the case of China, especially in the writings of Mao Zedong, the sense of a national perspective has been remarkably strong. The leaders of the Chinese Communist Party have found it possible to be both 'good Communists' and 'good Chinese', and have been sufficiently confident of their power in their own country to resist efforts by Moscow to subordinate the needs of China to those of the Soviet Union. Even so, their international thinking has been tuned more to revolutionary ideology than to nationalism in the 'bourgeois' sense. Their aim has often been to play an independent role, as the equals of Soviet leaders, in shaping a 'correct' international line for the world movement as a whole. This 'nationalism' of the Chinese

Communist Party has nevertheless exerted a profound influence on attempts, by American scholars in particular, to redefine the Communism of all other Asian countries (including Vietnam) in national terms.

In reality the Vietnamese case has been very different from that of the Chinese. Vietnam is a far smaller country than China, and since 1940 its internal affairs have never been settled entirely without reference to international conflicts and alliances. At no time have the leaders of the Party felt strong enough to act independently of *both* Moscow and Peking at once; and with the possible exception of the years 1963–5, they have not even dared to follow China in rebelling against the 'Moscow line' for the time being. To those who have read the periodic statements of the Vietnamese Party, from the 1950s to the 1970s, the final commitment of Hanoi to a close alliance against Peking in 1978 comes as no surprise. This need not mean that Vietnamese Marxists–Leninists have ceased to be conscious of their nationality; but more often than not their 'nationalism' found expression in a sense of pride that the Vietnamese revolution has been of major historical significance: a pride which grew considerably during the 1960s as Vietnam became the crucible of global conflict. Internally, Communist efforts to exploit the 'patriotism' of other Vietnamese groups were accompanied by the justification (in Inner-Party documents) that such tactics were necessary only so long as 'imperialism' was the principal enemy, and would be abandoned at a later stage. The Party of the proletariat had no intention of submitting itself to the leadership or authority of bourgeois nationalists, or of allowing the 'national democratic revolution' to be more than a well-controlled phase leading to 'socialist revolution' and full membership of the 'socialist camp'. Of all the Communist Parties in Asia, the Vietnamese has been the most conscious of its place in the wider perspective of world revolution, as well as of its own dependence on international support.

Having said this, however, we must be careful not simply to revert to the purely mechanistic view of 'world Communism' which prevailed in the 1950s. American thinking at that period was remarkably crude. The notion of a Communist conspiracy inside the United States was frequently projected onto the international plane to produce an image of the whole 'free world' threatened by a 'conspiracy' emanating from Moscow and Peking. In practice, the calculations of American decision-makers at the highest level were probably more sophisticated than their public rhetoric implied, but the political influence of anti-Communist lobbies in Congress established a framework of national assumptions within which policy had to be justified. Equally inadequate as a tool of analysis, although slightly more rational, was the academic image of Communism as a global organisation whose many tentacles all obeyed one centre of command in the Kremlin. (Perhaps the reason why so little attention was paid by scholars to the internal politics of such relatively minor Communist Parties as the Vietnamese was the belief that nothing of any consequence actually originated in Hanoi.) It is hardly surprising that liberal writers of the 1960s and 1970s reacted strongly against these oversimplified notions. By then the international relations specialists were more inclined to analyse Soviet and Chinese policies in terms of national interest, whilst political scientists – concerned primarily with the study of individual countries – found it easier to regard both Marxism and individual Communist Parties as merely one element in each national situation. Modes of explanation began to develop which allowed no place at all for the problem of Marxist–Leninist revolution as a global phenomenon, and the logical result was to dismiss the whole idea of international Communism as no more than a branch of the 'conspiracy theory' of politics.

Anyone who has read the more serious articles and speeches of Marxist–Leninist leaders themselves, at all periods since 1917, will appreciate that this 'liberal' conception fails just as completely as the 'monolithic' to come to grips with international realities. It is not necessary to invoke the much-derided 'orders from Moscow' in order to recognise the historical unity of the world revolution which has always been inherent in Marxist–Leninist thought. The idea of a 'world divided into two camps', put forward by Zhdanov in his denunciation of American imperialism in 1947, was not invented by Western cold warriors. It derived from Lenin's own appreciation of the international nature of imperialism and the fact that it could be defeated only by international revolution. The foundation of Marxist–Leninist thinking is its claim to be a science of revolution, which must be applied in each historical situation to identify the 'correct line' for the next phase of revolutionary action. As the world revolution has expanded since 1917, and especially since 1949, the pattern of Communist debate (and the scope for divergence of opinions) has become more and more complex; but imperialism as an essentially international phenomenon has never ceased to be the explicit enemy. The international Communist movement is in fact a wholly new type of political phenomenon, in which different schools of thought are liable at any one time to be debating the same fundamental issues at distant ends of the world.

Marxist–Leninist theory is in principle valid for all levels of social and political analysis, and even the most detailed aspects of grass-roots politics may have to be related to the global situation before conclusions can be reached. In the end each Party must decide its own strategy, on the basis of its ultimate responsibility to lead the revolution in its own country. But the 'correct line' at any given time may depend on global as much as on national and local circum-stances: no move can be made until the time is 'ripe', and 'ripeness' may depend on international as much as on national considerations. The two planes of analysis are thus interdependent, not mutually exclusive. Communist decision-making in the 1950s was not so much a matter of many elements in a single system obeying instructions from one source as of Party leaders in many different areas of the world all sharing the same ultimate framework of analysis. Within that framework there was scope for disagreement about the next course of action, and the existence of deep divisions within the leadership of the Communist International (Comintern) was evident as early as the 1920s. Thirty years later the question of Communist unity was itself an issue, giving rise to sharp conflict within the movement. But these ideological and tactical differences cut across those of nationality, so that it is unrealistic to analyse Communist politics as if 'the Russians', 'the Chinese' or 'the Vietnamese' were purely national Parties pursuing only national interests. Each Party embraced a wide range of ideological opinions, but was held together by the need for consensus and Party discipline. In Hanoi the Party consensus was bound to reflect international developments, both within and beyond the 'socialist camp'. Sometimes different Parties might decide on different 'lines' in any given situation, and the result might be active conflict within the international movement; but even in the case of the Chinese Communist Party ideology counted for at least as much as 'national' rivalry in shaping its relations with the Communist Party of the Soviet Union.

By the 1950s, and especially in the aftermath of the Geneva partition, the Vietnamese Communists were acutely aware that their own revolution occupied a vital place in the front line between the socialist and imperialist 'camps', and that any decision to continue the revolution south of the 17th parallel would have immediate global implications. They could not avoid taking into account the broader context of 'East–West' relations in contemplating the new stage of the Vietnamese revolution; nor could they embark on a programme of socialist construction in the North without substantial aid from China and the Soviet Union. Practically every year after 1955 one or another of the North Vietnamese leaders made his way to Peking and Moscow, and it is inconceivable that the 'advice' they received there would be completely ignored in Hanoi. In attempting to write a history of the Vietnamese conflict between 1955 and 1961 therefore, we cannot ignore the importance of Soviet and Chinese global strategies and their relations with the United States. Even without access to secret Party and government archives, it is necessary to consider in general terms the logical choices open to Soviet and Chinese leaders at various stages, using whatever clues can be found to indicate the character of the debate which must have gone on behind their public decisions.

Remarkably, there is still no comprehensive history of the global strategy of the Soviet Union in the period since the Second World War, and the present study cannot hope to fill that gap. The subject is one which has suffered disastrously from oversimplification at the hands both of 'Cold War' historians, who started from the notion that 'ideology' led inevitably to 'expansionism', and of 'revisionist' historians, who have argued that the United States itself was unilaterally responsible for the growth of tension between the Soviet Union and the West after 1945.[4] Other scholars, perhaps seeking to avoid the controversies surrounding the Cold War itself, have pretended that everything changed following the deaths of Stalin and Beria, so that for later periods it is enough to proceed from the principle enunciated by the Soviet premier Bulganin at the Geneva summit of 1955: namely that the Russians and their allies ought now to be seen simply as nation-states, without reference to the revolutionary origins of their governments or to the ideology of Marxism–Leninism. For the reasons already put forward, none of these approaches is likely to lead to an adequate historical analysis of the actual decision-making of the Soviet Union or of other Communist countries. Some alternative conceptual approach is necessary.

In this respect the apparent conflict between Stalin and Zhdanov in 1947–8 seems especially instructive. At the risk of introducing yet another oversimplification, it is possible to regard those two leaders as representatives of opposing schools of thought whose origins went back to the 1920s. Zhdanov's views, expressed in the speech with which he launched the Communist Information Bureau (Cominform) in September 1947, assumed a continuing world revolution which would be pursued by Marxist–Leninist Parties in one country after another – without regard to the restraints of international law or specific formal agreements. The Soviet Union, he believed, should dedicate itself to supporting such revolutions wherever they might break out, and should not be afraid to challenge imperialism whenever the opportunity might arise. The immediate strength of the United States and its allies might impose restraint in certain areas as a tactical necessity. But if restraint became a strategy, even as a means to protect the Soviet Union from dangers which might otherwise restrict its development then the ultimate aim of defeating imperialism on a world scale might not be achieved. Against that view, Stalin appears to have argued that the one hope of defeating the imperialists in the long run lay precisely in building up the economic and military strength of the USSR, if necessary sacrificing revolutionary opportunities in certain parts of the world to the more immediate goal.

Stalin had already taken the same attitude towards the Spanish Civil War in 1936–7, and had purged his regime of large numbers of Comintern activists who disagreed. In 1948 Greece became a comparable test-case: by expelling Tito from the Cominform at the same time as removing Zhdanov from power (even before the latter's sudden death), Stalin once again established the principle that an international equilibrium based on restraint was more important than 'national' revolution in those parts of Europe which the Yalta agreement had recognised as British and American spheres.[5] He also imposed tighter discipline over his own 'camp'. Thus in Europe after 1948 the Western doctrine of 'containment' was balanced by a Soviet strategy of constraint – leaving the two sides to build up military strength in their respective spheres and to play international games (like the Berlin Blockade) designed to win tactical advantage rather than to change the over-all balance of military or political forces. The line of 'containment', even when it cut across the city of Berlin, remained undisturbed; and the Greek Communists were left to surrender.

The Soviet leader may have aimed at a similar pattern of equilibrium in Asia. There, however, the situation was more complicated – not least because American use of the atomic bomb had brought the war against Japan to a more rapid conclusion than the Russians expected. In China the 'zone of operations' agreed on at the time of the Soviet invasion of Manchuria in August 1945 could not be converted into an area of permanent Communist control – mainly because neither Chiang Kaishek nor Mao Zedong was willing to see that happen. By 1947 the Communists and the Guomindang were locked in a struggle to decide which of them would control a reunified China. Two years later, having failed to restrain the Chinese Communists in the way he had restrained the Greeks, Stalin had no choice but to come to terms with Mao and make an alliance with him. The following year Moscow made no effort to impede the attempt by Kim Ilsung to draw the whole of Korea (which had also been partitioned in 1945) into a unified Communist state; and the resulting Korean War of 1950–3 brought Chinese and American armies into direct military conflict. By then too, revolutionary struggles had developed in Indochina and other parts of South-East Asia where the Chinese Communist Party presented itself as a model and guide. In all this the influence of Zhdanov was probably negligible, or at best short lived, but the same fundamental conflict between two schools of thought can be identified: on the one hand Stalinist restraint, on the other encouragement of expanding revolution. Not until after Stalin's death was the issue in Asia finally settled in favour of the principle which he (and also his immediate successors, Malenkov and Molotov) had already applied in Europe. That was the real significance of the international agreements which repartitioned Korea and settled the conflict in Indochina in 1953–4.

In itself Stalin's death resolved nothing. Soviet policy continued to be determined by interaction between the same two schools of thought. But as time went on the debate became complicated by the fact that the Soviet Union was developing powerful armed forces of its own, which made the policy of restraint less a matter of necessity and more a question of choice. At that point, during the middle and late 1950s, it is possible to identify a third school of thought which was to become increasingly influential in Soviet relations with Asia. It placed less emphasis than either of the other two on the pursuit of revolution in individual societies; much more on the pursuit of Soviet global power through the relatively conventional use of military strength and of *realpolitik* diplomacy – including even formal alliances with newly independent 'bourgeois nationalist' states in post-colonial Asia. This third approach seems to have predominated during the years 1955-8, whilst revolutionary struggle – whether along Maoist or Zhdanovist lines – went temporarily out of fashion. Meanwhile the United States redefined and reinforced its strategy of 'containment' during those years, seeking to draw as many Asian countries as possible into a series of regional defence pacts modelled on the example of NATO: the Baghdad Pact (later the Central Treaty Organisation), the Manila Pact (SEATO) and potentially a similar organisation in North-East Asia. In these circumstances Soviet (and also Chinese) strategy was directed not towards challenging the Western powers along the line of 'containment,' which now stretched across Asia from Turkey to South Korea, but rather towards winning over countries like India and Indonesia to a policy of neutrality and non-participation in the 'imperialist' pacts. During that period the Vietnamese Communists received little encouragement from their allies for an effort to undermine the Geneva partition or to challenge the neutrality of Cambodia and Laos. The change came only during 1958. Even then Hanoi's strategy consisted of mounting a revolutionary struggle inside South Vietnam, rather than making a frontal assault across the 17th parallel.

The resumption of armed struggle certainly did not occur because someone in Moscow – or Peking – took a simple decision that it should: there were no 'orders from Moscow' in that crude sense. But the years from 1958 to 1960 saw a distinct revival of the revolutionary international line in both the Soviet and Chinese Parties, which also made itself felt in several other areas of the world and led to a general heightening of East–West tension. These developments did not 'cause' the Vietnam War in a simple, mechanistic way. Nevertheless without any change in the international line Hanoi would not have been able to secure the kind of support it needed for an attempt to reverse the Geneva partition by revolutionary – and if necessary military – means. The result was a conflict whose significance, both in Communist and American terms, was directly comparable with the abortive Greek revolt of 1946-9.

Seen in these terms, United States policy in Vietnam was a matter of responding to the challenge posed by a new Communist strategy – which at that stage had the initiative. There need be little doubt now that the revolutionary movement inside South Vietnam was largely the product of Communist decision-making, and that if

Hanoi had decided otherwise it would probably not have grown up when it did. The propaganda image of the National Front for the Liberation of South Vietnam, as a purely southern movement created independently of Hanoi, need no longer be taken seriously. There is now an accumulation of evidence that the revolutionary movement which grew up inside South Vietnam from about the end of 1956 was a deliberate tactic decided on by the Vietnam Workers' Party, which had never applied partition to its own organisation and continued to follow a single 'correct line' laid down by one Central Committee in Hanoi. Since 1975 moreover, the growing tension between China and Vietnam has produced a number of revelations – concerning, for example, the degree of Viet-Minh dependence on Chinese aid – which have frequently confirmed assessments at the time by Western intelligence experts. The latter were persistently denied by Hanoi throughout the 1960s. On a number of points therefore, the historian can now feel himself on firmer ground in analysing the realities of Hanoi's decision-making.

Questions must still be asked about the formulation and effectiveness of the American response. Many critics of United States policy have blamed Dulles and his successors for overemphasising 'ideology' and for relying too mechanically on the doctrine of 'containment' in circumstances where it was not appropriate. To some extent the criticism may be valid. But Dulles' error lay not so much in misunderstanding the nature of Marxism–Leninism as in adopting an oversimplified view of the world. The real failure of American thinking in the 1950s was not its obsession with 'ideology' but rather its dependence on the mechanistic notion of 'two blocs' which could be permanently separated by a precise and defendable line across Europe and Asia. The illusion of a global partition creating two definable areas—one 'good', the other 'evil'—was a product not of the Cold War itself but of the Second World War, when Western propagandists found it expedient to treat the Axis powers and Japan as a single 'enemy' in control of a large part of the globe: in 1946–8 this concept of 'the enemy' was simply transferred to the 'Communist bloc'. In reality even the alliances of the Second World War were much more complex: Japan and Germany were far from totally committed to one another's aspirations, and there were serious differences between Britain and the United States. Stalin recognised the true complexity of the pattern of global 'contradictions' and based many of his decisions on the principle that the nature of imperialism made conflict inevitable amongst the other world powers; to a considerable extent he was right.

After 1948, the Western powers buried their differences in NATO and acknowledged the preponderant economic strength of the United States. But to transfer that unity to Asia and to expect all the newly independent states of post-colonial Asia to join together in the same common cause of 'containment' was hoping for too much. In attempting the task, Dulles achieved more than he had any right to expect – both in East Asia and the Middle East. The result, even so, was to create not a solid 'bloc' of countries, united into a single 'free world', so much as a series of individual allies whose economic and military dependence on the United States became too extreme. In Asia these included South Korea, Taiwan, the Philippines, Pakistan, Iraq and Iran – as well as South Vietnam and eventually Thailand. The strategy of 'containment' came to depend less on the unity of an alliance (as in NATO) than on the survival of these states as individual American allies. The weakness of the strategy lay in the fact that each of these close allies was vulnerable to the possibility of revolution. Even if it were a nationalist revolution, as in Iraq, the result would be to destroy a link in the American defence chain.

In the case of South Vietnam, perhaps the weakest link of all, the revolution was led from the start by the Communist Party and represented a challenge which the 'containment' strategy could not ignore, but which it was not well-equipped to overcome. Precisely how that challenge emerged during the years from 1955 to 1961, and how the United States sought to cope with it, is the principal concern of the chapters which follow. If it cannot be claimed for them that they offer a definitive interpretation, there is at least some hope that they will provide a framework for further research.

# 2 The Geneva Partition

Not every war carries in itself the elements for a complete decision and final settlement. But . . . with the conclusion of a peace a number of sparks are always extinguished which would have smouldered on quietly, and the excitement of the passions abates because those whose minds are disposed to peace . . . turn themselves away completely from the road to resistance. Whatever may take place subsequently, we must always look upon the object as attained, and the business of war as ended, by a peace.

Carl von Clausewitz, *On War*

Before I leave, I should like to express to you my deep appreciation for the work you have done here. It is thanks to the conciliatory work of the International Commission [of Supervision and Control] . . . that an important part of the Decisions of the Geneva Agreement – despite innumerable difficulties – has been executed in a practical manner . . . . Above all, in the course of an experiment which I am sure will constitute a remarkable precedent in the international plane, you have succeeded in creating – in particularly difficult circumstances – a climate of détente.

General Ely to the Chairman of the
International Commission of Supervision and Control.
June 1955

## I

A few days before the stipulated deadline of 16 May 1955 the regroupment of forces on either side of the 17th parallel was virtually complete: departing French troops handed over the Haiphong perimeter to the Viet-Minh at almost exactly the same time as Viet-Minh units left their last base area in the southern province of Quang-Ngai.[1] There can be little doubt that the strictly military terms of the ceasefire Agreement, signed by the French and the Viet-Minh at Geneva in the early hours of 21 July 1954, had been carried out with a precision worthy of congratulation on all sides. According to the Final Declaration of the Geneva Conference, also issued on 21 July but not actually signed by any of the delegations, 'the military demarcation line is provisional and should not in any way be interpreted as constituting a political or territorial boundary'. The same document insisted that the political future of Vietnam was to be settled on the basis of national elections to be held in July 1956. But the actual ceasefire Agreement handed over to the two 'parties' full responsibility for administering the two military zones in the interim. Since the French simultaneously issued a declaration acknowledging the 'independence of Vietnam' without specifying a particular regime, the practical effect was to establish two Vietnamese governments in Hanoi and Saigon, each of which proceeded to consolidate its control over half of the country.

In the international climate of May 1955 there was every reason to expect – despite the face-saving political clauses of the Final Declaration – that the partition of Vietnam would be of indefinite duration. It was not fundamentally different from those of Germany and Korea, which had likewise been military in origin and had been accompanied by pious statements about eventual political reunification. In the immediate situation the leading powers of both East and West were more anxious to see an end to the fighting in Indochina than to dwell on potential ambiguities in the settlement they had just negotiated. The possibilities for general disengagement and détente which seemed to be opening up in the world made it a moment of rare optimism in international affairs.

In Europe the Allied occupation of West Germany formally ended on 5 May 1955. A month later the first steps were taken towards establishing diplomatic relations between Bonn and Moscow, and there no longer seemed any danger of open conflict between the two Germanies, even though neither was yet willing to accept the legal existence of the other. Berlin remained a problem, but one which could be contained. Shortly afterwards the treaty of 15 May 1955 ended the occupation of Austria and recognised it as an independent neutral state. Other important changes at that time included the Warsaw Treaty of 14 May 1955, which established a new military alliance between the Soviet Union and its Communist neighbours in Eastern Europe. It was balanced by a trend towards a looser ideological unity amongst the countries of the 'socialist camp' – looser, that is, than the tight discipline imposed by Stalin after the expulsion of Yugoslavia from the Cominform in 1948–9. In late May and early June 1955 three Soviet leaders (Khrushchev, Bulganin and Mikoyan) visited Belgrade to make peace with Tito, thus absolving him of the ideological crime of 'revisionism'. Finally in July, again at Geneva, a summit conference of the 'Big Four' powers achieved, if nothing else, a further reduction in East–West tension. One reason for this change of mood in Moscow may have been a decline in the influence of Molotov, who suffered a serious political setback in February 1955 and by July was being openly criticised. Some observers have suggested that he tried to secure the premiership on the resignation of Malenkov but was defeated at the last minute by a coalition of Khrushchev, Bulganin and Zhukov.

In Asia, even the confrontation between the United States and the People's Republic of China had become less tense. Following an outbreak of fighting for some offshore islands in late January 1955, countered by a Congressional resolution reaffirming United States support for Chiang Kaishek's regime, Peking decided for the time being to adopt the line that Taiwan could be 'liberated by peaceful means'. Zhou Enlai used that expression in a report to the National People's Congress on 17 May 1955, and went on to reiterate a suggestion he had made a month earlier at Bandung for some kind of meeting between diplomatic representatives of China and the United States. The outcome was the start of Sino-American ambassadorial talks in Geneva on 1 August.[2] In practice China appeared to accept the partition of Vietnam, just as it had to accept the impossibility of liberating Taiwan and the continued partition of Korea. The survival of Chiang Kaishek's regime was itself seen by both sides as the partition of a single country rather than the creation of a new one. The one thing on which Peking and Taipei agreed was the ultimate unity of China, but Communist demands for American withdrawal from Taiwan amounted to a statement of principle rather than a serious intention to seize the island. In the case of Korea, the early sessions of the Geneva Conference in April 1954 (before it turned to Indochina) had been devoted to the 'political discussions' promised at the time of the armistice a year earlier; but there too it was unrealistic to expect that reunification would be achieved.

The Chinese attitude to the Geneva settlement had been indicated by Zhou Enlai in a report to the Central People's Government Council on 11 August 1954, the day the ceasefire became complete throughout Indochina. His optimism about the new situation did not depend on faith in an eventual political settlement in Vietnam, with or without elections. It arose from the military provisions of the signed Agreements and from the undertaking of the states of Indochina not to join any military alliance. No foreign bases were to be allowed in South Vietnam, Laos or Cambodia, and only limited supplies of new weapons and personnel could be introduced. Consequently this area, which bordered so closely on South China, could not become an American or SEATO base contributing to the anti-Chinese strategy of 'containment'. At that stage too, it was possible for Zhou to envisage a continuing role for France in Indochina as an effective signatory of all three ceasefire agreements. The principal Chinese fear was that 'United States aggressive circles will not allow smooth and thorough implementation of the agreements', and that American action would eventually frustrate the objective of an 'area of collective peace in Indochina and its surrounding countries'.[3] But the latter objective did not necessarily require early Vietnamese reunification under the Viet-Minh. Zhou was probably much more concerned about Laos, which had a direct frontier with China.

TABLE 2.1   *The Geneva Conference and Documents*

---

### The Conference, 8 May–21 July 1954

| *Co-chairmen* | *Delegations from Indochina* | *Other delegations* |
|---|---|---|
| United Kingdom | Democratic Republic of Vietnam | France |
| Soviet Union | State of Vietnam | United States |
| | Laos | People's Republic |
| | Cambodia | of China |

### The Agreements and Declarations, 20–1 July 1954

| *Agreements* | *Declarations* |
|---|---|
| 1   *Relating to all three states of Indochina* | |
| (Note: Three separate International Commissions of Supervision and Control derived their authority from the ceasefire Agreements; they reported to the Co-chairmen.) | (a) *Final Declaration of the Conference* (13 articles, not signed). |
| | (b) Two short *Declarations by France*, respecting independence of all three states; promising withdrawal of forces on request. |
| | (c) *Declaration by the United States* taking note of the Agreements and of Articles 1–12 of Final Declaration; stating also its position on the issue of elections. |

2 *Relating to Vietnam*

*Ceasefire Agreement*, of 47 articles, signed by representatives of French Union command (H. Deltiel) and the Viet-Minh command (Ta Quang Buu), setting forth terms of ceasefire, regroupment, temporary administration of zones, movement of civilians etc.

(*Note*: On 22 July, Ngo Dinh Diem made a statement in Saigon protesting at the Agreement and Declaration in so far as they covered Vietnam.)

3 *Relating to Laos*

*Ceasefire Agreement*, signed by same representatives as that for Vietnam (with the Viet-Minh acting for the Pathet Lao), covered withdrawal of all foreign forces (except 1500-strong French mission), and concentration of Pathet Lao forces in Phong Saly and Sam Neua provinces.

*Two Declarations by Royal Laotian Government*
(a) promising to integrate all citizens into the national community; allowing the Pathet Lao a role in administration of Sam Neua and Phong Saly pending elections;
(b) promising not to join any alliance contrary to Agreement.

4 *Relating to Cambodia*

*Ceasefire Agreement*, signed by representatives of Cambodian command (in effect, France) and of Viet-Minh (acting on behalf of Khmer Resistance forces), covered withdrawal of all foreign forces and demobilisation of Khmer (i.e. pro-Communist) forces.

*Two Declarations by Government of Cambodia*
(a) promising to integrate all citizens into the national community and allowing all to vote in elections;
(b) promising not to join any alliance contrary to the Agreements.

---

SOURCE  *Further Documents Relating to the Discussion of Indochina at the Geneva Conference* (London: HMSO, 1954) Cmd 9239; see also *Documents Relating to British Involvement in the Indochina Conflict 1945–1965* (London: HMSO, 1965) Cmnd 2834.

II

The Viet-Minh thus found themselves obliged to accept the partition of their country, although they were no more pleased with it than the new premier of the State of Vietnam, Ngo Dinh Diem, who openly denounced the Geneva Agreements as soon as they were signed. Ho Chi Minh accepted the settlement as a matter of international Communist discipline, and also because the military dependence of the Viet-Minh on China (and ultimately the Soviet Union) would not have allowed them to fight on alone in the face of greater United States involvement. But some Vietnamese Communist leaders resented the decision especially deeply, even though they remained silent. Twenty-five years later, in the 'White Book' of 1979, Le Duan finally brought their resentment into the open, directing it specifically against Peking.[4] He alleged that, during the months leading up to the Agreement, Zhou Enlai had brought pressure to bear on the Viet-Minh to accept a ceasefire at a time when they had the military advantage and ought to have continued the struggle until final victory. There seems to be general agreement amongst students of the diplomacy at Geneva that Zhou Enlai did indeed take the initiative in promoting a settlement, by urging the concessions which made agreement possible. But no mention was made in 1979 of the Soviet position, which had also been in favour of compromise at Geneva. Since Vietnam was essentially an Asian problem, the Soviet leaders probably took the view that Zhou should resolve it in his own way if a solution was possible – leaving the Russians free to present themselves to the Vietnamese as advocates of a 'harder' line than the one actually adopted.

The Viet-Minh probably also resented Chinese policy towards Cambodia and Laos at the Geneva Conference. Pham Van Dong's original proposals had envisaged a settlement based on three agreements, one for each Indochinese country, to be signed by representatives of their respective 'united front' organisation: the Viet-Minh, the Lao Issara and the Khmer Issara. The two latter organisations, although virtually dominated by the Viet-Minh, would in this way have secured international recognition. Dong also proposed that there should be no ceasefire without a political settlement for the whole of Indochina. In the end, however, the Communist powers conceded that the agreements for Laos and Cambodia should be signed only by the French and the Viet-Minh, both of whom were then obliged to withdraw from the two countries (except for a small French force in Laos) leaving behind non-Communist governments committed to a policy of national unity and diplomatic neutrality. This suited Chinese objectives very well, but was anathema to those Vietnamese Communists who believed that the Indochinese revolution was one and indivisible.[5]

The Americans, having decided against direct military intervention in spring 1954, also had no choice but to accept the partition of Vietnam and the neutrality of Laos and Cambodia. In public they deplored the 'loss' of half of Vietnam to Communist rule and dissociated themselves from the Final Declaration. In private they probably welcomed the return of stability to Indochina, and proceeded to concentrate on the analogy which could now be drawn between Vietnam and other post-war partitions in Germany and Korea. There too, military arrangements had opened the way to the development of separate states on either side of a dividing line, without any serious attempt at eventual reunification. South Korea and Taiwan became models for the creation of an American-oriented state in South Vietnam. On a regional level the Americans pursued an analogy between South-East Asia and Europe, which found reflection in the Manila Pact of 1954 and the inauguration of SEATO on 19 February 1955. Although only two independent states of the region were persuaded to join the Pact – Thailand and the Philippines – the ultimate objective of United States diplomacy was a collective security arrangement that would be as effective in its own region as NATO had been in Western Europe.

Two concepts were fundamental to American thinking about SEATO: first, that South-East Asia was a single region; and second, that strategic deterrence was the best means of 'containing' Communism. The regional perspective had been implicit in the first American assessments of the 'Communist threat' in Indochina as early as 1948, and had been reinforced by the Communist victory in China the following year. The partition of Vietnam was seen by the Americans not as one stage in the evolution of a 'national' Vietnamese Revolution, but as the 'loss' of one important area of the region. What had to be defended was the rest of mainland South-East Asia; and beyond that, the maritime countries farther south. However, the lesson of Korea was that wars on the Asian mainland were too costly for the United States to bear alone. SEATO was designed to provide a temporary bulwark against attack by land, but the ultimate deterrent was the use of nuclear weapons against the Communist powers themselves. Since America's allies could not be relied upon to carry an equal share of the burden in a conventional war, the only alternative was 'massive retaliation' against Communist 'aggression' anywhere in the world. This concept required one essential condition: a precise line on the map, the violation of which could immediately be recognised as 'aggression' and could be countered by an appropriate response. It was there that the Geneva settlement failed to meet American strategic needs and for that reason would eventually break down.

In Vietnam, it is true, a line had been drawn at the 17th parallel which could not be violated directly without a full-scale military invasion. But the situation was somewhat different from that prevailing in Germany or (after 1953) in Korea. The partition of Germany had been accompanied by a military occupation, with Soviet troops remaining in the eastern zone, British and American troops in the western zones. Berlin was partitioned in the same way. The official end of the occupation of the Federal Republic in May 1955 did not affect the continued presence of Western troops under a treaty signed the previous year, whilst Soviet divisions were still present in East Germany. It was thus impossible for either side to violate the 'iron curtain' without an immediate riposte, and the two Germanies had no opportunity to pursue political objectives by military means independently of their allies. In Korea, Chinese troops remained north of the 38th parallel until 1958 and American divisions stayed in the south much longer. The two Korean regimes therefore also had little alternative but to accept whatever was decided internationally. But there was no comparable occupation of either half of Vietnam by armies directly under the command of the great powers. Chinese aid to the Viet-Minh had not involved the overt presence of PLA units, or even a separate force of 'volunteers', and after 1955 the North was completely the domain of the PAVN. Likewise in the South the American presence was limited to the few hundred men of the MAAG and TERM missions, whilst the French in 1955–6 handed over formal military control to the ARVN. It might be difficult, therefore, for the Chinese and the Americans to restrain their respective Vietnamese allies from continuing the conflict in any form that did not amount to overt 'aggression'.

From the point of view of the deterrent strategy, the Geneva settlement was even less satisfactory in Laos and Cambodia than in Vietnam. Chinese willingness to see these two countries treated separately, and to allow their existing governments (both still formally monarchies) to continue in legal control of the whole territory, was in one sense a concession. The only conditions were that in each case they must integrate the people into a single national community, and must at the same time avoid participation in any military alliance (such as SEATO). That meant, however, that they could not be drawn fully into what the Americans referred to as the 'free world', and could not be defended on the basis of United States aid. Cambodia, which had no common border with North Vietnam or China, was not immediately subject to any real or imagined threat. Sihanouk was in any case eager to adopt a policy of neutrality. But Laos presented greater problems. It was a vast and thinly-populated country, whose borders with China and Vietnam were not only long but also remote – and in some places not very clearly defined. Precise national boundaries were in any case a relatively recent innovation in this part of Asia: the product of mapping exercises by colonial officials less than a century before, and quite alien to the traditional ways of thinking of the Laotians, Thais and Vietnamese. The frontier between Laos and Communist North Vietnam was all but impossible to defend. Added to that, the Geneva Agreement required the concentration of Pathet Lao forces (which had been heavily assisted by the Viet-Minh) into the northern provinces of Phong Saly and Sam Neua, whilst an accompanying Laotian government declaration allowed the Communists to administer those two provinces pending general elections. The result was neither *de facto* partition, drawing a sharp line across the country, nor genuine national unity of a kind that would enable the government in Vientiane and its armed forces to patrol – even in principle – the border between Laos and either China or North Vietnam. In the long run national unity could be achieved only through a political compromise by bringing the Pathet Lao into a coalition government: a prospect which alarmed the Americans and which would certainly undermine any attempt to make Laos a member of the 'free world' with a precise, defendable frontier.

Both its own history and the logic of the post-Geneva situation in Indochina made Laos a natural 'buffer state', whose neutrality might actively help to keep enemies apart. The one principle that could not easily be applied to it was that of the precise line necessary to the concept of deterrence, capable of defining the limits of 'aggression'. Nevertheless the Americans, anxious to encourage Thailand to remain a member of the 'free world', could not afford to

MAP 1  *Indochina after the Geneva Agreements of 1954*

abandon Laos altogether and so allow the Mekong River to become
the line defended by SEATO. In the event it proved difficult for
them to resist the temptation to draw Laos, and if possible even
Cambodia, into the SEATO framework. In June 1955 the

Americans established a separate MAAG in Phnom Penh; in December the same year a 'Programmes Evaluation Officer' in Vientiane began to channel aid to the Royal Laotian Army. The Americans were careful not to take any action which openly defied the terms of the ceasefire; but their ultimate objective was barely compatible with aspects of the Geneva settlement which the Chinese regarded as especially important.

## III

During the years 1955–6 North Vietnam was left with no choice but to carry on a 'diplomatic struggle' for the implementation of the political terms of the Geneva settlement. Its case was by no means watertight, since the Geneva documents were extremely vague in their references to a political settlement and to nation-wide elections. In the actual ceasefire Agreement there was only one mention of elections and no reference to a date: Article 14(a) allotted responsibility for administration of the two military zones to the respective parties, 'pending the general elections that would bring about the unification of Vietnam'. It was the (unsigned) Final Declaration which stated categorically that elections would be held in July 1956, and that preliminary consultations should begin on 20 July 1955. Apart from specifying that they would be by secret ballot and supervised by the states represented on the International Commission (India, Canada and Poland), the Declaration left open the precise form the elections would take. Together with other aspects of the eventual political settlement, that remained to be worked out through consultations between the authorities in Hanoi and Saigon.

Whether such negotiations would ever take place depended on what happened in Saigon, but in that respect too the Geneva documents were ambiguous. The ceasefire Agreement implied a continuing French responsibility for administration of the South; but a unilateral French Declaration (also made at the Conference) recognised the independence of Vietnam, without specifying whether this referred to the Democratic Republic in the North or to Bao Dai's State of Vietnam in the South. Already on 4 June 1954 the French had initialled a treaty granting full independence to the latter; and although it was never ratified, there was nothing in the

Geneva documents to challenge its status 'pending the elections'.[6] As Bao Dai's prime minister, therefore, Ngo Dinh Diem had some claim to temporary authority in the South; but he himself, with the full backing of the United States, refused to recognise the Geneva settlement at all. By mid-1955 any future political settlement depended on Diem's acquiescence in North–South consultations. But he rejected all proposals for a meeting on the grounds that free elections were impossible so long as a Communist regime was in control of the North. In this Diem was following the precedent of the United States attitude to all-German elections in 1946, and to the abortive discussions on Korea in the spring of 1954.[7]

In practice it was extremely unlikely that internationally super-vised elections, with all political groups participating freely, could actually be held in the circumstances of 1955–6. Whilst it was possible to quote no less a figure than President Eisenhower to the effect that Ho Chi Minh would 'win' an election, there was never anything to suggest that in the run-up period before elections the Viet-Minh regime would be willing to stand down and campaign on the same basis as all other political groups in both North and South. For the terms of the Declaration to be fulfilled adequately in the North, moreover, it would have been necessary to restore full civil rights to the landlords and rich peasants – not to mention purged Communist cadres – who were being systematically im-poverished and imprisoned (in some cases killed) during the later phases of 'land reform' from early 1955 to mid-1956. There was no suggestion from Hanoi that such a move was seriously con-templated, and North Vietnamese diplomacy was probably based on the safe assumption that Diem would never agree to consul-tations and that their bluff would not be called. On the other hand, if it ever proved possible to hold elections *without* strict international supervision and with the existing administrations in the two zones virtually determining the outcome, the North had the advantage: since its population was somewhat larger than that of the South, it would secure an automatic victory even if everyone in the South voted for Diem and Bao Dai.

Hanoi nevertheless found a measure of international support for its 'implementation' line, particularly from the Indian government whose representative presided over the International Commission. A statement of the Democratic Republic on 6 June 1955, calling for talks between the two Vietnamese administrations, was followed on

14 June by an Indian *aide-mémoire* to Britain and the USSR (as Co-chairmen of the Geneva Conference) urging them to take some initiative to bring consultations about.[8] India thus helped to keep alive the notion that a political settlement was possible in principle and might ultimately emerge in practice. But even the Russians were not eager to encourage beyond a certain point Hanoi's demand for strict 'implementation' of the political terms of the Geneva Declaration. Diplomatic support did not necessarily imply a serious desire to change the situation. In July, shortly before the deadline for the start of consultations between the two 'parties', Ho Chi Minh and Truong Chinh led a delegation to Peking and Moscow. They found it much easier to obtain promises of economic and technical aid than positive support for steps towards early reunification.

The international line now favoured by Khrushchev and his allies had two aspects, neither of which was helpful to North Vietnam. On the one hand, they sought improved relations with the West in order to stabilise the situation in Europe; on the other, they were pursuing a diplomatic offensive to win friends among the 'genuinely independent' (but still 'bourgeois nationalist') countries of South and South-East Asia. Whereas the ousted Molotov might have wanted to restrict positive Soviet support to states where Communists were already in power – as in North Vietnam – Khrushchev was eager to make overtures to Egypt, India and Indonesia, in order to wean them away from total dependence on the West.[9] The result was that during 1955–6 the Soviet leaders were more interested in helping such potential friends as Sukarno to preserve their 'genuine independence' than in upsetting the temporary stability of Indochina, and thus provoking a direct confrontation with the United States.

The Chinese in the meantime were making their own approaches to the Americans, which led to a series of meetings between their respective ambassadors in Geneva between August 1955 and December 1957.[10] By 10 September 1955 the two sides had reached an agreement on the repatriation of nationals, which seemed like a first step towards the easing of tension. There followed a period of several months (to mid-1956) during which they discussed the question of 'renunciation of force', with obvious reference to the status of Taiwan. Although no final agreement emerged, the Chinese had no wish during that phase to support military actions –

in Indochina or elsewhere – which might lead the Americans to abandon the talks altogether.

China was, however, willing to give greater encouragement than the Russians to North Vietnam's diplomatic moves. That was already evident in mid-1955, when the communiqué at the end of Ho's Peking visit was much stronger in tone than the one issued a week later in Moscow.[11] On 25 January 1956, in a letter to the Geneva Co-chairmen, Zhou Enlai protested vigorously against Ngo Dinh Diem's blatant disregard of the Final Declaration and called for the reconvening of the Conference itself. The occasion for that move was a request by Diem to France to complete its withdrawal from South Vietnam, in accordance with a promise made at Geneva. The United States had by then replaced France as South Vietnam's principal source of aid and had taken over the task of training its armed forces. That process was completed when the last French military units finally left Saigon towards the end of April 1956. The question raised by the Chinese letter was whether this change might not require a general reassessment of the situation by the countries originally represented at Geneva. If nothing else, it seemed necessary to take some action to oblige Diem to assume the legal responsibilities of France under the signed Agreement of 1954. Diem refused even to do that; hence the Chinese protest.

Whether any international action would be taken depended on Britain and the Soviet Union. The British view, expressed in a Note to Moscow on 9 April, was that at this stage neither side in Vietnam seriously intended a return to the use of force, and the Note rejected allegations that the United States was trying to build up Diem's army for an eventual campaign against the North. Beyond that, London insisted that maintaining the peace in Vietnam was of 'paramount importance', and that the question of a political settlement could not be allowed to undermine the ceasefire.[12] The Soviet position was equally cautious. When Khrushchev and Bulganin visited London later the same month (18–26 April 1956) Indochina does not appear to have figured prominently on their agenda. It was dealt with in supplementary talks at deputy foreign minister level, between Lord Reading and Gromyko, and the outcome was a large measure of agreement. Letters dated 8 May 1956, from the Co-chairmen to all the countries and parties concerned, amounted to an acceptance of the new situation: the International Commission would be allowed to continue in being in

both halves of Vietnam, without any new definition of the legal
responsibilities of Saigon.[13] China's proposal to reconvene the full
conference was thus set aside and Peking does not appear to have
pursued the idea farther at that stage. In effect the Communist
powers were acquiescing in the indefinite perpetuation of 'two
Vietnams', thus giving the Geneva partition the same practical
status as those of Germany and Korea. Only the North Vietnamese
had any real determination to prevent that situation from
crystallising.

# 3 The United States and Ngo Dinh Diem

We have been exploring ways and means to permit our aid to Vietnam to be more effective and to make a greater contribution to the welfare and stability of the government of Vietnam. I am accordingly instructing the American Ambassador to Vietnam to examine with you, in your capacity as chief of government, how an intelligent programme of American aid given directly to your government can serve to assist Vietnam in its hour of trial. . . . The purpose of this offer is to assist the government of Vietnam in developing and maintaining a strong viable state, capable of resisting attempted subversion or aggression through military means.

President Eisenhower to Ngo Dinh Diem,
23 October 1954

The main point I made was that we had to accept the fact that Vietnam is now a free nation – at least the southern half of it is – and it has not got a puppet government. . . . One can only hold free Vietnam with a government that is nationalistic and has a purpose of its own, and is responsive to the will of its own people. . . . And we have got to co-ordinate our policies to the acceptance of the fact that it is really a free and independent country.

John Foster Dulles, 17 May 1955,
on his recent talks in France

I

By the end of the three-hundred day implementation period
stipulated in the Geneva Agreements it was already clear that
United States influence in the southern half of Vietnam was rapidly
superseding that of France. On 11 May 1955, at the end of three
days of talks with the French prime minister and the British foreign
secretary, Secretary of State Dulles indicated that his government
could no longer adhere to a joint Franco-American policy towards
Vietnam. He persuaded the French to continue supporting the
administration of Ngo Dinh Diem, if only to prevent differences
over Indochina from damaging relations generally between
Washington and Paris. But in Saigon itself there was little hope of
long-term collaboration between the former colonial power and the
new patrons of 'free Asia'. Dulles might insist publicly that Diem
was not merely a 'puppet' of the United States, but he was unwilling
to allow the emergence there of any government which might wish
to preserve exclusive ties with France.[1]

Historians looking for the 'origins' of United States involvement
in Vietnam have usually identified it in the decision, taken in the
spring of 1950, to assist France in its war against the Viet-Minh. But
the degree of continuity between the French war and the conflict of
the 1960s is more apparent to students of decision-making in the
United States than to those concerned with the political evolution of
Vietnam. During 1954–5 South Vietnam took its place alongside
other Asian states to which the Americans were willing to make a
moral as well as a material commitment; and this happened in
conditions of relative peace, rather than in the pressing circumstances of war. It is this positive commitment to a 'new nation',
rather than Truman's emergency decision to aid the French, which
constitutes the real starting-point for an understanding both of
American objectives in Vietnam and the eventual failure to achieve
them.

Truman's decision arose from the need to defend South-East Asia
as a whole against a type of revolutionary warfare which had
recently brought the Communists to power in China and was still
being waged in Burma, Malaya and the Philippines, as well as in
Indochina. American thinking in 1950 was essentially regional. If
Indochina claimed a large share of material support it was because
the 'threat' seemed especially great in that quarter; and since
French forces were fighting the war there, Washington had no

TABLE 3.1  *Origin of United States military missions in Indochina*

| | Vietnam | Cambodia | Laos |
|---|---|---|---|
| **1950** | 16 Feb.: French request for US military assistance programme announced.<br>10 Oct.: MAAG inaugurated, Saigon.<br>23 Dec.: Formal Military Agreements between US and France, Vietnam, Cambodia and Laos. | | |
| **1954** | 1 June.: Saigon Military Mission established under Col. Lansdale (clandestine). | 20 Oct.: French withdrawal completed. | 19 Nov.: French withdrawal completed except for 1500 men. |
| | 13 Dec.: Ely–Lawton Collins Agreement on US role in training Vietnamese armed forces. | | |
| **1955** | 1 Feb.: Establishment of TRIM.<br>11 Feb.: US took over (from France) financial and training responsibilities. | 16 May: US–Cambodia military assistance agreement. | |
| | | 13 June: MAAG Cambodia inaugurated. | |
| | 1 Nov.: Redesignation of MAAG, to cover only Vietnam.<br>18 Nov.: Gen. S. T. Williams replaced J. W. O'Daniel as commander, MAAG. | | |
| | | | December: Programmes Evaluation Office set up in Vientiane. |

**1956**    19 Jan.: South Vietnam asked
              French Union forces to
              withdraw.
          1 June: Establishment of US
              TERM, later merged into
              MAAG Vietnam (May
              1960).

SOURCES  US Army, *Command and Control 1950–1969* (Washington, D.C., 1974)
   Vietnam Studies Series; *Pentagon Papers*, Gravel Edition (Boston, Mass., 1971)
   vol. i, chs ii and iv.

choice but to channel its military and economic assistance through
the French government. But that was not an ideal state of affairs
from the American point of view, and after 1954 it was changed as
rapidly as possible.

A nationalist government in Vietnam, independent of France,
had been the ultimate American objective as early as 1943, when
Roosevelt first suggested that the French colonial regime should be
dismantled once the Second World War was over. Only the
complexity of the political situation in Europe after 1945, and
perhaps also events in China, had obliged Truman to reconsider
that idea and to give priority to ensuring the stability of France
itself. By 1950 Roosevelt's vision of a post-war Asia of sovereign
states, emerging from the dissolution of the European and Japanese
empires, had been overtaken by the fear that newly independent
countries might easily fall prey to Communist revolutions. For that
reason, whilst still putting pressure on the Dutch to grant independence to Indonesia in 1949, the Americans allowed France to shun
negotiations with Ho Chi Minh's DRVN. Instead they encouraged
the creation of a non-Communist regime under the ex-emperor Bao
Dai. Despite the fact that the resulting 'associated state' was still
completely dominated by the French, the United States gave it
international recognition in February 1950 and embarked on a
programme of military assistance. But when the scale of the war
reached a level which only the Americans themselves could sustain,
Washington was able to insist on greater independence for the State
of Vietnam. That point was finally reached in 1954. While the
Geneva Conference was still in progress, on 4 June 1954, France
initialled a formal treaty recognising Vietnam's complete independence; simultaneously the State of Vietnam, by a separate act,
adhered to the French Union. When the Geneva Agreement

handed over administration of the military zones of Vietnam to the two 'parties', it was this newly-independent Vietnamese regime which effectively took over responsibility for the southern half of the country and made its capital in Saigon. Nevertheless, like the Democratic Republic created by the Viet-Minh in 1945 (which the French had ceased to recognise), the State of Vietnam claimed to be the sole government of a united people and was recognised as such by the Western powers. Having gained full independence, it thus lost control of half the country almost immediately.

It might still have been possible, in view of its economic interests there, for the former colonial power to retain a measure of political influence in Vietnam; just as the British still had a stake in the defence and security of the territories which later became Malaysia and Singapore. But Dulles was determined to exclude the French. In his eyes their failure to defend Indochina effectively, despite its strategic importance for South-East Asia as a whole, disqualified them from a primary role in the future security of southern Vietnam. Negotiations between General Lawton Collins (sent to Saigon as a special presidential envoy in mid-November) and the French commander General Ely produced the agreement of 13 December 1954, transferring to the United States responsibility for training and financing the Vietnamese armed forces. After two months' hesitation by Paris, the new arrangements came into operation on 11–12 February 1955.[2] Meanwhile South Vietnam abandoned the French Union and became financially independent of France by a series of agreements signed on 29–30 December 1954, which dissolved the customs union embracing all three Indochinese states, established a national bank, and instituted separate exchange control arrangements. This insistence on the removal of French-imposed restrictions on the Diem regime might in itself be construed as a further example of American anti-colonialism. In the long run, however, the Americans wanted much more: they would be satisfied only with a South Vietnam fully committed to the cause of the 'free world'.

A decade earlier it may have seemed that an Asia of sovereign countries – held together only by membership of the United Nations and by the international monetary arrangements created at Bretton Woods, each following the principle of the 'open door' in its foreign relations – would be enough to satisfy American political and economic interests. But the effect of the Communist victory in China, immediately followed by the Korean War, convinced the

United States that it needed positive allies and must create a system of collective security for the nations of the 'free world' in Asia. That in turn meant ensuring not only national independence from colonial rule but also the emergence in each country of a regime willing to identify itself with American strategy. Such a transition was easily achieved in South Korea, Taiwan and the Philippines. The situation was more complicated in other countries, and might even require covert American intervention.

We now know (as a result of disclosures in the 1970s) that the CIA had already undertaken a clandestine operation to restore the Shah of Iran by means of a *coup d'état* in August 1953. In Guatemala, the radical Arbenz government was overthrown by a CIA operation precisely at the time when Diem was forming his first cabinet in Saigon in June 1954. In both those cases, Western economic interests had been directly involved. The Mossadeq regime had nationalised the Anglo-Iranian Oil company, whose concessions the intervention was designed to restore; the Arbenz regime had threatened the privileges of the United Fruit Company as well as seeking Soviet arms. The danger of 'international Communism' was invoked on both occasions, but the immediate threat was to Western enterprises. In South Vietnam, however, probably for the first time, the Americans used their capability for clandestine operations to establish a pro-American regime in a country where their own business community had no immediate stake, for reasons which had to do entirely with global strategy.

## II

Initial American difficulties in South Vietnam arose partly from the way in which the French had exercised political control since 1946. The creation of a 'national' government – first the 'French Republic of Cochinchina' of June 1946, later the 'Associated State' under Bao Dai – represented only one aspect of French policy. Since neither of those semi-autonomous regimes had been allowed to develop its own police and security network, power on that level remained in the hands of the French Sûreté or of the Deuxième Bureau. The key role was played by a Corsican, Major Antoine Savani, whose knowledge of the political underworld of French Cochinchina was probably unrivalled.[3] He operated on the principle of winning over grass-roots organisations, notably the religious political sects which had at one time or another been alienated by the Viet-Minh, and allowing them to control their own areas as semi-independent fiefs. He then provided financial support for their paramilitary units. It was not a method which fitted well with idealistic American theories about 'modernisation' or 'revolution' in Asia. But it was effective, to the extent that even in 1954 the Viet-Minh still found difficulty in applying their own principles of grass-roots mobilisation in many southern provinces. Similar tactics were used by the French in parts of northern Vietnam, where a Catholic bishop and his paramilitary forces defended Phat-Diem against the Viet-Minh for several years.

By mid-1954, therefore, three significant political networks, operating at grass-roots level in South Vietnam, controlled areas which had only nominally been transferred to the provincial administration of the Associated State. Their leaders in some cases used their position to participate in 'national' politics; others were merely local warlords. None of them could be forced to obey the commands of the Bao Dai regime, since their power had depended on direct relations with the French Expeditionary Force and its intelligence officers. Let us examine each in turn.

## The Cao-Dai

The Caodaists (or adepts of the supreme spirit, Cao-Dai) had signed an agreement in January 1947 giving them administrative and paramilitary control over large parts of the provinces of Tay-Ninh and My-Tho. The 'new religion' they had established in the mid-1920s had deep roots in the Sino-Vietnamese tradition of Taoist spiritism and apocalyptic Buddhism, being in reality a merger of older sects. It was divided into a number of branches, with headquarters in different places, and periodic and often conflicting attempts were made to restore 'unity'.[4] The most important centre by 1954 was that at Tay-Ninh, presided over by Pham Cong Tac who had become associated with the Japanese in the 1930s and had been exiled by the French to Madagascar in 1941. On his return in 1946 he and the Caodaist commander Tran Quang Vinh had been drawn into an alliance with the French Expeditionary Force, which over the next seven or eight years allowed them to expand their paramilitary army from twelve to over 50 'mobile brigades': more than 16,000 fighting men and 18,000 reserves. But even the Tay-

Ninh Caodaists were not completely united. In addition to the main army commanded by Nguyen Thanh Phuong (under Pham Cong Tac), a dissident force led by Trinh Minh The had by 1954 abandoned the French alliance and taken to the maquis; it eventually began to collaborate with the American CIA. Meanwhile at least two other Caodaist groups had joined the Viet-Minh after 1945. The leader of one of these (Cao Trieu Phat) moved to Hanoi in 1955 to represent the Caodaists in the Fatherland Front. The other pro-Communist group was the Tien-Thien ('Former Heaven') sect led by Nguyen Buu Tai, who later established his own 'holy see' near Ben-Tre in 1957. By that time, as we shall see, Pham Cong Tac's branch of the religion was in sharp decline.

## The Hoa-Hao

The Hoa-Hao Buddhists (named after the village where their religion had been 'founded' in 1939 by Huynh Phu So) controlled significant parts of the area formerly known as West Cochinchina, notably in the provinces of Chau-Doc and Long-Xuyen. They too had antecedents: especially the Buu-son Ky-Huong movement which had organised a rebellion against the French in 1916.[5] Like the Caodaists they had developed ties with the Japanese during the occupation and had acquired a paramilitary element towards the end of the Second World War. Their alliance with the Viet-Minh following the 'August Revolution' had been shattered when the Communists murdered Huynh Phu So in March 1947, making it relatively easy for Savani to draw some of their 'generals' (for example Tran Van Soai) into his network. Another Hoa-Hao leader – Le Quang Vinh, known as 'Ba Cut' – remained in the maquis and refused to rally to the French or to Bao Dai at any stage; possibly he was still in touch with the Viet-Minh.

## The Binh-Xuyen

The secret society known as Binh-Xuyen had also quarrelled with the Viet-Minh in 1947–8 and was thereupon invited by Savani to collaborate with the French, helping to maintain security in the underworld of Saigon–Cholon. By 1954 its leader Le Van Vien (Bay Vien) controlled all the gambling establishments in the city as well as its opium dens and brothels, whilst his nominee Lai Van Sang was director-general of the Saigon police. It was hardly the most orthodox way to run a city, but it effectively prevented the Viet-Minh from developing a strong urban movement to balance their mobilisation of the rural peasantry.

This direct French participation in grass-roots politics, essential to the security of the State of Vietnam down to 1954, did not accord well with American notions of an independent 'new nation' in South Vietnam; still less with their desire to eliminate French influence once and for all. The Americans themselves, despising the French, were still ignorant of the Vietnamese. Their principal model of an ex-colonial country was the Philippines, where a Communist-led agrarian rebellion in the early 1950s had been effectively defeated by a combination of constitutional develop-ment, under a Philippine government, and a variety of covert operations organised by the CIA under Colonel Edward Lansdale. What the Americans failed to take into account was that in Vietnam they were no longer dealing with a former colony of their own, whose political leaders were used to American methods and values and whose 'tradition' was in any case deeply influenced by Spanish Catholicism. They faced the task of taking over a French colony – if necessary by force – and introducing it to a whole new way of political life. The transition would almost certainly be traumatic, the opportunity for serious errors of judgement very great.

Many Americans were later convinced that they made their first error in choosing to support Ngo Dinh Diem and his brother as the only possible leaders for the new South Vietnam. Bao Dai, as well as being an ex-emperor, was too pro-French; consequently the Americans failed to see that he was probably the one man who could have served as an effective figurehead, allowing decision-making to pass to the hands of Western-educated, modernising Vietnamese. From the American point of view many of the latter were also unacceptable since their education had oriented them towards France. There were several Vietnamese 'polytechnicians', as well as graduates of the other *grandes écoles* in Paris; but few of them rose to prominence in the years after 1954. In effect the choice of Diem gave the Americans the worst of both worlds. A former mandarin, who had quarrelled with Bao Dai after serving briefly in a 'reformed' imperial administration at Hue in 1933, Diem represented the old Vietnam rather than the new; one writer dubbed him 'the last

Confucian'. At the same time, lacking any advanced education or understanding of technical matters, he was too weak a personality to lead a government of men more talented than himself. His supposed strength lay in his anti-French background, and in his Catholicism, which seemed to guarantee an anti-Communist line; perhaps also in his pro-Japanese orientation before 1945.

After the Japanese coup of 9 March that year, when Bao Dai had been encouraged to proclaim independence from France, there had been a possibility that Diem might be chosen to head the new government at Hue; but he had been passed over because of his antipathy towards Bao Dai and his loyalty to another branch of the imperial family.[6] In 1954–5, however, it soon became clear that Diem was in no position to dominate all other political groups with previous Japanese connections. During the Second World War Japan's encouragement of Vietnamese nationalism had not reached a stage where the many disparate groups with Japanese links could be united into a single movement under one recognised leader. By allowing Admiral Decoux's colonial administration to continue in being until March 1945, Japan had left the French free to impede nationalist as well as Communist political activities. In that respect Vietnam differed markedly from Indonesia where the Japanese military authorities had eliminated the Dutch and had promoted various national and religious organisations – with the result that Sukarno's stature was firmly established by the end of the war. That simple difference goes far towards explaining why in Vietnam it was the Communists, with their clandestine network, who had been in the best position to exploit the opportunity created by Japan's surrender in August 1945. French policy since 1946 had also tended to fragment rather than to unify Vietnamese nationalism at the grass-roots. Diem was thus very far from being a Sukarno; only Ho Chi Minh could aspire to such a role in Indochina.

It was as Catholics that the Ngo Dinh family had been able to make a significant mark on Vietnamese political life in the early 1950s. Diem's brothers, especially Nhu, had played the leading role in creating a movement of Catholic intellectuals and had cultivated links with the nascent trade union movement. Their secret Can-Lao Party, officially authorised in September 1954, drew its initial strength from two older groups of intellectuals: the Tinh-Than ('Spirit') group, founded in 1947; and the Xa-Hoi group, more specifically the creation of Ngo Dinh Nhu in about 1952.[7] The latter group also included Tran Quoc Buu, principal leader of the

Catholic trade unions. There was a deliberate attempt to relate the small and highly disciplined Can-Lao, with its own ideology of 'personalism', to the growth of mass organisations, and it is not impossible that Nhu was imitating the relationship in North Vietnam between the Communist Party and the National United Front, later the Fatherland Front. The organisation in the South which corresponded to the latter was the National Revolutionary Movement, established in October 1954. Other movements created by Diem were designed specifically to unite civil servants, women and youth. The Can-Lao also maintained its own network within the national army, not unlike the Communist 'political department' in the PAVN. This use of Catholicism as a political base for anti-Communism was to some extent modelled on developments in France itself, where Catholic mobilisation had contributed substantially to the defeat of Communist aspirations after 1945. But Catholicism was a much more important element in French national life than could ever be the case in Vietnam, where Christians accounted for only 5–10 per cent of the population and were always more or less alienated from the mainstream of traditional culture and religion. Diem himself might be both Confucian and Catholic, but in any case by this time Confucianism was dead. It could be argued that conversion to Christianity need not make a man any less patriotic; but neither did it make Catholicism a basis for other men's patriotism, or for uniting the country at large. In that respect Vietnam was also very different from the Philippines, where again Christianity was of central importance.

One possibility for the political development of South Vietnam seems to have been ruled out from the start: namely the encouragement of military rule. The creation of a national army, structurally separate from the French high command, had been strongly advocated by the Americans in 1952 as part of the price for their expanding military assistance. It might not have been entirely illogical in 1954 to allow the military a more important role, once full independence had been achieved. At least one precedent could be found in the American support of Nasser in Egypt following the coup of 1952: a case where the United States had encouraged military rule as a way of reducing, if not eliminating, British imperial power. The Vietnamese chief-of-staff, Nguyen Van Hinh, may at one stage have expected to be given a similar role, and on one occasion – as if to hint as much – showed Colonel Lansdale a cigarette case he had been given by the Egyptian General Naguib.[8] But the Vietnamese officer corps was still French-oriented and potentially loyal to Bao Dai; it could have moved to centre-stage only in the context of Franco-American collaboration. As it was the Americans were anxious to secure full control of the army for Diem before entrusting it with any political role; and to that end Diem used the Can-Lao. Not until 1963 did Washington reconsider its attitude to the Vietnamese military as a possible alternative to the Diem regime.

## III

Ngo Dinh Diem was officially appointed prime minister by Bao Dai on 19 June 1954, after the head of state agreed to his demand for virtually absolute control of the government. Exactly a year later, on 19 June 1955, three leading Bao Dai supporters who by then had declared war on Diem finally abandoned the fight and retreated to Phnom Penh.[9] In the interval, however, there were a number of occasions when it looked as though Diem was finished and would be replaced by some other leader.

Diem's initial government included several ministers drawn from other political groups, including the sects, and his army chief-of-staff was Bao Dai's appointee Nguyen Van Hinh; the Binh-Xuyen's nominee Lai Van Sang still controlled the police. This uneasy balance of political forces was unlikely to last long and the first crisis came quickly. On 11 September 1954 Nguyen Van Hinh resisted an attempt to dismiss him and send him abroad. Then on 16 September, a conference of sect leaders decided to withdraw their representatives from the government. Bao Dai (still in France) had meanwhile been having consultations with the Binh-Xuyen leader Le Van Vien, who returned to Saigon on 20 September with instructions to form a new cabinet. Apparently deserted by everyone except his immediate following and his American backers, Diem nevertheless went on to form a second, more narrowly based government four days later. What mattered far more than the attitude of Vietnamese politicians was the grudging acquiescence of France in Diem's survival in office: Franco-American talks in Washington on 27–9 September reaffirmed official French support.

During October, however, it became clear that not all

Frenchmen were willing to show comparable restraint in Vietnam itself, where even elements in the French army appear to have been willing to encourage Nguyen Van Hinh. A second crisis came to a head in the week before 26 October – the date said to have been fixed for a *coup d'état* – but the French high commissioner General Ely once again allowed the Americans to forestall it.[10] On 23 October Eisenhower wrote a formal letter to Diem promising full United States support, provided he made progress towards modernising the country; privately, the Americans said they would cut off funds if the army ousted his government. Uncertainty about Hinh's future ended in late November, when he accepted the inevitable and withdrew to France. Two generals took over his responsibilities, holding separate posts: Le Van Ty as chief-of-staff, Nguyen Van Vy as inspector-general, with the latter in effective command. The question of the army had not yet been finally resolved but it no longer represented an immediate threat to the regime.

The next challenge to Diem's position, coming towards the end of 1954, arose from doubts in certain American quarters about his suitability to remain as premier once the French had handed over many of their responsibilities to the United States and allowed Vietnam to leave the French Union. If Diem had been chosen as merely an interim leader, with no more than a transitional role, that would have been the time to remove him and to find an alternative. Even Eisenhower's special envoy General Collins appears to have agreed with Ely that that would be the best course, the man suggested as a possible successor being Phan Huy Quat, a leader of the Dai-Viet party. Collins was still urging a change as late as 7 April 1955; but it is evident from Dulles' reply to his letter of that date that the secretary of state (and his brother Allen Dulles, head of the CIA) had already made up their minds to support Diem as the one leader who could be relied upon to supplant French influence. In the meantime a campaign was launched to win recognition and support for Diem amongst the American public. Cardinal Spellman himself made a much-publicised trip to Saigon in January, to present Diem with the first contribution of Catholic Relief Services towards meeting the needs of refugees then streaming from the North. An editorial praising Diem in the *New York Times* on 29 January was followed by similar articles in other influential journals.[11] By February it was unlikely that the Americans would withdraw their support, despite French protestations or Collins' doubts.

The transfer to the United States of financial and training responsibility for the Vietnamese national army, which finally took place on 11–12 February, had two consequences. It gave Diem and the Americans firmer control over a sufficiently large number of military units to be able to challenge pro-French elements to a trial of strength; and it gave the United States power over the financial subsidies previously paid by France to the sects. Lines began to be drawn for the next round of conflict when, in early March, the leaders of the Cao-Dai, Hoa-Hao and Binh-Xuyen groups formed a 'united front of nationalist forces' to support the claims of Bao Dai and to force Diem's removal. The one sectarian leader who, after some hesitation, remained outside the front was Trinh Minh The (apart, of course, from the pro-Viet-Minh Caodaists and the Hoa-Hao forces under Ba Cut, which were anti-French as well as anti-American). On 21 March the united front issued an ultimatum to Diem, who rejected it three days later; at which point he made his first attempt to seize control of the police headquarters from the Binh-Xuyen, but failed. The street fighting which ensued on 29–31 March was halted when Ely negotiated a ceasefire. Not until 24 April did Diem feel strong enough to dismiss the police director (Lai Van Sang), thus throwing down the gauntlet to the Binh-Xuyen. The virtual civil war which followed for control of Saigon and Cholon can be represented as a conflict between Diem's forces (mainly the national army, but with some support from Trinh Minh The) and the Binh-Xuyen; or alternatively as a 'proxy war' between the CIA (Lansdale) and the Deuxième Bureau (Savani).[12] While the fighting was still going on, a Revolutionary Committee was set up by some of Diem's supposed supporters on 30 April – possibly with the aim of pushing him aside once the Binh-Xuyen had been defeated. Its lynchpin seems to have been Trinh Minh The and it collapsed when the latter was killed during the last stage of the fighting on 3 May. Meanwhile a small group of colonels (including Duong Van Minh) decided now to commit themselves firmly to Diem, which enabled him to eliminate the last pro-Bao Dai general Nguyen Van Vy and to establish firmer control over the army.

The events of early May thus gave Diem the opportunity he needed to assert his power once and for all. It would appear that a State Department decision to withdraw American support, taken on 27 April, was rescinded as soon as the outcome of the battle in Saigon became known. Shortly afterwards, at a ministerial meeting in Paris on 8–11 May, Dulles finally made clear his intention to abandon any attempt at a joint Franco-American policy. By then there was little point in France making a stand against Diem, and they accepted defeat for themselves and for Bao Dai.

Diem (and Lansdale) were now in a position to confront the religious sects, whose power lay in various provinces of Cochinchina. Among the Caodaists Trinh Minh The was already dead, making it easy to incorporate his following into the national army. It also proved possible to buy off Nguyen Thanh Phuong, leaving only Pham Cong Tac and his 'palace guard' in opposition at Tay-Ninh; the latter were disarmed by Phuong's men in a *coup d'état* at the holy see in early October. The Hoa-Hao leaders presented a more serious problem. On 23 April, and again around 25 May, they rejected attempts to buy them off. Tran Van Soai then took to the maquis, where he was joined by Nguyen Van Hinh and Nguyen Van Vy. But on 5 June the national army began a campaign to recover the main Hoa-Hao stronghold in Long-Xuyen province, and a fortnight later the dissidents gave up the fight. One reason may have been the non-arrival of a shipment of arms, supposedly promised by Savani; but it seems probable that some kind of deal was struck before the final battle was joined, under which Hinh, Vy and Soai withdrew to Phnom Penh on 19 June. The areas formerly controlled by Soai and most other Hoa-Hao leaders were left in peace by Diem, without any final *rapprochement*, whilst the one remaining sect leader (Ba Cut) fought on alone until his capture and execution in April 1956. Meanwhile Diem's own troops also occupied Tay-Ninh, forcing Pham Cong Tac to flee to Phnom Penh where he died in 1958.

The events of 1954–5 illustrate dramatically the way in which American power was exercised in the international arena at that time. At least three levels of operation have to be taken into account. On the level of constitutional formalities, public speeches and official formal aid programmes, South Vietnam acquired the status of an American ally with its own policies, its own interests and a place within the 'free world'. On that level the United States commitment to South Vietnam in 1955 was not fundamentally different from its commitments to other states in 'free Asia'. Yet this development was made possible on the diplomatic plane, only by negotiations between the American secretary of state and the French prime minister which did not need to be made public or even formalised in any treaty; whilst at grass-roots level what actually happened on the ground still depended on the outcome of street fighting or of secret attempts to buy off opponents, and on the manipulative skill of men like Savani and Lansdale. In the 'game of nations' none of these three levels – nor the relationship between them, which is normally secret – can be ignored.

Having defeated Savani's Vietnamese clients, however, Lansdale made no attempt to imitate French methods by developing his own *ad hoc* arrangements with local groups in control of semi-independent 'fiefs'. The American model required the establishment of a central government capable of modernising itself to the point where its own administration and security apparatus could control the country effectively at all levels. 'Modernisation' was inseparably linked to American financial and technical aid, which in the field of administration and security was provided through police-training and field administration programmes run nominally by Michigan State University under the direction of Wesley Fishel.[13] Such assistance was officially requested by Diem in May 1955; an initial programme was approved by Washington the following October. It involved the creation of the 'civil guard': a police organisation with some military training, along the same lines as that which had succeeded in the Philippines. Under this and later programmes practical problems were defined in methodological terms and appropriate 'solutions' devised. It is hardly surprising that such theoretical advice from American experts sometimes ran into opposition when it reached Diem or Nhu, who had their own ideas about how to maintain political control of their own country.

By July 1955 Diem had gained a considerable measure of control over South Vietnam. At that point, according to the Geneva Declaration, he ought to have been entering into consultations with Hanoi to prepare for nation-wide elections. Instead Diem set about organising his own referendum in the South to remove Bao Dai and to replace the State of Vietnam by a Republic with himself as president. Three days after the referendum, on 26 October 1955, he proclaimed the Republic of Vietnam. Bao Dai was thus finally eclipsed, slightly more than ten years after his original abdication in favour of the Democratic Republic in 1945. Diem made no attempt to secure ratification of the Franco-Vietnamese independence treaty of 4 June 1954; it is in any case unlikely that the French Assembly would have confirmed it, now that he had withdrawn from the French Union. The formal basis of the Republic was the referendum itself. Diem's next move was to produce a draft Constitution, which was then 'debated' (and of course approved) by a Constituent Assembly elected in March 1956; it was finally promulgated in October 1956.

Both the referendum and the elections were stage-managed by the Can-Lao and the National Revolutionary Movement, leaving anti-Diem forces little opportunity to express their opinion. But in a society where the majority of the population were illiterate peasants, and where there was no tradition of democratic representation, it is unlikely that any election could have been conducted according to the standards of sophistication prevailing by that time in, say Japan or India, or for that matter the Philippines. Diem could also point to the fact that North Vietnam held neither a referendum nor elections during this period. The rump of the first National Assembly, elected in 1946, reconvened in Hanoi in 1954; elections for a second Assembly were not held until 1960, following the adoption of a new DRVN Constitution. Even then serious opposition to the Communist regime was not allowed to express itself through the ballot box; only candidates approved by the Party were allowed to participate.

Having once exposed himself to the electoral process, such as it was, Diem did not take further risks in that direction for some time. The Assembly in Saigon prolonged its existence until 1959, whilst he himself did not have to face re-election until 1961. His continuing success, however, such as it was, depended on factors beyond his own control. The survival of his regime was not a question merely of 'legitimacy' in his own half of the country; nor even of an effective security system. The essential vulnerability of South Vietnam lay in the fact that the partition was based on an international ceasefire agreement, the validity of which was unaffected by Diem's own refusal to recognise it. So long as the partition was accepted by all the major world powers – including Moscow and Peking – as an imperfect but acceptable solution to a dangerous problem, so long Diem would remain safe. But a change in the world political climate or in Communist international strategy might at any time produce a serious challenge to the continuing existence of a separate South Vietnam. If that time should come, Diem's survival would not be guaranteed by the Geneva settlement, whose somewhat nebulous political terms he had persistently ignored; it would depend on the power of the United States to protect him.

TABLE 3.2    *The two Vietnams: constitutional development, 1945–61*

| Democratic Republic of Vietnam (1945–76) | State of Vietnam (1949–55) Republic of Vietnam (1955–75) |
|---|---|
| **1945** 25 Aug.: Abdication of Bao Dai. 2 Sept.: Democratic Republic proclaimed independence. | |
| **1946** 6 Jan.: National Assembly elections. 2 Mar.: Coalition Government, appointed by Assembly. 6 Mar.: Franco-Vietnamese Agreement 6 July–10 Sept.: Fontainebleau Conference: no agreement. 14 Sept.: Franco-Vietnamese *modus vivendi*. 28 Oct.–10 Nov.: National Assembly, 2nd session: Constitution approved; new government appointed. 19 Dec.: Abortive Viet-Minh rising, and withdrawal from Hanoi. | |
| | **1948** 5 June: Ha Long Bay Agreement (France and Bao Dai) on creation of unified State of Vietnam. **1949** 8 Mar.: Elysée Agreement, creating 'Associated State'. |
| **1950** 18 Jan.: DRVN recognised by People's Republic of China. 30 Jan.: DRVN recognised by Soviet Union. | **1950** 29 Jan.: Agreements ratified. 7 Feb.: Associated State recognised by US and Britain. |
| **1953** Dec.: National Assembly held 3rd session (in maquis) | |
| | **1954** 4 June: Treaty granting full independence (initialled). 22 July: Ngo Dinh Diem rejected Geneva Agreements. |
| **1954** 21 July: Geneva Agreement and Declaration; DRVN given control of the North. | |

29–30 Dec.: Agreements granting full economic independence to the States of Indochina. Vietnam withdrew from French Union.

**1955**  20–26 Mar. and 15–20 Sept.: National Assembly held 4th and 5th sessions; new government appointed.

**1955**  23 Oct.: Referendum in South Vietnam, creating Republic, with Diem as President.

**1956–9** Six further sessions of National Assembly held.

**1956**  4 Mar.: Constituent Assembly elections.
26 Oct.: Constitution promulgated.

**1959**  Dec.: New Constitution adopted by 11th session of National Assembly.

**1959**  30 Aug.: National Assembly elections held.

**1960**  8 May: National Assembly elections.
July: Second National Assembly met; new government appointed.

**1961**  9 Apr.: Presidential election; Diem re-elected.

# 4 Hanoi and Reunification

The American imperialists' policy of intervention is disastrous for our people and for world peace. They are sabotaging the Geneva Agreements and plotting to perpetuate the division of Vietnam: to drag South Vietnam, Cambodia and Laos into their military blocs in preparation for the renewal of hostilities, to transform South Vietnam into their colony and thus enslave our compatriots there.

Manifesto of Vietnam Fatherland Front,
10 September 1955

When we say that the socialist system will win in the competition between the two systems – the capitalist and the socialist systems – this by no means signifies that victory will be achieved through armed interference by the socialist countries in the affairs of the capitalist countries . . . . We have always held, and continue to hold, that the establishment of a new social system in this or that country is the internal affair of the peoples of the countries concerned.

N. S. Khrushchev at the 20th Congress of the CPSU,
February 1956

I

Even if the resistance war had not been brought to an end in 1954 and there had been no Geneva partition, the Viet-Minh would have faced special problems in the South. Throughout the preceding decade the Communist movement in the southern half of the country, especially the Nam-Bo, was much weaker than in the provinces which became North Vietnam. Two reasons can be invoked to explain the contrast, each associated with a specific stage in the history of the Party or of the revolution.

During the 1930s, under the leadership mainly of Tran Van Giau and other Moscow-trained cadres, Communist strength had been steadily increasing in Saigon and the provinces of the Mekong delta. By late 1940, after the French had been defeated in Europe and the Japanese had moved into northern Indochina but had not yet advanced to the South, there may have been some reason to hope that an open rebellion against the colonial regime might succeed; or at least achieve more than the short-lived 'soviets' of ten years before. But when the 'Nam-Ky' rising was launched, on 23 November that year, the French had little difficulty in suppressing it; its leaders being either executed or imprisoned. Consequently by mid-1941 when the Japanese began their move into southern Indochina, there were few parts of the Nam-Bo where the peasantry was under predominantly Communist leadership. In the North, by contrast, Truong Chinh's clandestine network not only survived but expanded during the years of occupation. In the South the field was left open to the leaders of the Cao-Dai and Hoa-Hao sects – sometimes collaborating with the Japanese – to build up their own mass following.[1] The most the Communists could achieve, during the years 1944–5, was to rebuild their network in certain areas. Thus at the time of the August Revolution the southern members of the Party were still obliged to work through a united front of sectarian and nationalist groups over which they had very limited control.

Although the provisional government established in Hanoi on 2 September 1945 could command the support of revolutionary committees throughout the country, it needed time to establish firm political control over the population at all levels. In the North circumstances once again favoured the Viet-Minh. The Chinese nationalist forces occupying Indochina north of the 16th parallel allowed Ho Chi Minh sufficient room to manoeuvre, and there was an interval of several months before the French returned in strength to Haiphong. But southern Indochina, designated at Potsdam as an area under Mountbatten's South-East Asia Command, was quickly occupied by British forces who permitted the French to re-establish the colonial administration on 23 September 1945. Although it took some time for French forces to recover all provincial centres in Cochinchina and southern Annam, the provisional revolutionary committee in Saigon collapsed immediately. In such circumstances the rudimentary coalition created by the Viet-Minh in the South could not survive. Some sectarian leaders, already alienated by the Communists, were willing to come to terms with Saigon and accepted French money to build up their own paramilitary brigades.

The second reason for Communist weakness in the South by 1954 stemmed from the Communists' own review of strategy in South-

East Asia in the second half of 1951. The Korean War had by then reached something like stalemate: a significant achievement for the Chinese People's Volunteers, commanded by Peng Dehuai, but one which nevertheless left Korea still divided at virtually the same point as in 1945. Soviet support made it unlikely that the Americans would extend the war to China or employ nuclear weapons; but massive nuclear superiority on the Western side meant that the Communist powers had little to gain by raising the stakes in the global confrontation. They were not yet strong enough to provide (the kind of support required by North Korea – or any other lesser Communist state – to win in a direct conflict with the United States. Stalin's motives for limited détente were bound up with a belief, expounded in his *Economic Problems of Socialism* of 1952, that further conflicts *within* the imperialist camp were inevitable. He predicted an eventual rebellion by the Western European countries and Japan against American economic domination, which would deepen the crisis of capitalism and lead to new wars. In the meantime the Soviet Union and its allies should pursue a policy of 'peace'. Communist willingness at that stage to enter into talks in Korea was accompanied by a review of strategy in areas of South-East Asia where armed struggle was still going on.

Despite American fears to the contrary, the Chinese probably took a firm decision in late 1951 or early 1952 against intervention in Indochina by PLA combat units (as opposed to military advisers). They confined their additional support to the supply of weapons and technical specialists necessary to enable Viet-Minh mainforce units to withstand assaults by American-assisted French divisions, Dien-Bien-Phu being the culmination of that strategy. But in areas beyond northern Indochina, even including the southern half of Vietnam, there seems to have been a decision towards the end of 1951 against substantial Chinese military support for revolutionary struggles.

It is impossible to know whether to believe reports put out by Taipei Radio that the senior Chinese official Gao Gang convened a meeting of South-East Asian Communist leaders about that time at which he insisted on revolutionary 'self-reliance' in all countries except Vietnam.[2] (In other words, in future the Parties elsewhere in the region must finance their own struggles and fight solely with weapons captured from the enemy.) Whether that meeting took place or not, such a decision was in accord with the logic of the new situation. Only by concentrating military assistance at one point –

namely the struggle of the Viet-Minh against the French – could the Communist side hope to make any progress at all. Whether that decision meant consigning other movements to eventual defeat, only time would tell. In the event, it proved relatively easy for the authorities in Malaya, Singapore and the Philippines to restore and maintain public security after 1954–5; whilst in Burma, even though the war did not die away altogether, Communist capabilities declined rather than expanded during the 1950s. In other areas of Asia, Communist Parties now began to participate in legal political activity and in parliamentary elections: notably in India from late 1951, and in Indonesia from April 1952.

The Chinese decision not to intervene directly in Indochina probably also explains the increasing emphasis on the political dimensions of the Viet Minh struggle, which was apparent from the autumn of 1951. Articles by Vo Nguyen Giap about that time indicated a new desire to combine the military and political aspects of the struggle more effectively, by mobilising the masses in order to bring in recruits for the revolutionary armed forces. The principle of 'self-reliance', much favoured by Truong Chinh, would lead gradually to the policy of agrarian reform in liberated areas: a policy which was already being implemented during 1953–4 – before the Viet-Minh had won firm control of the North. The new emphasis on political struggle was especially pronounced in the South. In late 1951 the regional edition of *Nhan-Dan* carried a series of articles by Le Duc Tho, who appears to have been sent south specifically to impose the new line and to have carried out a thorough overhaul of the Party in Nam-Bo, an exercise which may have brought him into conflict with Le Duan, as the regional Party secretary and political commissar.[3]

In particular, Le Duc Tho criticised the southern leadership for having paid too much attention to purely military affairs and too little to the political movement; he even found shortcomings in the military sphere itself where in future more effort must be made to develop guerrilla warfare rather than attempting large-scale operations. There was a remarkable similarity between these ideas and the decisions taken at a plenum of the Malayan Communist Party in October 1951.[4] In both cases the recipe was for a 'self-reliant' struggle, which did not pose an immediate military threat to the colonial administration either in Kuala Lumpur or in Saigon. The inauguration of the new political line in the Nam-Bo was followed in January 1952 by news of the death of Nguyen Binh, commander of

Viet-Minh forces there since 1946. He was accorded a funeral with full honours somewhere in the maquis, but it has often been suggested since then that his death was a political elimination. Possibly he opposed the decision to give lower priority to armed struggle in his own region.

The combined effect of these developments between 1940 and 1952 was to ensure that by the time of the Geneva ceasefire Communist strength was much smaller in the southern half of Vietnam than in northern areas. The one important exception was the region of Quang-Ngai and Binh-Dinh, in southern Central Vietnam, where a significant liberated zone had been established as early as 1945 after the famous Ba-To uprising. In late 1953 the Viet-Minh were still able to launch a major military thrust from that area towards Laos. There was also a liberated zone in the Ca-Mau area of Nam-Bo (farthest from Saigon), whose guerrilla forces were beginning to challenge the French position in the Mekong delta. But whilst the Viet-Minh had to abandon those areas in 1954, the Communists were still a long way from being able to mount a final campaign to take over the whole of the South.

## II

The Viet-Minh leaders who had been fighting south of the 17th parallel must have resented the partition with special keenness. Pham Hung and Nguyen Duy Trinh, together with Le Duc Tho, went north with the 80,000–90,000 troops who had to be withdrawn from the liberated zones of the South. Le Duan remained behind to lead the 5000–10000 cadres and soldiers secretly left in place, and did not finally go north until 1957.[5] These leaders may have argued strongly against accepting the Geneva partition at all, since it meant abandoning the political and military mobilisation that had been achieved in the early 1950s.

Many years later the Vietnamese 'White Book' of 1979 would criticise the Chinese for insisting on a settlement at Geneva, and for bringing an end to the fighting, at a time when the Viet-Minh were supposedly moving rapidly towards final victory.[6] In reply the Chinese rejected the implication that they had positively en-couraged the partition of Vietnam. The military realities of 1954 had left no alternative, since without an agreement the war would have escalated to a new level of violence. There would have been no French withdrawal, and a much greater level of American involvement, which in turn would have required greater commitment from the Chinese. The Vietnamese 'White Book' played down the extent of Viet-Minh dependence on Chinese military aid, and it was left to the former Vietnamese Politburo-member Hoang Van Hoan (by 1979 an exile in Peking) to reveal that during the early 1950s the Viet-Minh had been assisted by a Chinese advisory mission headed by General Wei Guoqing and that the celebrated victory of Dien-Bien-Phu had only been achieved – as Western intelligence experts have always alleged – because the Vietnamese could rely on Chinese technical support.[7] Without such assistance during the years 1952–4, some of it consisting of advanced weapons captured from the Americans in Korea, the Viet-Minh would have been quite unable to counter the increase in French firepower resulting from the American aid programme inaugurated in 1950. If the war had continued beyond 1954, with direct United States intervention, this dependence on Chinese aid would have been even greater. Conceivably the war might eventually have been lost, whereas in 1954 it was at least being won in the North. In short, the Chinese were unwilling to make Indochina a cause for prolonged military confrontation with the United States; and without Chinese aid the Viet-Minh would have faced disaster.

The decision to compromise at Geneva was undoubtedly correct, and at the time the Vietnamese themselves admitted as much. In his speech to the 6th Plenum of the VNWP held on 15 July 1954, while the Geneva Conference was still in progress, Ho Chi Minh explained why the Agreements had to be accepted. He noted that 'some people, intoxicated with our repeated victories, want to fight on to a finish at all costs'. Such people were guilty of a 'leftist deviation' which led them to 'see only the trees, not the whole forest': that is, 'they see only the French, not the Americans'.[8] Ho did not regard the regroupment into two zones as more than a temporary expedient; but the realism with which he accepted it at all suggests that he and his colleagues knew that Communist success south of the 17th parallel would require a whole new phase of struggle which might have to be indefinitely postponed.

It is important at this point to understand one of the fundamental differences between the Vietnamese and Chinese revolutions. In China, following the defeat and withdrawal of the Japanese in 1945, the revolutionary conflict between the forces of Mao Zedong and of

Chiang Kaishek had been settled on the battlefield. The two sides were able to draw on a certain amount of material assistance from outside, but essentially the war was one between Chinese armies, which neither Stalin nor the United States could influence in the direction of diplomatic compromise. Negotiations between the two sides never amounted to more than an interval between decisive rounds of fighting.

In Indochina, however, despite their seizure of power at the time of the Japanese surrender, the Viet-Minh were not militarily strong enough to resist the return of the French. The August Revolution of 1945 was primarily a political movement, with very limited military capabilities. As such it collapsed in the face of the British occupation of the South in September 1945, and of French determination to control the North in 1946. It developed into a fully-fledged armed struggle against French forces only during 1947–8, and despite early successes in relatively remote areas it acquired the ability to operate effectively on a large scale only after Mao's victory and the arrival of Communist divisions in Yunnan and Guangxi. The possibility of Chinese support for the Viet-Minh led France to seek aid from the United States during 1950, which meant that long before the war reached a decisive stage it had become an international conflict. This dependence of both sides in Indochina on external support made it extremely likely that the war would end in a military stalemate, capable of being resolved only through international negotiations. The Chinese might argue in principle that their own revolution was a model for other parts of Asia but, in practice, international circumstances made it virtually impossible for revolutions in the colonial countries of South-East Asia to end in outright military victory for Communist guerrilla armies. Thus the Dien-Bien-Phu campaign made sense only as one element in a strategy which also included political and diplomatic struggle. It presupposed both political activity in French-controlled Vietnam and in France itself, to undermine the enemy's will and win sympathy for the Viet-Minh, and also diplomatic activity, to hold out the possibility of a negotiated solution which would allow the French to withdraw. The Soviet and Chinese decision in favour of 'peaceful co-existence' in 1953–4 led to negotiations on Indochina sooner rather than later, making it inevitable that armed struggle would be at least temporarily abandoned in areas beyond northern Indochina.

## III

Ho Chi Minh's journey to Moscow and Peking in July 1955 failed to secure support for any immediate challenge to the partition, leaving Hanoi only a limited range of options in the South. Nevertheless an attempt was made to devise a strategy which would combine the continuing demand for 'implementation' of the political settlement with a series of political and (clandestine) military moves. The period between the 8th and 9th Plenary Sessions of the VNWP Central Committee (that is, from August 1955 to April 1956) stands out as a distinct and important phase in the evolution of Hanoi's response to partition.[9] The 8th Plenum appears to have identified several moves which might contribute to eventual reunification. One of these was to broaden the united front (the Lien-Viet of 1946, reorganised in

TABLE 4.1    *The diplomatic and political struggle for reunification, 1955–6*

| | Diplomatic struggle | Struggle in South Vietnam |
|---|---|---|
| **1955** | 6 June: Pham Van Dong's statement on DRVN willingness to hold a consultative conference on elections. | |
| | 27 June–7 July: Ho Chi Minh and Truong Chinh visited Peking; communiqué gave some verbal support to DRVN position. | |
| | 12–18 July: Ho and Truong Chinh in Moscow; main emphasis on economic aid. | |
| | 16 July: Broadcast by Ngo Dinh Diem, virtually rejecting elections while North was under Communist control. | |
| | 19 July: Message from Pham Van Dong to Ngo Dinh Diem, requesting him to nominate a representative for consultations; no reply. | |
| | 9 Aug.: Saigon government declaration on impossibility of free elections in the North. | Early August: Report (unconfirmed) of first visit to South by Van Tien Dung. |
| | 17 Aug.: Letter from Pham Van Dong to Geneva Co-chairmen seeking their intervention to secure implementation of political terms of settlement. | 13–20 Aug.: VNWP 8th Plenum, said to have approved use of 'tactical' violence in South. |

TABLE 4.1 *(Contd.)*

| Diplomatic struggle | Struggle in South Vietnam |
| --- | --- |
| 10 Sept.: Programme of VNFF: new organisation for the whole country, based on decision to broaden the united front (formerly Lien Viet). | |
| | 10 Oct.: Hoa-Hao leader Ba Cut announced formation of 'Vietnamese National Liberation Front'. |
| | 15–17 Oct.: Meeting of VNWP Nam-Bo Committee (presumably Le Duan) with Hoa-Hao leaders Ba Cut and Tran Van Soai, to discuss formation of southern branch of Fatherland Front. |
| 31 Oct.: Letter from Zhou Enlai to British and Soviet foreign ministers supporting DRVN position. | |
| | Dec.: Nam-Bo Committee of VNFF formed, with Le Duan as chairman. |
| | Dec.: Reports indicating reorganisation of Viet-Minh forces in the South, under a new commander (Tran Quang); possible second visit to South by Van Tien Dung. |
| **1956** 25 Jan.: Zhou Enlai called for re-convening of the Geneva Conference to overcome Diem's disregard for agreements. | Jan.–May: ARVN forces conducted 'Operation Nguyen Hue' in Plain of Reeds and Western Nam-Bo. |
| 14 Feb.: Pham Van Dong's letter to Geneva Co-chairmen on similar theme. | Mid-Feb.: Tran Van Soai negotiated terms allowing his men to surrender to Diem. |
| | 19 Feb.: ARVN troops occupied Tay-Ninh, ending potential Cao-Dai resistance. |
| | 18 Mar.: Le Duan's proposals for expansion of military struggle, and 14-point plan for military consolidation in both Nam-Bo and Cambodia. Overruled by Party Centre in Hanoi. |
| 3 Apr.: French gave formal notice of their withdrawal from Vietnam. | Early Apr.: Further Nam-Bo regional conference of VNWP, accepting impossibility of violent struggle; approving plan for political struggle in villages. |

TABLE 4.1 *(Contd.)*

| Diplomatic struggle | Struggle in South Vietnam |
|---|---|
| 9 Apr.: Pham Van Dong to Geneva Co-chairmen, insisting that Diem regime take on France's legal obligations. | 13 Apr.: Ba Cut captured by Diem forces (executed in June). |
| | 19–24 Apr.: VNWP 9th Plenum: confirmed decision for political, not armed struggle in South. |
| 8 May: Message from Geneva Co-chairmen, following meetings of Reading and Gromyko in London: emphasis on need to keep the peace in Indochina; Co-chairmen and ICSC to continue their responsibilities. | |
| 11 May: Pham Van Dong to Ngo Dinh Diem, repeating demand that he appoint representative for consultations, and calling for normalisation between the two zones. | |

PRINCIPAL SOURCES *Documents Relating to British Involvement in the Indochina Conflict 1945–65* (London: HMSO, 1965) Cmnd 2834; and C. A. Thayer, 'The Origins of the National Front for the Liberation of South Vietnam', PhD thesis, Australian National University, Canberra, 1977.

1951) and to rename it the Vietnam Fatherland Front. At its inaugural Congress in early September, the VNFF established the aim of uniting all political parties in the North behind a political programme whose central theme was national reunification.

The new Front was also intended to function clandestinely in the South, where by December 1955 Le Duan had organised a regional committee including two leaders of the Hoa-Hao sect (Ba Cut and Tran Van Soai) who had already begun to align themselves with Viet-Minh 'veterans' in the South.[10] Ba Cut had never surrendered; Tran Van Soai had been obliged to retreat to Phnom Penh but had now returned. Operating in their own right, without acknowledging any link to the Communists, the Hoa-Hao could continue to challenge the Saigon regime without any risk of Hanoi being accused of ignoring 'peaceful co-existence'. The question was whether they were strong enough to destabilise the South and prevent Diem from carrying out his referendum of 23 October 1955 and subsequent plans for elections to a constituent assembly in March 1956. In the event they were unable to do so. Between January and May 1956, Duong Van Minh's 'Operation Nguyen Hue' (in the Plain of Reeds and the western provinces of Nam-Bo) virtually destroyed the Hoa-Hao forces as an instrument of the Fatherland Front. Tran Van Soai himself negotiated a second surrender in February, whilst Ba Cut was captured on 13 April 1956 and later executed. Diem's forces meanwhile took possession of the Caodaist 'holy see' at Tay-Ninh, forcing Pham Cong Tac to flee to Cambodia in February, and a group of Cao-Dai military forces still opposing Diem was defeated in the field at about the same time. By mid-March 1956 it was clear that the 8th Plenum strategy had not yielded satisfactory results. Diem had held the Assembly elections according to plan, making his regime look stronger than ever, whilst the Hoa-Hao forces were all but defeated, and the Tay-Ninh Caodaists were no longer capable of mounting an effective challenge even if they had been willing to join the Fatherland Front. The only forces capable of mounting an effective armed struggle now were those directly commanded by the Viet-Minh.

The Communists themselves appear to have reorganised and consolidated their political and military structure in the South during the last quarter of 1955. The number of Viet-Minh troops (as opposed to local supporters) remaining south of the 17th parallel after May 1955 was variously estimated between 5000 and 10 000. Some of these may have assisted in the predominantly Hoa-Hao campaign of late 1955 and early 1956; others are believed to have regrouped in the Plain of Reeds, to be reorganised by a military delegation from the North. One apparently reliable report indicates that around fifty cadres who had originally gone north earlier in the year were reinfiltrated into the South in October. It is less certain whether we should believe allegations that General Van Tien Dung himself (chief of staff of the PAVN) undertook two missions to the South to supervise the reorganisation.[11] In any case Le- Duan presumably remained in over-all charge of political affairs. In March 1956 he is believed to have submitted to Hanoi a long-term plan for an armed struggle that would have embraced Cambodia as well as Nam-Bo; but the Politburo rejected his proposals, probably in April.[12] One reason why he was overruled may have been that his ideas clashed with Chinese thinking: certainly his concept of a single arena of armed struggle extending into Cambodia did not accord with Zhou Enlai's encouragement of Cambodian neutrality under Sihanouk. Le Duan probably belonged to the school of thought within the Party which foresaw long-term difficulties if Cambodia and Laos were allowed to develop relations with Peking independently of Hanoi, and whose aim was an integrated revolution throughout Indochina, under firm Vietnamese leadership. But that line did not prevail in the spring of 1956.

The debate about Le Duan's proposal took place against the background of a visit to Hanoi by the Soviet deputy premier Mikoyan from 2 to 6 April.[13] Shortly before his arrival, *Nhan-Dan* (31 March 1956) indicated Vietnamese approval of the resolutions adopted by the 20th Congress of the CPSU the preceding February, which Truong Chinh and Le Duc Tho had attended. But it is unlikely that the Vietnamese approved wholeheartedly every aspect of Khrushchev's report to the Congress, which had defined an international line based on the principles of 'peaceful co-existence' and 'peaceful transition'. Mikoyan's task was probably to convince the Vietnamese of the validity of the Soviet line, even if that meant sacrificing their own immediate objectives. The absence of any joint statement after his visit was taken as a sign of continuing disagreement. On another level, however, his visit was welcomed. He had just come from Burma, where he negotiated a long-term agreement on the exchange of rice for industrial machines, and it is believed that a substantial part of the rice went to solving North Vietnam's food problems. In the end the Vietnamese had to accept that economic survival and the socialist construction of the North must take priority over a more aggressive policy in the South.

The VNWP 9th Plenum (19–24 April 1956) coincided precisely with Khrushchev's visit to London – during which little attention was paid to the Vietnam issue – and also with the announcement that Stalin's Cominform was to be dissolved. The latter move, which made possible a visit by Tito to Moscow in June, symbolised clearly the decision in favour of 'de-Stalinisation'. Whilst it would be inappropriate to represent the Vietnamese as obeying 'orders from Moscow', they were obliged to accept the logic of an international line based on Moscow's perception of the world situation as a whole, rather than on the perspectives of a single national revolution. Within the VNWP leadership, 'hardliners' like Le Duan had therefore to submit to the discipline of a majority led by Ho Chi Minh and Truong Chinh. Shortly afterwards the meeting of Gromyko and Lord Reading in London produced the messages of 8 May already noted (in Chapter 2), which left the world in no doubt that the Communist powers were willing to allow the partition of Vietnam to continue. The only action left open to Hanoi at this stage was to demand 'normalisation' of relations between North and South, which Pham Van Dong proceeded to do in a letter to Ngo Dinh Diem on 11 May. He did so more as a propaganda move than in the expectation of any actual progress towards reunification.

## IV

The actual programme for the South adopted by the 9th Plenum, in keeping with the constraints of 'peaceful transition', focused upon three political objectives: to win over all types of people to the Fatherland Front, especially better-off farmers, rich peasants and 'patriotic' landowners; to organise local youth groups with a view to the eventual recruitment of militia forces; and to gain control (by legal means) of village administrative committees wherever possible.[14] Since Diem's own intelligence reports are our main source for this information, it is hardly surprising that during the summer and autumn of 1956 the Saigon regime adopted a number of measures designed specifically to counter these Communist objectives.

In June the village council elections introduced three years earlier, but not always effectively implemented, were abolished, Diem's purpose being to make it impossible for members and sympathisers of the Fatherland Front to stand for election and to win office by manipulating local grievances. A similar change was made for the municipal councils in August. Also during this period the government began discussions with its American advisers on the question of land reform. Ordinance no. 57, promulgated on 22 October 1956, imposed a limit of 100 hectares on the amount of land any one person could own; it also ordered the redistribution of formerly French-owned riceland to better-off tenants. Land reform of this type was designed to win over precisely that element in the rural population to which the Fatherland Front programme was addressed: namely the rich and middle peasants. The same principle had been applied successfully in Japan after 1945 and in Taiwan since about 1953, and it was no accident that Diem's chief adviser in this field (Wolf Ladejinsky) was a veteran of those two land reform campaigns.[15] But progress in South Vietnam was very slow; it took until 1959–60 for actual redistribution to take effect, and even then it was relatively easy for Vietnamese (as opposed to French) owners to circumvent the legal limit on size of holdings. Later on, when Diem was in trouble, critics would argue that an important reason was the failure of Ordinance no. 57 to deal with the real agrarian problems of the South. But if its purpose was to help the richer peasants and substantial farmers, rather than the poor peasants who were supposed to benefit from Communist-sponsored land reforms, it was not wholly inappropriate. In theory it could have led to the transfer of over 600,000 hectares, which would at least help to satisfy the land-hunger of those most actively seeking to cultivate more land or to own their existing holdings.

A further element of Diem's policy was the campaign to denounce Communists, which led to the arrest and imprisonment of a great many suspects – many of them probably innocent of any actual deeds against the government. Diem faced the problem of many urban-based governments in predominantly rural societies when seeking to establish a tighter political grip on the countryside: namely how to ensure that officials were both loyal to the centre and also effectively in control of their localities. In most areas, however, he did not have to cope with active guerrilla forces in the countryside. The natural inclination of most peasants was probably to obey the government so long as its security forces were relatively strong.

By the middle of 1956 therefore, two years after the Geneva Agreement, those Communists remaining in the South had to admit that Diem was becoming stronger and their own position weaker as time went on. Whilst Le Duan's plan to resume armed struggle had been overruled, the current programme of political action was unlikely to succeed. 'Peaceful co-existence' in the world at large, combined with 'peaceful transition' as the only permissible form of struggle inside South Vietnam, would probably leave Vietnam permanently divided. The one approach still open to Le Duan and those who thought like him was to foster a southern-based revolution against Diem, which no outside force could prevent from developing and which ultimately Diem himself would be unable to resist. In the first instance this need not depend either on diplomatic support or material assistance from outside, or on its own armed forces. The Party would merely seek to identify the 'contradictions' within South Vietnamese society, and exploit them in order to build up a political movement capable of revolutionary action. Such a revolution would gain strength from the achievements of socialist construction in the North; it would also encourage the attention and sympathy of 'peace-loving' people in the world at large. Without challenging the current international line of 'peaceful co-existence', it need not be confined to legal forms of struggle. It would be, above all, a revolutionary and not just a 'reformist' movement.

This line was represented by a document circulating amongst Party cadres in the South towards the end of 1956 and early 1957, whose author is now known to have been Le Duan.[16] Entitled 'The Path of the Revolution in the South', it marked the beginning of a new phase in the southern struggle, not so much because it advocated a major intensification of activities as because it defined revolution itself as the long-term goal. In short, there was to be no final abandonment of the struggle for ultimate reunification despite the international pressures evident earlier in the year. Le Duan estimated that in the end Diem's power base would prove too weak to resist a revolutionary movement; and that his dependence on political violence would become so great that he would sooner or later be destroyed by his own inability to maintain order. In the meantime Party branches at grass-roots level in the South would organise a network capable of leading the revolution to success once the time became ripe for an open bid to seize power.

# 5 Laos and Cambodia: the Search for Neutrality

The Government of the Democratic Republic of Vietnam considers that the settlement which is due to take place between the Royal Government of Laos and the 'Pathet Lao', by virtue of the Geneva Agreements, is a question of internal order which (they) are entirely free to solve in the best way possible in the higher interests of the country and people of Laos.

> Joint statement of Pham Van Dong and Katay Don Sasorith,
> after meeting at Bandung,
> 23 April 1955

Peace in Indochina is indivisible, a fact recognised during the discussions of the Geneva Conference and confirmed by the spirit of its Final Declaration.

> Ung Van Khiem, deputy foreign minister of the DRVN,
> 31 May 1958

My Canadian colleague himself has used the term 'interdependence' to describe the relations between the three states in Indochina at the time of the Geneva Conference. In the Geneva Agreement itself, especially the Final Declaration of the Geneva Powers . . . one would find that this question of interdependence among the three states correctly reflects the views of the Geneva Powers while framing the Geneva Agreement. The position of the Indian delegation is that . . . the three International Commissions have to continue till a political settlement is completed in all three countries, namely Cambodia, Laos and Vietnam.

> Statement of Indian delegate
> to the International Commission in Laos,
> 23 May 1958

# I

The form of the Geneva Agreements enabled Laos and Cambodia to escape the kind of partition imposed on Vietnam. The French and the Viet-Minh committed themselves to military withdrawal, which left the existing governments of the two countries free to claim international recognition and to make a smooth transition to full independence. France had permitted both countries to develop as 'Associated States' within the French Union, under Constitutions originally promulgated in 1947, with the result that by 1954 they both had elected national assemblies and legally established governments. In Cambodia the position of Sihanouk, who was king and prime minister until his abdication in 1955, was strengthened by the achievement of independence. He welcomed the idea of neutrality as a positive advantage. In Laos, although the Pathet Lao were left in effective control of two northern provinces, international recognition was automatically given to the government of Prince Souvanna Phouma in Vientiane, whilst the king continued to reign in Luang Prabang. In principle therefore, Laos too was free to pursue a policy of neutrality as a potentially unified kingdom.

TABLE 5.1   *Laos and Cambodia: constitutional development, 1945–55*

| | Laos | | Cambodia |
|---|---|---|---|
| **1945** | 8 Apr.: Proclamation of independence by King Sisavang Vong (at Japanese instigation). 17 Sept.: The king accepted that the French protectorate continued in force; and was 'deposed' by the Lao Issara. | **1945** | 13 Mar.: Proclamation of independence by King Sihanouk. Sept.: Return of French. |
| **1946** | 15 Mar.: French forces reoccupied Vientiane; defeat of Lao Issara. 27 Aug.: *Modus vivendi*, making Laos a unified state within the French Union. | **1946** | 7 Jan.: *Modus vivendi*, making Cambodia an 'autonomous state' within the French Union. |
| **1947** | 10 May: Constitution promulgated. Nov.: Elections to National Assembly. | **1947** | 6 May: Constitution promulgated. Nov.: Elections to National Assembly |

**1948** September: National Assembly dissolved.

**1949** 19 July: Franco-Laotian Convention establishing 'Associated State'.

27 Oct.: Lao Issara government, in exile in Bangkok, dissolved itself. (Souphanouvong went to the Viet-Minh area; Lao Issara continued as basis for Pathet Lao.)

**1949** 8 Nov.: Franco-Cambodian Treaty, establishing 'Associated State'.

**1951** Sep.: New National Assembly elected.

**1952** June: Sihanouk, still king, also became prime minister.

**1953** Mar.: Sihanouk visited France to seek full independence.

**1953** 22 Oct.: Treaty giving Laos full independence within French Union.

**1954** 21 July: Government declaration on national unity and neutrality, following Geneva Agreement.

November: Katay Don Sasorith replaced Souvanna Phouma as premier.

**1954** 21 July: Government Declaration on national unity and neutrality, following Geneva Agreement.

**1955** Series of inconclusive talks between the two sides, including Rangoon meeting of Katay and Souphanouvong (30 Sept.–11 Oct.).

**1955** 7 Feb.: Referendum supported Sihanouk's demand for total independence.

2 Mar.: Sihanouk's abdication.

11 Sept.: New National Assembly elected.

26 Sept.: Sihanouk became premier and proclaimed full independence.

25 Dec.: Elections in ten provinces controlled by Vientiane.

The effect of the Geneva settlement was thus to bring Cambodia and Laos into the category of Asian states whose governments faced a choice between what the Communist powers called 'genuine independence' and 'alignment with imperialism'.

The Chinese approach to such countries was defined by Zhou Enlai in his speeches and private conversations during the Afro-Asian Conference at Bandung in April 1955. He presented an image of reasonableness calculated to win over as many Asian countries as possible to a recognition that China posed no threat to its neighbours, and that they had no need to join any American-sponsored anti-Chinese alliance. He was appealing not only to countries like Burma and Indonesia, which had already taken up a neutralist position and refused to join SEATO, but to Thailand and Pakistan, whose governments had signed the Manila Pact, and also to Laos and Cambodia. At that stage it was by no means a foregone conclusion that Thailand would remain committed to the United States, and Chinese efforts to influence the government of Phibulsonggram were not necessarily doomed to fail. Twenty years later it was revealed that following Zhou Enlai's conversations with the Thai foreign minister at Bandung there was a serious attempt at Thai–Chinese *rapprochement*, involving an unofficial and highly secret Thai mission to Peking which was received by Mao Zedong himself on 21 December 1955 .[1] The message of the Chinese leader was that Thailand should remain neutral rather than align itself with SEATO. It is still not clear how seriously that option was considered in Bangkok, but some time during 1956 Phibulsonggram sent one of his close associates to meet the Chinese ambassador in Rangoon and to sign a 'people-to-people' agreement. One overt consequence of this secret diplomacy was a decision by Thailand to lift its earlier embargo on sales to China of rice and other non-strategic goods in June 1956. Not until after the Thai *coup d'état* of September 1957, when Phibulsonggram was forced into exile, did the Americans succeed in persuading Bangkok to reverse this 'thaw' in Thai–Chinese relations.

The application of China's 'Bandung' strategy to Cambodia and Laos was even more successful. The United States had hoped to draw these countries into the defence arrangements centred on SEATO, even though the two states were precluded from seeking full membership of the Pact. But some leaders in Vientiane, as well as Sihanouk in Phnom Penh, were wary of a commitment to SEATO and were willing to respond to Chinese initiatives. In

Cambodia, Sihanouk overcame the opposition of those generals and politicians who wanted to rely mainly on American aid and to develop the armed forces and economy along Western lines. During a visit to Manila at the beginning of 1956, he made it clear he had no intention of collaborating closely with SEATO, despite the inclusion of Cambodia as a 'protocol' area under the Pact. As if to reaffirm this commitment to neutrality, the prince soon afterwards visited China (13–21 February) and by June had entered into trade and aid agreements with Peking. That summer he also began to develop relations with the rest of the Communist world, touring the Soviet Union, Poland, Czechoslovakia and Yugoslavia.[2] In November 1956 Zhou Enlai himself visited Phnom Penh and was taken to see the ancient temples of Angkor, which led to a further strengthening of economic ties, including the establishment of a permanent Chinese economic mission in the Cambodian capital. It was noticeable, too, that whereas the Chinese protested strongly against Ngo Dinh Diem's legislation restricting the activities of Chinese residents in South Vietnam during 1956–7, they turned a blind eye to similar regulations issued by Sihanouk.

Sihanouk's strategy for the defence of Cambodian independence was thus diplomatic rather than military; but it depended on two conditions. First, it assumed continuing close relations between the United States and his two immediate neighbours, Thailand and South Vietnam – without either of them actually declaring war on Cambodia. Second, it assumed a continuation of the international Communist strategy of support for 'genuinely independent' regimes, despite their 'bourgeois nationalist' character. For the time being, both conditions were fulfilled; but it did not lie within Cambodia's power to ensure that they would continue indefinitely.

In Laos the situation was more complex. The Geneva Agreement had allowed the fighting forces of the Pathet Lao to continue in existence, and to take over the provincial administrations of Phong Saly and Sam Neua. But the terms of the ceasefire required the eventual reintegration of those two provinces into the national administrative framework, and of the Pathet Lao military units into the Royal Army, under the auspices of a single government established through national elections. Thus, although there was no formal partition into two military zones, it was impossible to achieve a settlement without negotiations between the government and the Pathet Lao. The one important difference from Vietnam was that in the interval the existing government in Vientiane was recognised as legitimate so long as it respected the Agreement: the fact that the Pathet Lao had not been allowed to participate at Geneva or to sign the Agreement meant that they had no legal standing except within the national polity as a whole.

Talks between the two sides went on for much of 1955, but without significant progress.[3] The chances for compromise had been considerably diminished by the assassination of the Vientiane defence minister in September 1954, leading to a government crisis and the emergence of the right-wing Katay Don Sasorith as prime minister in place of Souvanna Phouma. Katay insisted that the obligation to hold national elections could be fulfilled within the terms of the existing Laotian constitution, without depending on agreement between the two sides. Although he agreed to postpone elections from 10 June to 25 December 1955 (and in the interval went to Rangoon to meet Souphanouvong) the elections were held on the latter date in the ten provinces controlled by the government, with the Pathet Lao refusing to participate. Even so the results did not confirm Katay in power. He was unable to secure the required majority in the new Assembly and was therefore obliged to return the premiership to Souvanna Phouma in March 1956. At that point there was again a possibility of compromise with the Pathet Lao. An important development occurred in mid-July 1956 when the Assembly in Vientiane sent a delegation to Bangkok to invite the senior prince of the Lao royal family, Phetsarath, to return home. He had withdrawn to Thailand after the French defeated his efforts to win full independence in 1945–6, but as the elder brother of both Souvanna Phouma and Souphanouvong he was the one man capable of reconciling the prime minister and the Pathet Lao leader. Although he did not actually return to Laos until the following March, his public acceptance of the invitation was sufficient to bring about a meeting between the two younger princes. On 5 and 10 August 1956 they signed agreements establishing joint committees to discuss the reintegration into the national polity of the Pathet Lao fighting forces and of the two provinces under their control.[4]

It is not clear whether Chinese diplomacy played any part in this *rapprochement*, but it was certainly welcomed by Peking. Shortly afterwards, between 20 and 26 August, Souvanna Phouma led a Laotian delegation to China and followed Sihanouk's example in reaffirming his country's neutrality. But the internal politics of Vientiane made cultural and economic relations with China a more delicate issue for Laos than for Cambodia. Acceptance of Chinese aid would be vigorously opposed both by rightists in the cabinet and by the American ambassador to Laos, J. Graham Parsons. With the Pathet Lao insisting on an aid agreement with Peking as a condition for further progress towards national integration, it is not surprising that at the end of 1956 there was still no final implementation of the Geneva Agreement. Parsons himself later admitted that he had worked very hard to prevent the formation of any government of national union.[5]

## II

American strategy towards Laos and Cambodia was based on the principle that as states on the frontiers of the 'free world' both would ultimately be drawn into the defence arrangements of the Manila Pact. Only if it embraced all non-Communist countries of the region would SEATO be able to function effectively as a component of the system of global deterrence, designed to 'contain' Communism against further military expansion. The Manila signatories had already designated Laos and Cambodia as countries to be defended under the Pact, even though the Geneva Agreements precluded their actual membership of the organisation; a step taken without even consulting Sihanouk or Souvanna Phouma. In the long run, the American objective was to strengthen those political elements in each country which favoured a tacit alliance with the United States. An NSC document of September 1956 indicates clearly what was involved: the 'courses of action' recommended for Cambodia included the encouragement of 'individuals and groups who oppose dealing with the Communist bloc'.[6] The same principle applied to Laos.

There were two ways in which the United States might hope to find political allies in Laos and Cambodia. One might be described as 'traditional', the other as 'modern'. Traditionally, both kingdoms had been caught between the conflicting ambitions of more powerful states on either side, which had sought to dominate them by supporting the cause of their respective allies in 'internal' disputes. The Vietnamese had first begun to expand into what is now southern Vietnam in the early seventeenth century, and to challenge the Thai position built up in Cambodia during the two preceding centuries. The result was that in the eighteenth and nineteenth centuries Cambodia was torn by frequent civil wars between opposing royal factions, one looking towards Bangkok, the other towards Hue. For a short while around 1836–40 the country was virtually partitioned by the Thais and Vietnamese, with the latter annexing more than half the Cambodian provinces. The French conquest interrupted that process and thus preserved the separate identity of Cambodia; but the French did not succeed in uniting the royal family, within which factionalism continued into the twentieth century. Norodom Sihanouk himself had close ties with the French, who had placed him on the throne in 1941. But his cousins were not wholly reconciled to his control of the country, and the Americans eventually found an ally in his rival Prince Sirik Matak – who would in due course engineer Sihanouk's overthrow in 1969–70.

In Laos, no one traditional centre of power had completely dominated the country. By the eighteenth century there were in effect three separate kingdoms, each sending tribute in different directions: Luang Prabang, which paid tribute to Peking; Vientiane, whose rulers had originally been installed with Vietnamese support and acknowledged the suzerainty of Hue; and (in the far south) Champassak, whose rulers looked towards Bangkok. Siam aspired to dominate the whole country, however, and towards the end of the eighteenth century managed to impose its own vague suzerainty over all three centres. Following a revolt by Vientiane in 1827 the Thais defeated a Vietnamese-backed prince and sacked the city, annexing part of its territory. By 1880 they had almost succeeded in establishing firm control over Luang Prabang as well. Once again it was the French who prevented the disappearance of a separate kingdom by imposing their own protectorate over all three of the Mekong principalities in 1893. The kingdom of Luang Prabang still survived in the mid-twentieth century, but under a royal family which may still have had some natural inclination to look towards China. But in the south the traditional élite continued to look towards Thailand, and it was there that the Americans were able to use their Thai connections to cultivate allies who opposed both the Chinese connection and any expansion of Vietnamese influence in Laos.

The 'modern' form of American influence in the two countries consisted of the use of military and economic assistance to strengthen their civilian administrations and armed forces, and to tie them into the American global system. In Cambodia, where a small MAAG had been allowed to continue alongside the American embassy, a small group of generals (including Lon Nol) welcomed such modernisation – without necessarily being exclusively 'pro-American'. But their political influence was limited by Sihanouk's refusal to enter into defence arrangements with SEATO, or to receive substantial quantities of United States aid. The prince's acceptance of Communist economic and technical assistance enabled him not only to remain internationally neutral but also to defeat potential opposition at home. The result was that American tactics failed in Cambodia.[7]

United States aid made a much greater impact in Laos. A 'Programmes Evaluation Office' (a disguised MAAG) was set up late in 1955 to assist the training of the Royal Laotian Army, although the French still maintained a garrison in Vientiane and provided formal military training. Although the military capabilities of the Vientiane armed forces were not great, they gradually acquired a political status comparable with that of Lon Nol in Cambodia. But their influence was much greater, and in the power struggles of 1957–8 the Americans were able to look to young military officers to play an active part in orienting Laos towards an alliance with Thailand and the United States. Notable among them was Colonel Phoumi Nosavan, a native of southern Laos and a relative of the Thai defence minister, Sarit Thannarat (who seized power in Bangkok in September 1957). In such circumstances, although progress was eventually made towards the formation of a coalition government in Laos during the second half of 1957, it was difficult for any government in Vientiane to establish sufficiently firm control over the situation to defy the Americans and embark on a policy of strict neutrality.

One possible interpretation of the 'origins' of the second war in Vietnam is that it arose not from anything the Americans did in South Vietnam – which Hanoi might dislike but could not effectively counter – but rather from the consequences of American policy in Laos. If Laos had remained neutral and relatively stable, it might have achieved a modern revival of its traditional pattern of relationships without presenting a threat to any of its neighbours. But the United States could not fit such a pattern into its global strategy: it needed Laos to be committed to the 'free world'. Having decided to block Chinese ambitions in Laos, the Americans created a situation in which the only chance for stability depended on the complete success of their own policy. But their political allies there, whilst strong enough to disrupt the efforts of Souvanna Phouma to create a stable coalition, were unable to dominate the political scene to the extent of carrying a unified Laos into the American camp. The result was that the American presence, without being powerful enough to prevent further Communist intervention in Laotian politics, seemed to threaten both Chinese and North Vietnamese interests in Laos.

### III

It is now evident that Chinese strategy in Laos in 1956–8 may not have been entirely to Hanoi's liking. At the very least, the North Vietnamese were divided in their attitude towards the rest of Indochina. The Communist decision at Geneva to abandon the initial demand for full participation by the Khmer Issara and Pathet Lao seems to have been the responsibility of Zhou Enlai; and although Ho Chi Minh himself accepted the decision without protest, others in the Vietnamese Party probably opposed it. This clash, moreover, seems to reflect two quite different perceptions of the Indochinese revolution.

Ho himself, as a former Comintern official with general responsibility for the South Seas area in the years 1927–31, saw the Vietnamese revolution as one component in a historical sequence which would ultimately destroy colonial rule throughout the region. But the means to that end lay through a series of 'national' revolutions, and it was noticeable that when he unified the various Communist groups at Hong Kong in February 1930, he designated the new organisation the *Vietnamese* Communist Party. (Shortly afterwards he is said to have been involved in launching the Malayan Communist Party in Singapore.) It seems to have been Ho's opponents who had preferred the label *Indochinese* Communist Party in 1929, and who returned to that name in October 1930.[8] Although there is no evidence of any Communist activity in Laos and Cambodia at that period, the difference seems to have had more than nominal significance. Whilst one school of thought envisaged a South-East Asian revolution in which each national Party would conduct its own affairs, the other preferred to concentrate on the aim of overthrowing French colonial rule –

treating French Indochina as a single entity which would generate one coherent revolution.

From the point of view of those who believed in an integrated Indochinese revolution under Vietnamese leadership, China's policy towards Sihanouk and Souvanna Phouma during 1956 must have appeared as a threat to their own long-term aims. It was Le Duan who in early 1956 proposed a new armed struggle in both southern Vietnam and Cambodia, as a single arena of conflict. Although he was overruled by Hanoi, the fact that he could think in such terms suggests that he already favoured an *Indochinese* revolutionary perspective, which would make him unsympathetic to Zhou Enlai's approach. Something like a compromise between the two points of view seems to have emerged when the Party was allowed to re-emerge under the name of the *Vietnamese* Workers' Party. This left room for separate Party organisations to develop in Laos and Cambodia. Immediately following the Second Congress of the VNWP in February 1951 three national united fronts came into being, held together by a joint liaison committee which publicly celebrated its first anniversary on 3 March 1952.[9] Vietnam was represented by the Lien-Viet front of 1946 (renamed the Fatherland Front in 1955), whilst in Laos the Communists took over the 'Lao Issara' label previously used by the Bangkok government in exile. (They applied it to their own united front from August 1950.) In Cambodia the 'Khmer Issara' also had deep roots, but was linked to the Viet-Minh by mid-1951. It was these Laotian and Cambodian fronts which demanded the right to attend the Geneva Conference and sign any agreements reached, which would have given them a measure of international recognition; but their claims were rejected.

Much less is known about the Party organisations underlying the Cambodian and Laotian united fronts. In 1981 the (pro-Vietnamese) People's Revolutionary Party of Kampuchea claimed to have held its First Congress in June 1951, under the leadership of Son Ngoc Minh and Tou Samut.[10] Three years later, when the Khmer Issara dissolved its armed forces after the Geneva Agreements, the People's Party (Pracheachoun) surfaced as a legal organisation and took part in elections for the National Assembly. But its underground network was broken up by Sihanouk on at least two occasions between then and 1960. In the meantime it would appear that several thousand Khmer Issara forces retreated to North Vietnam, where they remained ready for an eventual resumption of armed struggle. Sometimes known as the 'Khmer Viet-Minh', they later became the pro-Hanoi element in the Khmer Rouge; but a rival faction led by Saloth Sar (Pol Pot) became increasingly opposed to Vietnamese domination of the movement and looked towards Peking. Therein lay the origins of the bitter conflict which emerged twenty years later for control of Democratic Kampuchea.

In Laos, documents found in later years show that a Lao People's Party (Phak Pasason Lao) was secretly established on 22 March 1955 but little is known of its activities. Nine months later, on 6 January 1956, the Lao Issara transformed itself into the Lao Patriotic Front (Neo Lao Hak Sat), which eventually sought recognition as a political party entitled to put up candidates for election. What is somewhat unclear is whether these organisations had closer links with Hanoi or with Peking. Another captured document referred to the Vietnamese Party *re-establishing* close relations with the Lao People's Party in May 1959, which suggests that during the preceding four years the relationship was less intimate than the Vietnamese would have liked.[11]

The ambivalence of Vietnamese Communist attitudes towards Laos was reflected in an apparent change in their view of the Geneva Agreement itself between 1955 and 1958. When he met the then Laotian prime minister Katay at Bandung, Pham Van Dong insisted that the question of negotiations between Vientiane and the Pathet Lao was an 'internal' one which the Laotians must be free to resolve without outside interference.[12] But in 1958 the North Vietnamese argued that 'peace in Indochina is indivisible' and that it was impossible for Laos to fulfil its Geneva obligations independently of the reunification of Vietnam. This later perception, however, had more to do with the idea of a single Indochinese revolution than with the actual contents of the Geneva Agreement on Laos. By that time, the whole situation, both in East Asia and in the Communist world, had begun to change fundamentally, and the possibility of a neutral Laos which had been opened up by the Geneva settlement was overtaken by events elsewhere in the world.

# Part II
## 1956–8

# 6 Vietnam and the Communist World Crisis

> At bedrock of the relations of the world socialist system and all the Communist and Workers' Parties lie the principles of Marxism – Leninism, the principles of proletarian internationalism which have been tested by life . . . .
>
> Marxism–Leninism calls for a creative application of the general principles of the socialist revolution and socialist construction, depending on the concrete conditions of each country . . . .
>
> The theory of Marxism–Leninism derives from dialectical materialism. This world outlook reflects the universal law of development of nature, society and human thinking.
>
> Moscow Declaration, November 1957

## I

The crisis which erupted in North Vietnam during 1956 must be interpreted on two levels: as an internal conflict within Vietnam, and as one element in the international Communist crisis which followed Khrushchev's attack on Stalin at the 20th Congress of the CPSU. The two aspects should not be regarded as contradictory alternatives between which the historian is free to make his own choice. The Vietnamese Communists themselves were always conscious of both their national and their international responsibilities and have been remarkably sensitive to changes of international line in Moscow.

In Stalinist terms North Vietnam, as a Democratic Republic under the dictatorship of a Workers' Party, had a status in the socialist camp very similar to that of the countries of Eastern Europe. In the 1950s its revolution was passing through the same phase of 'socialist transformation' which Eastern Europe had experienced in the late 1940s. The same could be said of China, which was to some extent a model for Vietnam, but differences of size made that comparison only partly appropriate. China was sufficiently large, and its Communist Party sufficiently long-established, to justify a sense of independence from Moscow if not of complete equality; whereas North Vietnam, like Poland or Hungary, was bound to experience a degree of dependence on one or both of the major Communist powers and to adjust its policies accordingly. The Vietnamese response to the 'de-Stalinisation' of 1956–7 exhibits remarkable parallels with events in Eastern Europe.

In spring 1956 the problem of international co-operation between Communist Parties in different countries was a matter of special concern to the Soviet leadership, following the dissolution of Stalin's Cominform which had been agreed at the time of the 20th Congress in February and was formally announced on 17 April. The question of whether some new organisation should take its place was still being debated, and in a conversation with the Yugoslav ambassador to Moscow on 2 April Khrushchev revealed that one proposal under consideration was to create four new regional organisations: respectively for Eastern Europe, Western Europe, the Americas and Asia.[1] We have no means of knowing whether the plan was actually implemented. Certainly the existence of such a network was never publicised; any formal and public organisation would doubtless have been opposed by Tito, whose visit to Moscow in June 1956 was conditional upon the abolition of the Cominform. Nor would it have been acceptable to the Chinese if it meant greater discipline from Moscow. But the conversation itself indicates the direction of Soviet thinking, and Moscow's interest in closer relations with Asian Communist Parties was not something that could be ignored. On the same occasion Khrushchev mentioned particularly the absurdity of having no formal relations between the CPSU and the PKI in Indonesia. He also alluded to Mikoyan's current visit to Asian countries, during which the Soviet deputy premier was to raise this question with various Party leaders; on that same day (2 April) Mikoyan was arriving in Hanoi.

Shortly before his visit, the North Vietnamese endorsed the formal resolution of the CPSU Congress after hearing a first-hand account of its proceedings from Truong Chinh and Le Duc Tho. The implications of the new Soviet line were no doubt analysed in some detail, both in talks with Mikoyan himself and at the VNWP

TABLE 6.1    *Events in Eastern Europe and North Vietnam, April–August 1956*

| Eastern Europe | North Vietnam |
| --- | --- |
| **April 1956** | |
| | 31 Mar.: VNWP Politburo issued a communique fully supporting the resolutions of CPSU 20th Congress, (attended by Truong Chinh and Le Duc Tho). |
| | 2–6 Apr.: Mikoyan visited Hanoi; absence of formal joint statement noted. |
| 17 Apr.: Dissolution of Cominform announced by *Pravda*. | 19–24 Apr.: VNWP 9th Plenum: Ho Chi Minh emphasised theoretical weaknesses, need for more criticism from below. |
| 18–26 Apr.: Khrushchev, Bulganin visited London. | |
| 23 Apr.: Polish government invited criticism by Diet; followed by amnesty of 30,000 political prisoners. | (Decision against new armed struggle in the South?) |
| **June–August 1956** | |
| 1–23 June: Tito's visit to Moscow. | June–July: Van Tien Dung in USSR. |
| 20 June: Khrushchev–Tito declaration. | |
| 27 June: Hungary: Petofi Circle demanded end to censorship of press. (Suppressed by Rakosi, 30 June.) | 26 June: Decision to reduce armed forces by 80 000 men; but report of anti-aircraft training. |
| 28 June: Poland: Poznan riots–revolt suppressed. | |
| | 10 July: *Nhan-Dan* editorial reaffirming support for CPSU 20th Congress. |
| 17 July: Hungary: Rakosi replaced by Geroe and Kadar as Party leaders; Mikoyan and Suslov in Budapest. | 18 July: Council of Ministers communiqué, affirming basic completion of land reform. |
| 18–20 July: Poland: rehabilitation of Gomulka by Central Committee; Zhukov and Bulganin in Warsaw. | 18–22 July: VNFF Central Committee session; decisions to seek implementation of Geneva Agreements, to consolidate North, to broaden the Front. |
| | 30 July: Phan Khoi's letter criticising Party leadership in the cultural field. |
| | 2–4 Aug.: Local congresses to review land reform. |
| | 18 Aug.: Ho Chi Minh's letter to rural cadres on successful completion of land reform; recognises some errors. |
| | 29 Aug.: First issue of non-Party journal *Giai Pham Mua Thu* ('Literary Works of Autumn'). |

Central Committee's 9th Plenum (19–24 April). The absence of any published communiqúe at the end of the visit may have reflected disagreement on international issues, as well as on the more specific question of South Vietnam. In the end, however, the 9th Plenum appears to have endorsed the line of the 20th Congress and to have accepted a policy of restraint towards the South. Both these decisions must be seen against the background of a profound sense of uncertainty which must have pervaded the whole Communist world when Stalin came under attack. Khrushchev's 'secret speech', together with his public redefinition of the international line, were not necessarily welcome in all quarters – either in Moscow itself or in Peking and Hanoi; but no Party could afford to ignore the change (and perhaps conflict) taking place within the Soviet leadership.

One aspect of de-Stalinisation which came to the fore at precisely the same moment in Poland and North Vietnam – and also in China – was that of encouraging criticism from below. It was an important theme of Ho Chi Minh's speech at the 9th Plenum on 24 April, although at that stage he did not elaborate upon its implications for agrarian policy.[2] Almost simultaneously the Polish government invited criticism from the Diet and decreed an amnesty for several thousand political prisoners. In China too an important meeting of cadres heard Mao's speech of 25 April 1956, 'On the Ten Major Relationships', which marked the end of 'socialist upsurge' for the time being and the adoption of a more 'moderate' approach to socialist construction. In early May another speech by Mao anticipated the slogan 'Let a hundred flowers bloom, a hundred schools of thought contend' – implying greater freedom of debate.

A second stage in North Vietnam's adjustment to the new situation came on 18 July with the publication of a statement by the Council of Ministers to the effect that the 'anti-feudal task' was now basically complete. No details were given of the state of affairs on the ground, and it is by no means certain that the fifth phase of agrarian reform *had* been allowed to run its full course before the brakes were applied. Once again the Vietnamese move coincided precisely with changes in Europe, after disturbances in Poland and Hungary at the end of June. In Warsaw the anti-Stalinist Gomulka was re-habilitated on 18 July in the presence of Bulganin and Zhukov; whilst in Budapest, Mikoyan and Suslov supervised the replacement of the Hungarian Party leader Rakosi. There seems to have been no such direct Soviet intervention in Hanoi; nevertheless the question of replacing Truong Chinh may already have arisen. The conduct of agrarian reform was reviewed at a series of provincial conferences in early August, during one of which the leading activist of the Hanoi municipality appears to have made a self-criticism.[3] A further stage in the conflict within the Vietnamese leadership began on 18 August when Ho Chi Minh circulated a letter to cadres openly admitting that 'errors' had occurred during land reform.

This gradual slowing down in the socialist transformation of North Vietnam was accompanied by a more tolerant attitude towards criticism of the authorities by non-Communists within the Fatherland Front. During the 1940s there had been a deliberate effort to draw the 'national bourgeoisie' and even 'patriotic landlords' into the anti-imperialist struggle by abandoning the slogans of agrarian revolution. The united front of 1946 (the Lien-Viet) had included two non-Communist political Parties: the Democratic Party founded in 1944 and the Socialist Party of 1946, some of whose leaders were allowed to play a part in the administrative work of the Front and even to become government ministers. That policy had continued into the 1950s. But from 1953–4 peasant mobilisation and land reform (soon to be followed by the transformation of trade and handicrafts) challenged the very existence of the bourgeoisie and rich peasantry as a class. Now, the opportunity for more open criticism produced an inevitable reaction. A publication entitled 'Literary Works' (*Giai-Pham*) appeared as a single volume in March 1956 and later grew into a series, lasting from the end of August until mid-December that year. In September there appeared the still more outspoken *Nhan-Van* ('Humanities') – not to be confused with the Party daily *Nhan-Dan* – sponsored by the veteran nationalist Phan Khoi.[4] The initial target of these journals was literary censorship by Party officials; but as time went on they began to satirise the bureaucracy at large and by autumn they were attacking land reform specifically.

Such criticism, however, coming from outside the Party, is not sufficient cause to explain the major crisis in the Hanoi leadership which had emerged by the time of the Central Committee's 10th Plenum sometime in September 1956. Saigon's specialists in psychological warfare were free to interpret events in North Vietnam as a revolt of the masses against Communist oppression, placing special emphasis on public criticism of both land reform and the bureaucracy; and it was in their interests to emphasise the disillusion prevailing amongst non-Communist politicians who had chosen to live in the North. But the real crisis arose within the leadership of the Party. Once that had been resolved it was not too difficult for the government to reimpose press censorship as a first step towards handling what Mao Zedong called 'contradictions among the people'. The historian's problem is to understand, if possible, the issues which divided the Party itself at this critical juncture.


## II


At any given time the lines of debate within the Vietnam Workers' Party probably reflected parallel differences in Moscow and Peking; but that was never the whole story. Understanding the full complexity of Hanoi politics requires a knowledge of the Party's own past history and of individual relationships (and rivalries) which had grown up over several decades. By the mid-1950s the Party embraced a wide diversity of revolutionary experience and international contacts which made its position unique in the 'socialist camp'. The major power-struggle going on in the Politburo by 1956, although probably occasioned by the more general trend of 'de-Stalinisation', had to be resolved as a crisis within the Vietnamese Party. Events elsewhere might serve to strengthen or weaken the position of individual leaders in relation to their rivals; the final outcome was probably decided in Hanoi.

Ho Chi Minh had spent periods of exile both in the Soviet Union and in China from the 1920s, and it was his earlier status as Comintern delegate that had made him undisputed leader of the Party since 1945. But it would be a mistake to regard the history of Vietnamese Communism, as some Western writers have done, as no more than an extension of Ho's biography. When he returned to Vietnam in 1945 not long before the August Revolution, Ho was dependent on the support of colleagues who had nurtured the movement inside the country during his absence, and who had survived numerous French attempts to suppress it. They were men who had joined the Party at different times, had been active in different provinces, had become defenders of ideological and tactical points of view that were often in conflict. Not all of them were closely associated with Ho himself and the task of maintaining a consensus amongst them was not easy. Ho had the advantage of age, having been born in 1894 (or possibly earlier) making him at least eleven years senior to the next youngest leader Hoang Van Hoan.[5] But his views were not necessarily identical with those of other leaders, and age alone did not guarantee that he would get his way at all times.

Factional conflict in the Party had a long history, going back even to the time of its foundation in 1929–30, and each subsequent phase of Party history produced new differences and rivalries. At the same time, tight bonds were created by shared revolutionary experience – notably the harshness of imprisonment on the island of Con-Son (Poulo Condore) where many of those who led the Party in the 1950s spent the period 1931–6. As the movement expanded in the late 1930s and 1940s, there was also room for rivalry between groups working in different areas of the country. The Cao-Bang base area created by Ho himself with the assistance of Hoang Van Hoan, Vo Nguyen Giap and Pham Van Dong between 1942 and 1945, was distinct from Truong Chinh's network in lowland Tongking; whilst both were separated from key areas of revolutionary support in the Centre and South. The two former groups were also more open to Chinese influence, whereas southern-based Communists were more likely to have links with the French Communist Party and with Moscow. Other lines of division emerged in the 1950s as it became necessary to assign responsibility for particular spheres of activity to different leaders. Some conflicts can best be understood in terms of the opposing interests of institutional entities within the revolution: the Party, the Front and its mass organisations, the government administration, the armed forces. Some leaders began to establish specific power bases within an expanding system, so that rivalries between them may have been partly personal, partly ideological, but also partly institutional. We have seen too how one group of leaders became especially identified with the struggle in the South, which had to be abandoned after the Geneva Partition.

It is not easy to reduce these various aspects of the power struggle to a single coherent pattern. The following attempt to distinguish between three groups within the leadership as it existed in 1955–6 may make the situation slightly less confusing. The first group was closely associated with Ho Chi Minh himself, and its main areas of responsibility lay in the fields of government, diplomacy and military affairs. The second group consisted of men who had spent most of their revolutionary careers in Bac-Bo (Tongking), and who after 1950 became important in the Party machine and the mass organisations. The third group comprised those whose main experiences in the early 1950s had been in southern Vietnam, but only two of these were actually born south of the 17th parallel, and Le Duc Tho may properly belong with the 'Northerners'.

| *Ho's Group* | *'Northerners'* | *'Southerners'* |
|---|---|---|
| Ho Chi Minh | Truong Chinh | Le Duan |
| Hoang Van Hoan | Hoang Quoc Viet | Pham Hung |
| Pham Van Dong | Le Van Luong | Nguyen Duy Trinh |
| Vo Nguyen Giap | Le Thanh Nghi | Le Duc Tho |
| | Nguyen Chi Thanh | |

This represents a more complex pattern than that presupposed by American analysts in the 1960s, who habitually identified only two 'factions' in Hanoi, one 'pro-Chinese' and the other 'pro-Soviet'. Several members of the Politburo, it is true, had had a special relationship with the Chinese Communist Party at one time or another: notably Ho himself, Hoang Van Hoan, and probably also Nguyen Chi Thanh – who according to one account was trained in Yenan in the early 1940s. (By the time of the Sino-Vietnamese conflict of 1978–9 when Hoang Van Hoan actually 'defected' to Peking, Ho and Thanh were both dead.) Other leading figures, especially Truong Chinh, were ideologically imbued with 'Maoist' ideas but were probably less closely identified with the Chinese Party as such. What is remarkable is that, apart from Ho, no member of the Vietnamese Politburo of 1956 appears to have been trained in Moscow before the Second World War. Such a group had existed but had been banished from the top leadership during the August Revolution, and some who later became identifiably 'pro-Soviet', notably Le Duan, seem merely to have been those least close to the Chinese Party. In any case no individual Vietnamese leader should be seen purely as an instrument of 'the Russians' or 'the Chinese' in a nationalistic sense. Faced with the Sino-Soviet 'split', the natural inclination of most Vietnamese leaders was to promote harmony between Moscow and Peking rather than to allow themselves to become permanently divided by conflicting international loyalties. Their aim was to achieve their own consensus in accordance with the international line of Marxism–Leninism at any given time, and so establish a basis for disciplined action within the

Party. Very seldom did an individual leader challenge that consensus to the point of having to be permanently excluded from the Politburo.


# III


At the core of the power struggle of 1955–6 lay the agrarian issue.[6] Originally decreed by the Party and the National Assembly at the end of 1953, land reform was in full swing during 1954–5 and its early phases were carried out in an orderly way (in areas already liberated from the French) as a means of recruiting peasant support for 'people's war'. It involved two stages of mass mobilisation: the first restricted to the regulation and reduction of rents and interest rates, the second involving actual redistribution of land. By the autumn of 1955 the first four phases of agrarian reform, covering both stages of the process in the affected areas, had been completed across a substantial part of North Vietnam; but much remained to be done. The critical period came with the fifth phase, from November 1955, which had to be undertaken more rapidly. At that point the two stages of mobilisation were combined, and the campaign incorporated additional measures against 'counter-revolutionaries' who were deemed to be sabotaging the programme. This speeding up of agrarian reform was in keeping with the current trend in China, where a speech by Mao at the end of July 1955 heralded a 'socialist upsurge' in the Chinese countryside. At the end of October another Chinese instruction inaugurated the more rapid socialist transformation of industry and handicrafts. In both countries the 'mass line' of rapid change remained in force until the spring of 1956.

It was during this fifth phase that land reform began to get out of hand. There is little need in the present context to enter into the question of 'excesses' committed against landlords and better-off peasants, some of whom had been loyal supporters of the Viet-Minh and even members of the Party. With the limited evidence so far available it is impossible to settle the issue whether larger or smaller numbers of people were executed. But some indication of the seriousness of the situation can be gleaned from a report of 25 November 1955 when Chinese and Soviet cultural groups, which had been on tour, suddenly left the country after two members of the

Chinese delegation had been killed in an incident outside Hanoi.[7] The campaign seems to have been especially violent in the Hanoi suburbs where one would expect the rich peasant element to be strongly represented. It was also very complex in 'Interzone IV' (the provinces of Thanh-Hoa and Nghe-Tinh) where the Viet-Minh had held power since 1945–6 without previously disturbing the relationships of production at grass-roots level. One of the points made by Vo Nguyen Giap in his speech of 30 October 1956 criticising the conduct of land reform was that it had failed to distinguish between the landlords and rich peasants as a class and the many individuals who had supported the resistance, and had even sent their sons to fight with the Viet-Minh. The latter had in some cases been imprisoned during land reform, or even worse; and their position in the villages had been taken over by 'new' cadres drawn from the poor peasantry.[8]

The long-term goal of socialist transformation was not, however, the only aspect of the agrarian reform – and probably not the most controversial. As well as the confiscation and redistribution of land, the campaign involved a revolutionary transformation of local administration. Until the reorganisation approved by the Central Committee's 8th Plenum in August 1955, government affairs had been largely dominated by the group in the leadership most closely associated with Ho Chi Minh. Ho himself, who ceased to be prime minister at that time, had long been grooming Pham Van Dong for that office; whilst another of his associates of the early 1940s, Vo Nguyen Giap, had also played an active part in government as well as being commander of the PAVN. In the reorganisation, however, the prime minister's office was enlarged to include at least two senior leaders from outside Ho's own group: the 'Southerner' Pham Hung and the 'Northerner' Le Van Luong, an associate of Truong Chinh. As deputy minister of the interior, Luong was also effectively in charge of that ministry since his superior was a non-Party figurehead. Likewise Ho Viet Thang, as deputy minister of agriculture also under a non-Party man, had party responsibilities which included the creation of mass associations among the peasantry. Moreover Le Van Luong and Ho Viet Thang seemed bent on using their government positions to undermine Pham Van Dong's potential opposition to the acceleration of land reform.

In effect, Truong Chinh and his associates were mounting a bid for greater control of rural affairs at the grass roots by making the mass organisations (directly under the Party) more powerful than the established administrative hierarchy (under the Council of Ministers). The land reform campaign was by this time generating its own hierarchy of tribunals, closely associated with the peasant associations but outside the jurisdiction of local administrative committees. Once again we can turn to Giap's speech in October for confirmation that this was an issue of some consequence. He deplored the emergence of separate land reform tribunals, which had 'invaded the powers of Party committees and local authorities'. Although we have few details about what actually happened on the ground, the conflict may have been almost comparable with the Chinese 'cultural revolution' ten years later. The subsequent defeat of the land reform group at the VNWP 10th Plenum – which dismissed Le Van Luong and Ho Viet Thang from their Party and government positions as well as forcing Truong Chinh himself to resign as Party secretary-general – amounted to a reassertion of the authority of Pham Van Dong in the administrative sphere.

Finally, the land reform campaign may have involved a potential – if not actual – confrontation between the Party (with its mass organisations) and the armed forces. Following the Soviet model, the PAVN had its own political department of Party commissars presided over by Nguyen Chi Thanh. Within that framework Vo Nguyen Giap and other generals were trying to modernise and professionalise the army after Dien-Bien-Phu. But Truong Chinh's concept of peasant mobilisation implied a more 'Maoist' approach to military affairs, with continuing emphasis on the militia and 'people's war', and his ultimate aim may have been to subordinate the professional commanders not merely to the Party but to a new form of control through mass organisations. An article published on the eve of the fifth phase of land reform, signed by General Tran Do, emphasised that the task of building the army and strengthening national defence was one for the whole people, not for the armed forces alone. An even more serious criticism was implicit in another article, appearing on 2 April 1956, which accused the PAVN of tolerating 'rightist thinking' and 'landlord mentality'.[9] It is possible therefore that Vo Nguyen Giap, in announcing the official criticism of land reform at a public meeting on 30 October, may have had his own interest in reversing some of the more extreme changes of the preceding twelve months.

## IV

The critical 10th Plenum of the VNWP Central Committee met sometime during September 1956, possibly towards the end of the month, and it was then that the decision was finally taken to replace Truong Chinh as secretary-general and to remove Le Van Luong and Ho Viet Thang from their government and Party positions. Such important changes were not agreed without a major political crisis and the decisions of the Plenum were not publicly announced until the end of October. For the time being Ho Chi Minh himself took charge of the Party Secretariat; and early in 1957 he recalled Hoang Van Hoan from Peking, where he had been ambassador since 1950, to assist him in Hanoi. Another associate of Truong Chinh, the 'Northerner' Hoang Quoc Viet, appears to have retained his place in the Politburo at the 10th Plenum, but by 1957 he too had been dropped.

Once again it is possible to observe parallel events elsewhere in the Communist world. In August 1956 a conflict in the Korean Workers' Party between Kim Ilsung and his enemies came to a head at a Central Committee Plenum in Pyongyang.[10] Kim defeated an attempt to depose him, but in the event was prevented from completely purging the opposition by the intervention of Peng Dehuai (former commander of the Chinese People's Volunteers in Korea). The Soviet deputy premier Mikoyan paid a secret visit to Pyongyang in early September to restore unity in the KWP. Then from 15 to 27 September the CCP held its 8th Congress in Peking; Mikoyan was present there too, whilst the Vietnamese were represented by Hoang Quoc Viet and a more junior figure To Huu. Soviet criticism of Stalin's 'cult of personality' was reflected in the removal of all personal references to Mao from the new CCP constitution: a decision for which Liu Shaoqi and Deng Xiaoping (who had succeeded Liu as Party secretary-general) would be severely criticised during the cultural revolution ten years later. A further indication that the 'Maoist' line had suffered a major reverse was the demotion of the radical Kang Sheng from full to alternate membership of the Chinese Politburo; nor was Peng Zhen so prominent as before.[11]

The Vietnamese decision to curb the influence of Truong Chinh and his radical line was thus in keeping with developments in China, whilst the failure to purge him completely had some parallel in North Korea. But the full complexity of the crisis in Hanoi remains shrouded in mystery, with crucial questions still un-answered after a quarter of a century. During October the decisions of the VNWP 10th Plenum were discussed by three consecutive meetings of leading cadres. Following the return of Hoang Quoc Viet from Peking early in the month, a conference of 760 Party officials met from 8 to 21 October to 'study' the resolution of the Plenum. A special meeting of the Fatherland Front was then given a report on land reform. Finally, between 23 and 31 October, a conference of military officers continued the process of 'studying' the resolution. Only towards the end of this latter meeting were the plenum decisions finally made public.[12]

The interval between the two most important of these con-ferences (21–3 October) seems to have been a turning point of considerable significance. It was also a critical moment inter-nationally: the crisis in Poland was resolved by restoring Gomulka to power, but the same few days saw the start of an even more serious crisis in Budapest and it was probably around 21 October that the Soviet leaders finally made up their minds on a firm line there. The outcome was the Hungarian rising and Soviet military intervention in early November. Another important development was the Soviet government statement of 30 October defining the basis of future relations between Communist states, which permitted a new period of Sino-Soviet harmony and may also have assisted the Vietnamese in resolving their own problems.

One other event which occurred on 21 October, however, is less easily fitted into the international picture. On the 22nd Hanoi Radio reported the death the previous day of General Nguyen Son, perhaps the most 'pro-Chinese' of all Vietnamese Communist military leaders, who had been virtually banished to China by Ho Chi Minh in the late 1940s. He had already spent much of the 1920s and 1930s in exile there and was said to have taken part in the Long March as a soldier in the Chinese PLA. He returned to Vietnam during the August Revolution and played an active role in running northern Central Vietnam, but then clashed with Vo Nguyen Giap and was sent back to China. According to one account, his decision to return home again was made in August 1956 because he was suffering from cancer; the official obituary merely said that he died in hospital after a long illness. But the story circulating in Saigon three weeks later, told by refugees coming out of the North, implied a much more dramatic turn of events. According to that version Nguyen Son had been sentenced to death by the Party Central

TABLE 6.2  *Events in Eastern Europe and North Vietnam, October–November 1956*

| Eastern Europe | North Vietnam |
|---|---|
| 5 Oct.: Tito ended more talks with Khrushchev, in Crimea. | |
| 6 Oct.: Hungary: Central Committee agreed to state funeral for Rajk. | 8–21 Oct.: Congress of 760 Party cadres, to study resolution of VNWP 10th Plenum held in (late?) September. |
| 13 Oct.: Poland: Politburo agreed to restore Gomulka to power (on 19th). | |
| 19–20 Oct.: Poland: Central Committee met (8th Plenum); Gomulka again first secretary of Party. (Khrushchev, Mikoyan, Molotov and Kaganovich in Warsaw at time). | 21 Oct.: Death of Nguyen Son reported. |
| 22 Oct.: Hungary: Petofi Circle's ten-point programme for reforms followed by demonstrations on 23rd. | 22 Oct.: VNFF meeting heard report on land reform. |
| 24 Oct.: Nagy appointed premier. | 23–31 Oct.: Military conference studied 10th Plenum resolution. |
| 24–25 Oct.: Mikoyan and Suslov in Budapest: Kadar replaced Geroe. | |
| 30 Oct.: Soviet declaration on relations between socialist states, welcomed by Poland and China. | 30 Oct.: Announcement of VNWP 10th Plenum decisions, including replacement of Truong Chinh as Party secretary, removal of Le Van Luong, etc. Speech by Vo Nguyen Giap in Hanoi. |
| 30–31 Oct.: Nagy announced a multi-party coalition and Hungary's intention to leave Warsaw Pact. | 30–31 Oct.: VNFF meeting: 'self-criticism' by Truong Chinh. |
| 4 Nov.: Soviet troops intervened in Hungary: Nagy overthrown. | |
| | 2–14 Nov.: Disturbances in district of Quynh-Luu (Nghe-An). |
| | 7 Nov.: Council of Ministers decisions on rectification of land reform errors; abolition of special tribunals. |
| 11 Nov.: Speech by Tito, criticising Soviet action in Hungary. | |

Committee and had been arrested by Truong Chinh and Vo Nguyen Giap, who mobilised a military unit for the purpose; after that he had been taken to Hanoi and executed. If that story contained even a grain of truth, it suggests a crisis far more serious than the revolt of a handful of intellectuals and local groups of dissident peasants. The very fact of Nguyen Son's return to the country in the middle of August cannot have been entirely without political significance. At his funeral moreover, both Truong Chinh and Vo Nguyen Giap were conspicuous by their absence; Ho Chi Minh and Pham Van Dong placed wreaths on the coffin, but the oration was delivered by the second deputy minister of defence, Hoang Anh.[13] If Nguyen Son did indeed attempt a rebellion of some kind, it is likely to have centred on 'Interzone IV' (the provinces of Thanh-Hoa, Nghe-An and Ha-Tinh) where he had been military commander for a time following the August Revolution. Discontent amongst military units there would go far towards explaining the delicacy of the situation between the actual meeting of the 10th Plenum in September and the publication of its decisions.

A press conference to report the decisions of the 10th Plenum was finally held on 30 October 1956; on the same day a meeting of 10,000 people in Hanoi heard Vo Nguyen Giap outline the new situation and criticise the 'excesses' of land reform. Truong Chinh also made a self-criticism before a meeting of the Fatherland Front, at which a number of bourgeois critics of land reform had their say. The outcome was a 'rectification of errors' campaign, to be conducted by the Party itself, which was intended to correct mistakes village by village, district by district. Shortly afterwards there occurred the one acknowledged case of anti-Communist revolt against the Hanoi regime: the Quynh-Luu incident of 2–14 November 1956. It broke out in a Catholic district of Nghe-An province, where Ngo Dinh Diem was known to have connections, and it may even have been instigated from the South. But if reports in *Nhan-Dan* are at all credible, it was actually a very small-scale affair and easily suppressed. Its importance was probably much exaggerated in Saigon.[14]

## V

Things were returning to normal, therefore, by the time Zhou Enlai and General He Long visited Hanoi from 18 to 22 November 1956 at the start of a tour of Asian countries. The suggestion that their visit was prompted by desire to protect a 'pro-Chinese faction' against further victimisation by its 'pro-Soviet' rivals in the Hanoi Politburo is inherently unlikely. In any case Ho Chi Minh was at least as 'pro-Chinese' as Truong Chinh, from whom he differed essentially on ideological issues. Zhou's real purpose was probably to ensure that the outcome of the crisis did not damage Sino-Vietnamese friendship; that was certainly the main theme of his public statements during the visit.[15] But differences of nuance between his speeches and those of his hosts suggest that he failed to persuade the Vietnamese to follow China's strong line on the issue of 'great nation chauvinism', which already amounted to indirect criticism of the Soviet Union. The Vietnamese in turn could not persuade Zhou to support specific proposals for further action by the Geneva co-chairman to insist on a settlement of the reunification issue. Shortly after his departure *Nhan-Dan* (24 November) tried to revive the idea of reconvening the Geneva Conference, but without effect. At this point the diplomatic struggle may be said to have reached a dead-end except as a propaganda vehicle. But the North Vietnamese refused to abandon reunification as their ultimate objective.

Whatever may have happened in Hanoi during the crisis of October 1956, one of its consequences was a reaffirmation of the revolutionary struggle in the South. In his speech of 30 October, Vo Nguyen Giap attacked those who had conducted the agrarian reform as if the destruction of feudalism was the only thing that mattered and had failed to relate it to the tasks of the revolution as a whole. The 'socialist transformation' of the North was certainly important; but it must not become divorced from the need to complete the 'national democratic' revolution in the South. Giap went on to criticise the view that the reunification issue was merely a 'foreign relations struggle', not directly involving revolution. When his speech is related to Le Duan's document of November 1956 ('The Path of the Revolution in the South') it is clear that these two leaders were engaged in defining a new Party line on reunification, which was probably confirmed by the VNWP Central Committee at its 11th Plenum sometime before the end of December. The theme of the unity of the Vietnamese revolution was again stressed in a report to the National Assembly by Pham Hung, the leader in charge of Southern affairs in Hanoi, on 3 January 1957.[16]

If the international Communist line precluded the revival of full-scale armed struggle in the South, it was still possible to begin laying the foundations for a political revolution. A more vigorous revolutionary strategy seems also to have been approved by the second conference of the Nam-Bo regional Party committee at the beginning of 1957, calling for mobilisation of as many discontented elements in the population as possible. The aim was not to promote an immediate revolutionary struggle, but to concentrate on the specific grievances of such groups as workers in industry and on plantations, amongst whom there was an expansion of strike activity from late 1956. Richer farmers were also encouraged to protest against Diem's resettlement schemes and the shortcomings of his decrees on land reform, whilst small traders were organised to protest against restrictive regulations. At the same time, without reactivating its own armed forces, the Party appears to have supported moves by other dissident leaders to establish a 'joint staff' in December 1956. A mass break-out from Bien-Hoa jail in the middle of that month gave the dissident forces a new supply of weapons.[17]

The crisis of 1956 in North Vietnam was thus important not only for the North, where it certainly involved a major change of line, but also for the revival of the struggle in the South. In April it had seemed as if the partition of Vietnam might become an accepted fact of international life despite Hanoi's reluctance to accept it. By the end of the year the North Vietnamese had taken a clear decision not to abandon the struggle entirely. They would not openly defy the line of 'peaceful co-existence' but they would find ways to circumvent its consequences. In that sense the outcome of the crisis seems to mark a new starting-point in the evolution of the southern struggle: the first tentative step along the road to a new war.

# 7 Asia at the Crossroads

At present, overt aggression and militant subversion are less likely than
an intensified campaign of Communist political, cultural and economic
penetration in the area. The political instability, economic backward-
ness, export problems, and extreme nationalism of these countries
provide many opportunities for Communist exploitation by trade and
economic assistance, conventional political and diplomatic activity, and
extensive infiltration. This offensive now constitutes a threat to US
interests more subtle and more difficult to cope with than other threats.

US National Security Council policy document,
September 1956

I

Despite Le Duan's enthusiasm for the 'path of revolution', South
Vietnam ceased to be an area of international conflict during the
years 1955–7. In order to understand how this happened, and also
how the Vietnamese struggle eventually recovered its international
importance in 1958–9, it is necessary to consider events elsewhere in
Asia, and to relate them to the even broader, global strategies of the
United States and the Communist powers. Khrushchev's tour of
India, Burma and Afghanistan at the end of 1955 had dramatised a
new departure in Soviet policy towards Asia. Coming in the wake of
Zhou Enlai's diplomatic success at Bandung the previous April, it
heralded a new phase of political and economic competition
between the global powers which lasted until mid-1958. The
revolutionary line of the late 1940s and early 1950s now gave way to
a strategy of encouraging 'genuinely independent' nationalist
regimes to adopt a policy of neutrality and to reject American
demands for total commitment to the 'free world'. Among leading
advocates of this line in Moscow it seems reasonable to number
Khrushchev himself and perhaps also Marshal Zhukov, who
preferred to emphasise military strength and political alliances

rather than ideological discipline and international class war as the basis of Soviet policy. It was only during the year following Zhukov's fall from grace, in October 1957, that the pendulum began to swing back towards a more revolutionary international line.

The general effect of the change of 1955–6 was to shift the focus of East–West conflict in Asia away from countries already committed to either the socialist or imperialist 'camp' – and also from those which might soon be 'ripe' for Communist-led revolution – toward countries whose governments were seeking to remain neutral. The latter areas now became focal points of rivalry in a struggle for influence among the global powers. Although there was a strong possibility that the new Communist line would sooner or later lead to rivalry between the Soviet Union and China, the United States was more immediately concerned about the threat to its own power in those parts of Asia – especially South-East Asia and the Middle East – where it felt most vulnerable. A policy review approved by the NSC on 5 September 1956 defined the political, economic and diplomatic offensive of the Communist powers as a new type of challenge which must be met by an effective American response.[1]

One important aspect of 'peaceful competition' during 1956–8 was a new Communist economic strategy, designed to enable Asian countries to reduce their dependence on the capitalist world market in disposing of their primary produce. The Korean War and its aftermath had created a rising demand for raw materials from South-East Asia, but by 1956–7 the boom was giving way to a slump – aggravated by the fear of recession in the industrialised West. As prices fell, nationalist governments in Asia had every reason to take seriously Soviet and Chinese offers of bilateral agreements for the sale of their produce, if not at higher prices than on world markets then at least in direct exchange for manufactured goods and machinery. During 1956–8 an increasing number of such bilateral agreements were being reached and the United States was becoming seriously alarmed. The logical Western response was to expand economic and technical aid programmes in order to promote Asian development, and American confidence in their ability to compete successfully with the Communists in that sphere would be amply justified in the long term. But in the short term what was required was a boost in the demand for raw materials and food stuffs.

The key to the success of the capitalist economic recovery in Asia lay in promoting the industrial expansion of Japan, which became a vital aim of American policy after 1956. The resulting economic 'miracle' not only ensured the continuing political stability of Japan itself but also had an impact on South-East Asia. The growing Japanese demand for materials was accompanied by the negotiation of reparations agreements – to compensate countries of the region for war damage – which helped to finance a new pattern of economic relations in the region. Between 1954 and 1958 three such agreements were signed – with Burma, the Philippines and Indonesia – and in addition long-term Japanese loans were arranged on favourable terms.[2] Thailand, which had been Japan's ally during the war, secured the release of funds in Tokyo which had been blocked since 1945. The general effect, therefore, was to channel resources into South-East Asia in much the same way as Marshall Aid had been pumped into Western Europe in the late 1940s.

This economic dimension was not the only important feature of the Soviet 'diplomatic offensive' in Asia and the Middle East in the mid-1950s, however. Encouraging 'neutral' regimes to be genuinely independent also involved offers of military assistance, usually in the form of Soviet loans to buy more sophisticated weapons either from the USSR or from its East European allies. Moscow's first success in that direction was the announcement that Egypt was to purchase arms from Czechoslovakia in September 1955. Two years later, in September 1957, the Americans were even more alarmed by Soviet plans to sell weapons to Syria, in circumstances which seemed likely to lead to greater Communist participation in the affairs of that country. Whereas the United States had always regarded Nasser as a potential friend and had taken his side during the Suez crisis of 1956, they regarded Soviet designs on Syria as a direct threat to Turkey and Iraq as members of the Baghdad Pact. There followed a critical period of international manoeuvering in which the Americans finally became reconciled to a political union of Syria and Egypt, under Nasser's leadership, in the United Arab Republic. After that it was unlikely that either of the two countries would join the Baghdad Pact; but Syria was no longer in danger of being drawn into the Soviet sphere.[3] Whatever the rights and wrongs of that affair, it illustrates clearly the growth of United States concern about Soviet ambitions during 1957.

The provision of Soviet arms arose also in the case of Indonesia, whose President Sukarno visited the USSR in September 1956. An agreement signed about that time, ostensibly for a Soviet economic loan to Indonesia, later turned out to have been the first step towards the supply of East European weapons – which finally materialised at a critical moment in March 1958.[4] In the interval the question was whether Sukarno could gain sufficient control over the political process in Indonesia itself to overcome the reluctance of right-wing politicians to accept economic and military ties with the Soviet bloc. The Russians thus had a keen interest in the outcome of the political battle inaugurated by Sukarno's *konsepsi* speech of 21 February 1957, which was to culminate in his imposition of 'guided democracy' in July 1959. It would be absurd to pretend that those events represented nothing more than an international power game; but as so often in the recent history of South-East Asia, 'internal' politics were closely intertwined with 'international relations'. From the Soviet point of view, an important development was the visit to Indonesia by President Voroshilov in May 1957, during an Asian tour which also took in China, North Vietnam and India. It was probably about that time that Moscow persuaded the Chinese that the main responsibility for relations with Indonesia should lie with the Soviet Union, whilst the Chinese would be responsible for mainland South-East Asia – a division of labour which appears to have lasted until the spring of 1959. During his visit, Voroshilov spoke in support of Indonesia's claim to West Irian (Dutch New Guinea) which was to remain the focal point of Sukarno's anti-imperialism until the issue was finally resolved in his favour in mid-1962. The Russians did not, as we shall see, have things all their own way in Indonesia. But as in the case of Syria and Egypt, the Americans had to abandon the idea of persuading Indonesia to join the regional anti-Communist pact in this case, SEATO.

All this took place against a background of increasing concern in Washington about intelligence reports that Soviet scientists had succeeded in developing an intercontinental rocket. Although such

a move could not immediately change the balance of military power
in the world, it was likely to increase the confidence and prestige of
the Communist powers. Soviet preparations for a test programme
were first detected towards the end of 1956, and early the following
summer pictures taken by the experimental U-2 'spy-plane'
confirmed the existence of a site from which long-range tests were
being carried out.[5] A public Soviet announcement about the tests
was made in late August; but the most dramatic evidence came with
the launching of the first Soviet space satellites (*Sputniki*) on
4 October and 3 November 1957. Although the Americans responded by stepping up research, and launched a satellite of their
own as early as February 1958, it was evident that the Russians had
achieved at least a temporary advantage. The days of automatic
Western superiority in the field of nuclear weapons were over, and
theoreticians like Henry Kissinger were already beginning to
speculate on the implications of mutual deterrence.

American military strategists now began to question the feas-
ibility of relying on 'massive retaliation' as an appropriate deterrent
in all circumstances. In the long run it might once again be
necessary for the United States to have a capability at least for the
tactical use of nuclear weapons, which would require greater
dependence on its military allies across the world. In NATO the
eventual outcome was a series of agreements giving the United
States suitable sites for intermediate-range ballistic missiles in
various countries of Europe; it was also decided that West Germany
should play a more important conventional military role. In Asia, a
decision was taken as early as February 1957 (and acted upon in
May) to deploy Matador surface-to-surface missiles in Taiwan;
nuclear missiles were also placed in South Korea.[6] As far as is
known, there was never any intention to deploy atomic weapons in
South-East Asia, but moves were certainly made to increase
conventional military preparedness in that area.

## II

The question is bound to be asked whether the United States missed
an opportunity in its relations with China during 1956–8. A final
answer cannot be attempted until all the records of the Geneva
ambassadorial talks become available for research, but there are a

few small indications that some members of the Chinese political establishment – not least Zhou Enlai and foreign minister Chen Yi – were hoping for an improvement rather than a deterioration in Sino-American relations. It might be argued that their influence in Peking would have been strengthened if Dulles had responded more favourably to the proposals for an exchange of newsmen put forward by Wang Bingnan at Geneva on 14 February 1957. Instead, the United States insisted on the release of ten remaining American prisoners held in China and proposed a tightening rather than a relaxation of Western restrictions on trade.

It is generally thought that Dulles' San Francisco speech of 28 June 1957, in which he argued that Communism was no more than a passing phase in China, put an end to any remaining hopes of détente with Peking. On the other hand, the 69th ambassadorial meeting in Geneva on 8 August was followed two weeks later by a slight easing of the United States position on the question of allowing American journalists to visit China. Although that 'signal' was rejected by *Renmin Ribao* four days later, it is possible that a debate of some kind was still going on behind the scenes in Peking which the Americans were hoping to influence. The next ambassadorial meeting however, on 12 September, was followed by an exchange of public statements which implied that neither side intended to change its stand in the immediate future. As always the critical issue, on which no compromise seemed possible, was Taiwan. Further (unpublicised) exchanges must have taken place between then and the 73rd meeting of ambassadors on 12 December 1957; but after that the Americans virtually suspended the talks by failing to appoint a successor to U. Alexis Johnson in Geneva.[7]

From China's point of view, the failure to make any progress in direct contacts with the United States was less consequential than the success or failure of a parallel attempt to work out an economic *rapprochement* with Japan. There too, the Chinese ran into American opposition. The United States viewed the emergence of a new network of financial ties between Japan and other Asian countries as a major gain for the 'free world', which went a long way towards countering the Soviet and Chinese economic offensive. That purpose would not be served, however, if Japan also began to develop close economic relations with the People's Republic of China. It was natural for Japan to have strong economic links with Taiwan, formerly a Japanese colony (from 1894 to 1945). But some Japanese businessmen saw greater long-term advantage in trade with Peking, and even before the restoration of Sino-Japanese diplomatic relations in November 1955 three successive agreements had been made between 'private' trade organisations in the two countries. By mid-1957 a fourth agreement was contemplated on a much more ambitious scale, which if it had come to fruition would have provided steel for Chinese industrialisation and given Japan additional sources of coal and high-grade iron ore. But Dulles was determined to drive a wedge between the two major East Asian powers, and to isolate China from the rest of Asia; and in that aim he was firmly supported by Chiang Kaishek.

It was probably not only the Americans who opposed closer Sino-Japanese relations; for the result would also have been to make China less dependent on economic relations with the Soviet Union. A later Soviet account of the period claims that there was continual tension within the Chinese leadership throughout the 1950s, between those who wanted to remain close to the Moscow line (and the 'socialist camp') and those who believed China should find its own way in the world and should develop independent relations with Japan and the United States.[8] American policy itself tended to weaken the position of those Chinese leaders looking towards Japan, however, whilst a more active Soviet strategy in late 1957 and 1958 had the effect of strengthening those seeking to draw China away from a new relationship with Japan.

To analyse Chinese Communist politics in terms of a conflict between only two points of view may in fact be an oversimplification. There certainly were elements in the Party who attached most importance to solidarity with the Communist bloc, even though by this time they could not openly defend the idea of Chinese economic subservience to the Soviet Union. Likewise it is easy to identify a group, presumably led by Zhou, in favour of relations with Japan as a basis for rapid industrialisation without total dependence on Soviet Aid. Such a policy might also, in the spirit of the Bandung strategy, have drawn Japan itself away from complete dependence on the capitalist world. Against both ideas however, a third school of thought held that China should be as far as possible 'self-reliant', mobilising its own masses rather than relying on either fraternal aid or foreign trade. It is convenient to call this the 'Maoist' approach, although Mao's own position was not always clear. One of its principal advocates seems to have been Lin Biao, who would later became identified with a strongly anti-Japanese line and would become increasingly influential after his

promotion to the standing committee of the Party Politburo in May
1958. Although ostensibly opposed to Chinese imitation of Soviet
economic and military models, Lin advocated a line that would
leave China more dependent than ever on the Soviet nuclear
umbrella for its defence against the West.

We have no means of knowing whether China's internal power
struggle would have developed differently if at some critical point
the United States had made a major conciliatory move. Perhaps we
should regard Zhou Enlai's remarks of 25 July 1957, criticising
Kishi Nobusuke for sabotaging the projected Sino-Japanese trade
agreement and for his recent visit to Taiwan, as a cry for help rather
than a total rejection of Dulles' position. But Zhou may have been
losing ground within the leadership at that point, and the anti-
rightist movement which gathered momentum during August
probably worked against the possibility of closer relations with
either the United States or Japan. The campaign against the
principal literary victim of the movement, the woman writer Ding
Ling, began on 7 August – coinciding with a long-awaited decree on
socialist education in the countryside (8 August) and with the
decision-making which must have preceded the 69th Sino-
American meeting in Geneva.[9] The key figure in the movement at
that stage would appear to have been Peng Zhen, who had earlier
played a leading role in the anti-American campaign of 1951. At
that juncture it was unlikely that anything short of an actual
American withdrawal from Taiwan could have made much
difference to the direction being taken by Chinese politics.
Nevertheless Sino-Japanese negotiations did go ahead in the
autumn, and as we shall see an agreement was eventually signed in
March 1958; but the circumstances were not auspicious, and in the
end the *rapprochement* with Japan did not take place.


In Indochina, the Chinese continued to pursue their 'Bandung
strategy' towards Cambodia, Laos and Thailand. Relations with
South Vietnam deteriorated (if that was possible) when Ngo Dinh
Diem went ahead in May 1957 with plans to oblige Chinese
residents born in Vietnam to take Vietnamese citizenship immediately.[10] But the main focus of conflict was Laos, where Chinese
diplomacy finally began to bear fruit during 1957. After a
government crisis lasting from May to early August that year,

Souvanna Phouma (having resigned on 31 May) was reinstalled as premier on 8 August and finally received support from the National Assembly for a new programme to improve relations with the Pathet Lao. The latter welcomed the Prince's reappointment in a broadcast a few days later.[11] It is impossible to say whether the situation in Laos figured in Sino-American discussions at the Geneva ambassadorial meeting on 8 August; but it seems likely that the Americans were opposed to the action which Souvanna Phouma was now about to take.

Certainly the new situation alarmed pro-American elements in Thailand, where a public outcry against the rigging of assembly elections in February had been followed by a new period of instability within the leadership. As the year went on it appeared that Phao Siyanon's faction, which had supported the approach to China in 1955–6, was becoming estranged from the faction of army commander Sarit Thannarat. On 20 August 1957, after the outbreak of a corruption scandal, Sarit resigned from the government; a month later (17 September) forces loyal to him staged a coup which obliged Phibunsonggram and Phao to flee into exile. The coup itself came only one day after the start of preliminary talks between the two sides in Laos on 16 September.

The resumption of formal talks in Vientiane on 25 September 1957 led eventually to a summit meeting between Souvanna Phouma and Souphanouvong on 2 November, following which a joint communiqué set out principles for an agreement on several issues: the formation of a coalition government, to include two Pathet Lao ministers; the reintegration of the northern provinces into the national administration and of the Pathet Lao fighting forces into the Royal army; and the recognition of the Patriotic Front (*Neo Lao Hak Sat*) as a legal party entitled to put up candidates in supplementary elections. This was followed by a series of formal handover meetings, culminating in a ceremony in the Plaine des Jarres on 18 February 1958 at which two Pathet Lao battalions (1500 men each) formally accepted integration into the Vientiane army – but still under their own officers – whilst another 4280 men were disbanded.[12] Supplementary elections, affecting 21 out of the 58 seats in the National Assembly, were to be held on 4 May 1958. Meanwhile Souphanouvong entered the government, as minister in charge of the 1957–8 national plan; and Phoumi Vongvichit took over the ministry of cults. For a Communist to be in charge of religion in a Buddhist country must have seemed somewhat remarkable; but from a political point of view it was a clever choice, giving Phoumi access to the network of temples throughout the kingdom. The coalition did not last long enough for us to judge whether the participation of the Pathet Lao represented a sincere attempt to achieve national unity and stability, or whether it was merely – as the Americans certainly feared – the first move towards a Communist 'takeover' of the whole government.

### III

It is by no means clear how far the American intelligence community was aware of the extent of divisions within the Chinese leadership, or of the tension which existed between China and North Vietnam in relation to Laos and Cambodia. Nor is it easy to assess whether those tensions offered any real opportunity for a new departure in United States policy. But from the information so far available it would appear that Washington was mainly preoccupied with countering what it saw as a coordinated Sino-Soviet challenge to its own power in Asia. Moreover, the burden of the Moscow Declaration, issued by a meeting of all Communist Parties in November 1957 seemed to be that the Soviet Union and its allies (including China) were firmly united behind an anti-imperialist line. That, together with the successful launching of the first two Soviet space satellites, left the Americans feeling deeply concerned about the world situation at the end of 1957. It was inevitable that they would react strongly against what seemed to be significant political gains by the Communist powers in both Laos and Indonesia. Unfortunately, the *Pentagon Papers*, in their almost exclusive concentration on Vietnam, provide no details of the debate which must have been going on in American government and military circles at that point about how to deal with the new situation in South-East Asia. Very probably it was then that a division began to emerge between two schools of thought: those who believed in strengthening regional military pacts – at all costs – and those who preferred a 'moderate' approach. The latter sought to avoid alienating Asian regimes which refused to commit themselves to an American military alliance but which were still far from being oriented exclusively towards Moscow and Peking; whereas the more 'hawkish' view was that such countries ought to be persuaded to change their position – if necessary through clandestine American intervention in their internal affairs.

During the early months of 1958, Indonesia provided the acid test of American policy in Asia. The critical issue was whether Sukarno would survive and continue to strengthen his authority internally, whilst pursuing a policy of genuine independence in the world, or whether he would be forced to appoint a new right-wing government opposed to relations with the Communist powers and willing to cooperate more closely with the West. The Americans, and certainly the Japanese, were not necessarily opposed to Sukarno's quarrel with the Dutch, so long as other foreign enterprises remained secure. Indeed it was the reparations agreement with Japan, negotiated between October and December 1957, which gave the Indonesians both the confidence and the financial resources to embark on a more vigorous anti-Dutch economic policy towards the end of the year.[13] However, Sukarno's desire for closer relations with the Communist world, as well as with Yugoslavia and Egypt, was not compatible with United States strategy and it was logical for the Americans to ally themselves with his opponents inside Indonesia. There is now sufficient evidence to support the allegation that by early 1958 the CIA was committed to some kind of covert operation in support of open rebellion against Sukarno, although the details remain secret. In January, as Sukarno embarked on another foreign tour (to Cairo, Belgrade and Tokyo), his opponents gathered in Sumatra and on 15 February 1958 established a rebel government at Padang. Their objective was probably to force a new coalition government in Jakarta; with the Americans (together with the Taiwan Chinese and the Philippines) providing covert military support both in Sumatra and in Eastern Indonesia. But all depended on the attitude of Nasution and the Indonesian high command.

Sukarno's travels bore fruit. Whilst he himself visited Egypt and Yugoslavia, a separate military delegation went to Czechoslovakia, and as a result shipments of arms began arriving in Indonesia from Eastern Europe during March. Sukarno then went on to Japan, where he used high-level contacts dating from the 1940s to secure support from the Kishi government – despite the fact that some Japanese appear to have sided with the rebels. On his return home in mid-February the general staff of the armed forces rallied to

Sukarno's cause and in March loyal troops began landing in Sumatra to suppress the revolt. American covert support for the rebels was not adequate to defeat an all-out offensive by government forces: Padang was recaptured in mid-April, and by early May resistance in Sumatra had collapsed. On 15 April Jakarta established formal relations with Japan and the reparations agreement (duly ratified by both sides) came into effect.

Initially the United States appears to have responded to the Sumatra defeat by stepping up support for the other main centre of revolt in Eastern Indonesia. Bombing raids by unmarked planes on government targets in that area culminated in an incident on 18 May, when an American pilot was captured alive after being shot down over Ambon. But shortly afterwards United States policy towards Indonesia underwent a sharp reversal and the attempt to force a complete change of government in Jakarta was abandoned. The 'hawks' in Washington were probably forced to admit that continued support for the outer islands would merely lead to civil war, which might well offer greater opportunities to the Communists than a stable but neutral regime in Jakarta with Sukarno at its head. Even before the Ambon incident an American admiral had held talks with General Nasution on 10 May, and on the 22nd the United States decided in principle to sell small arms to the Indonesian armed forces.[14]

For the next five years and more, American policy towards Indonesia was typefied by the approach of the 'moderate' ambassador to Jakarta, Howard Jones, who had arrived in early March and was able to exploit his good personal relations with Sukarno and with prime minister Djuanda to American advantage. A formal agreement on arms sales was finally reached on 13 August. The PKI remained an influential force in Indonesian politics, but the Americans now began to compete with them by cultivating potential allies within the Indonesian armed forces. The elimination of Dutch interests, moreover, benefited the Japanese and the Americans rather than the Soviet Union or China, and the reparations agreement brought Indonesia into what would soon become an expanding Japanese economic sphere. The one Soviet success was that Indonesia refused to join SEATO and continued to pursue a 'neutralist' policy in the world at large. In this respect there was a close analogy between Sukarno's Indonesia and Nasser's United Arab Republic, proclaimed on 1 February 1958.

Precisely as the crisis in Indonesia came to a head, in March and April 1958, the issue of China's relations with Japan was also resolved – in a negative direction. A formal (but still technically 'private') trade agreement was finally signed on 5 March, which had it gone into effect would have permitted China's more rapid industrialisation on the basis of expanding trade and the supply of Japanese steel.[15] But almost immediately difficulties arose from Peking's insistence that a Chinese trade mission in Tokyo should be allowed to fly the flag of the People's Republic, even though Tokyo still recognised Chiang Kaishek. Kishi himself had long-standing ties with the Guomindang (KMT) and had taken the opportunity to visit Taipei in June 1957. Immediately following the agreement of 5 March, Taiwan suspended its own negotiations for new trade arrangements with Japan, and by early April the Japanese government was pressed into making a stand calculated to undermine the agreement with Peking. The direction events would take must have been clear even before the Nagasaki incident of 2 May 1958 when a right-wing 'fanatic' tore down the flag of the People's Republic at a trade exhibition. Two days later the Chinese themselves cancelled the fourth agreement, leaving the way open for signature of the Japan–Taiwan agreement on 21 May 1958.

This failure to take what might have become the first step towards Sino-Japanese *rapprochement*, which would in turn have permitted more rapid Chinese economic development independently of the Soviet Union, must count as one of the most important turning-points in the post-war history of Asia. It served to reinforce a pattern of relationships in which Sino-American détente became more remote than ever, forcing China either to fall back on Soviet assistance or to turn in upon itself. During the remainder of 1958 it tended towards the latter course. The second session of the 8th Party Congress (5–23 May 1958) approved the basic principles of Mao's 'great leap forward' and the creation of 'people's communes'. About the same time, the Chinese media embarked on a new campaign of ideological criticism directed against the 'revisionism' of Tito's Yugoslavia. Internationally, that represented a significant move away from Zhou Enlai's 'Bandung' strategy and marked the beginning of a return to revolutionary anti-imperialism: a development of great significance for the future of Vietnam.

## IV

The change in American policy which occurred in relation to Indonesia in May 1958 was not paralleled in Indochina, where it would seem that the 'hawks' continued to prevail. There is little to be gained by speculating whether the new coalition might have given Laos a period of much-needed stability had it been allowed to function for a number of years; perhaps Sino-Vietnamese rivalry would have wrecked it sooner or later. In the event it was wrecked by the Laotian rightists with the active support of Ambassador Parsons. In May, despite a rapid infusion of American economic aid into the provinces concerned, the supplementary elections produced disappointing results from the ambassador's point of view: out of 21 seats, nine went to the Patriotic Front, another four to its ally the Peace (*Santiphab*) Party. Only eight were won by supporters of Souvanna Phouma or by politicians farther to the right. The American response was to encourage the formation in June of a new political grouping outside the Assembly, made up of army officers and civilian officials sympathetic to the West, which called itself the Committee for the Defence of National Interests. More dramatically, on 30 June 1958 United States aid to Laos was suspended: officially in order to pressure the government into making monetary reforms; in reality to create difficulties for the coalition government. When Souvanna Phouma was obliged to resign on 22 July, he found it impossible to form another cabinet. His place was taken by Phoui Sananikone, a leader more acceptable to the Americans, who secured approval on 18 August for a government including four members of the Committee for the Defence of National Interests and no representatives of the Pathet Lao.

Another important development at this period was the eclipse – at least for the time being – of the International Commission which had been responsible for supervising the Geneva ceasefire in Laos. This was not in itself an American initiative and might have occurred even if the coalition had survived; but it worked to the advantage of the new government. As early as 20 March 1958 Souvanna Phouma had written to the Indian chairman of the Commission, arguing that in Laos the holding of the May supplementary elections would complete the political settlement for which the Geneva Conference had called; and that once the settlement had been implemented there was no need for the Commission itself to continue. The members of the International

Commission debated the issue in May and June and, despite the reservations of the Polish delegate, decided to adjourn *sine die* on 20 July 1958.[16] The North Vietnamese tried to insist that 'peace in Indochina is indivisible' and that the Geneva settlement could not be regarded as having been fully implemented in Laos before Vietnam itself had been reunified; but to no avail. The Chinese, indeed, probably welcomed the new move since it demonstrated more firmly than ever the separateness of Laos from Vietnam as an independent nation-state. But the collapse of the coalition and the emergence of the Phoui government can hardly have pleased Peking so much. It reinforced the North Vietnamese view that American policy in Laos would eventually have to be opposed by a new revolutionary struggle. It was now becoming less and less likely that Laos would move closer to China, and so fulfil Zhou Enlai's hopes of 1956.

Cambodia, on the other hand, was demonstrating more than ever its genuine independence of the West and its friendship towards China. Agreement on formal diplomatic relations with Peking was reached on 24 July 1958; to be followed by Sihanouk's second visit to the Chinese capital from 14 to 24 August.[17] He had to pay the price of offending Thailand, with whom his relations would henceforth deteriorate rapidly. But in international standing, which was the real basis of his political strength inside Cambodia, Sihanouk must have calculated that the gain outweighed the loss. From the Chinese point of view it meant that at least one country in Indochina (apart from North Vietnam) had been rescued from the tentacles of SEATO.

Given what was happening elsewhere in South-East Asia during 1957–8, it is perhaps not surprising that the United States began to strengthen its military relations with South Vietnam. Apart from the Philippines, that was the one country of the region whose government was completely oriented towards Washington – although Thailand also moved in that direction after the coup of September 1957. (Malaya, which became independent in August 1957, remained in the British sphere and did not seek separate membership of SEATO; Singapore was even more closely tied to Britain at this stage.) As a result, South Vietnam received a growing amount of attention from American military leaders during 1957, with visits to Saigon by the Far East commander (Lemnitzer) in January; by the army chief-of-staff (Maxwell Taylor) in March; and by CINCPAC (Admiral Stump) in September. From 5 to 19 May

1957, Ngo Dinh Diem paid a state visit to the United States which
also included military talks.[18] The main emphasis was still on
conventional military training for the South Vietnamese armed
forces, and the officer commanding MAAG from 1955 to 1960,
General Williams, would subsequently be criticised for failing to
develop counter-guerrilla techniques. At that stage American
motives for strengthening South Vietnam had more to do with the
global situation than with anything actually happening inside the
country. The internal security situation was remarkably calm
during 1957 and early 1958. But in terms of the international power
struggle, which would become more intense during the latter part of
1958, the very fact that South Vietnam was becoming more
important for the Americans made it also an area of greater interest
to the Soviet Union and China.

Vietnam also attracted a certain amount of attention from Japan
at this period. As far as reparations were concerned, it might have
been argued that it was the North which had been more severely
damaged in the Second World War; and some people in Tokyo may
have favoured the granting of reparations to Hanoi. If so, they were
overruled. The Japanese prime minister Kishi Nobusuke went to
Saigon in November 1957 – one of a series of visits he made to Asian
capitals during his first year in office – and protracted negotiations
followed for an agreement to pay reparations to South Vietnam.
Japan nevertheless still sought to maintain commercial relations
with North Vietnam, and an agreement to expand trade was signed
in Hanoi on 18 March 1958.[19] Nor did that arrangement, so far as is
known, suffer the same fate as the abortive trade agreement between
Japan and China made about the same time. But when the conflict
between North and South Vietnam became more acute the
Japanese found themselves siding with the Americans, and therefore with South Vietnam, and a formal reparations agreement with
Saigon was finally signed in May 1959. The sum involved was much
smaller than in the case of Indonesia or the Philippines, but one
notable result of Japanese investment was the Da-Nhim hydro-
electric dam in the mountains west of Phan-Thiet.

The contrast between United States policy in Indonesia and in
Indochina in the period from about May 1958 is quite striking, and
might even tempt some historians to conclude that if only the

'moderate' strategy adopted towards Indonesia had been applied to Laos and Vietnam the tragedy of the Vietnam War might have been avoided. In the case of Laos, it is certainly possible to argue that the Chinese (as opposed to the North Vietnamese) were not necessarily opposed to the emergence of a stable regime so long as it was genuinely independent and neutral; and that if the Americans had helped rather than hindered the fulfilment of that objective, North Vietnam would probably have been unable to cause trouble. One might even go further and suggest that the application of the 'cold war' principle to Laos in 1958 did more than anything else to undermine the relative equilibrium established in the Indochinese peninsula by the Geneva settlement. By helping to destroy the coalition of Souvanna Phouma and Souphanouvong the Americans played into the hands of those Chinese and North Vietnamese leaders whose aim was a new phase of revolution in South-East Asia. Leaving such speculative judgements on one side, however, it is probably fair to argue that in the actual circumstances of 1958 the adoption of a 'moderate' strategy in the case of Indonesia made it almost inevitable that the situation in Indochina would be interpreted in 'cold war' terms. If SEATO could not embrace the whole of South-East Asia, then close allies like South Vietnam and Thailand became all the more important for the maintenance of American power in the region. And the fear that Thailand might move away from the Western alliance had considerable bearing on American policy towards Laos.

What is not justified is the asumption that Indochina and Indonesia represented the same kind of problem for the Americans. The former area already included one fully-fledged socialist (that is Communist) state in North Vietnam, whose ambition to control the southern half of the country was very real. Vietnamese revolutionary aspirations did not depend on decisions taken in Washington; and if they were held in restraint during the years down to 1958 it was because of international Communist judgements about the situation in South-East Asia and the world at large. South Vietnam developed into a relatively stable, pro-American state during that interval; but its very existence could be seriously challenged at any moment if there were a significant change of line in Hanoi, Peking and Moscow. We must now consider the years 1957–8 from that point of view.

# 8  The Emergence of Le Duan

In 1957, when he was transferred from southern to northern Vietnam, Le Duan began ganging up with foreign anti-China forces and subscribed completely to their anti-China fallacies. However, he still did not dare to oppose China openly . . . .

Hoang Van Hoan, February 1981

Imperialism has become a system which exploits all the world's people, the weak and the small peoples, and keeps them in bondage. Without a superior international position the revolution for national liberation of the Vietnamese people cannot have a revolutionary theory capable of grasping the line of the growth and extinction of imperialism, cannot have powerful allied forces in the world and cannot triumph. It is precisely the unity of the world proletariat and the contradictions of imperialism which have created for the national liberation movement in Vietnam the conditions to overthrow imperialism and local feudalism.

Le Duan, August 1957

I

The same months which saw the collapse of the bid for Sino-Japanese détente were also critically important in the evolution of the Communist international line. The Conference of Marxist–Leninist Parties, held in Moscow in November 1957, was a significant turning point which inevitably had consequences for Vietnam. Hanoi-watchers have long been aware that a new political crisis developed in North Vietnam during the latter part of 1957. It was reflected in the disappearance of Vo Nguyen Giap from public view between late October and December, and in the failure of Ho Chi Minh to return home from the Moscow Conference at the same time as the rest of the Vietnamese delegation.[1] But on its own the Hanoi evidence is baffling. Only when the conflict in the Vietnamese Politburo is related to events elsewhere in the Communist world, does it become possible to make sense of what happened. Although many questions remain unanswered even now, it is clear that the crisis and its aftermath helped transform both the balance within the Party leadership and the evolution of Communist strategy in South Vietnam.

The fact that China was tending to develop its own solutions to the problems thrown up by the international crisis of 1956, and was abandoning the habit of taking the Soviet model as its main guide to action, did not in itself mean a Sino-Soviet 'split'. The Chinese were still anxious to preserve the fundamental unity of the world Communist movement, but on a basis which would allow each Party a measure of freedom to deal with its own particular situation. It was Zhou Enlai, during the course of a visit to Moscow in January 1957, who first proposed the meeting of Communist leaders which finally took place – under rather different circumstances – in November.[2] At that stage the Chinese may have been looking for an international line sufficiently broad to be acceptable not only in Moscow and Peking but also in Belgrade. The Russians, on the other hand, were probably anxious to prevent the Chinese becoming too independent – especially in their relations with Japan. The Soviet head of state Voroshilov visited China towards the end of April 1957, on a mission designed to reaffirm the special relationship between the two countries.

In Moscow itself the year 1957 saw what amounted to a two-stage conflict within the Soviet leadership: the first stage ending with the fall of the 'anti-Party group' in June, the second culminating in the dismissal of Marshal Zhukov in October.[3] The first conflict arose from a bid by Molotov and his 'Stalinist' allies to oust Khrushchev, in the aftermath of the apparent failure of 'de-Stalinisation' in Eastern Europe. It was a conflict too between those leaders who wanted to preserve the established, highly centralised system of state control, and those in favour of Khrushchev's proposals to decentralise the economy and so increase the power of the Party Secretariat. Khrushchev's plan was accepted at a plenum of the CPSU Central Committee in February and formally approved by the Supreme Soviet in May; but on 18–19 June 1957 the first secretary was confronted by a revolt in the Party Presidium, where his opponents succeeded in mustering a majority of votes against the reforms. Khrushchev survived only because he was able to convene another meeting of the Central Committee (22–29 June) at which he successfully appealed to the larger body against the majority in the Presidium. The result was a decision to expel Molotov and several others from the Central Committee and to promote in their place a group favouring the increased power of the Party Secretariat as opposed to the State administration. In the fullness of time it would become evident that these men were far from being wholehearted supporters of Khrushchev on all issues; in particular F. R. Kozlov would emerge as his leading opponent within the Secretariat. But on this occasion they took his side and obliged Molotov to withdraw.

Another decisive factor in Khrushchev's victory was the support of Zhukov and the army; the latter was by this time a full member of the Presidium and a powerful figure in his own right. The leadership conflict moved into a new phase when the Party bosses attempted to subject the armed forces to their own discipline, thus challenging an order issued by Zhukov on 12 May 1957 to the effect that professional commanders could not be overruled by Party commissars. The Party-oriented majority in the Politburo now decided that Zhukov must be removed, before the army became more powerful than the system it was supposed to serve. The Marshal returned from a tour of Albania and Yugoslavia, between 5 and 25 October 1957, to find himself stripped of power and replaced as defence minister by Malinovsky. In the meantime an article in the army newspaper *Kraznaya Zvezda* on 19 October had reaffirmed the principle of Party control of the armed forces. Khrushchev himself may have been less than happy with the outcome of this second conflict, in that Zhukov had been willing to bring military pressure to bear in support of ideas they both shared. But as chief of the Secretariat he could not argue against the logic of the decision, even though it may have reduced his own ability to dictate the Party line. Although the leadership in Moscow was at pains to insist that Zhukov's fall had nothing to do with his conversations with Tito, one of the more noticeable changes that followed was a gradual reversal of the attempt at *rapprochement* between Moscow and Belgrade – a development perhaps more to the liking of Suslov than of Khrushchev himself.

In China during the same period a 'rectification campaign' (or *zheng-feng* movement) was heralded by Mao Zedong's famous speech of 27 February 1957, 'On the correct handling of contradictions among the people'.[4] After a good deal of inner-Party debate the campaign got under way in May and June, leading to the climax of the 'hundred flowers' movement, which had started in the aftermath of de-Stalinisation the previous year. Criticism of Party and State organs by members of the 'bourgeois' political parties was allowed to reach its peak, leading to at least one violent incident on 13 June. Thereafter the authorities began to crack down, so that an 'anti-rightist' campaign was well under way by the time of the Central Committee's Third Plenum (20 September–9 October 1957). The campaign sought to identify and remove 'rightists' in the government and armed forces – and eventually to purge the Party itself. It also insisted that officials must engage in manual labour and it called for a 'socialist education' movement in the countryside. Behind the scenes there was almost certainly a continuing struggle for control of policy, but in China there was no attempt to identify an 'anti-Party group' or to expel anyone from the Politburo.

Mao had defeated the challenge of the Stalinists Gao Gang and Rao Shushi in 1954–5. At this stage, although he may not have been strong enough to prevent the defeat of some of his ideas, he was able to establish a consensus which his colleagues, whatever their doubts, were obliged to accept. Nor was there any question at this stage of the People's Liberation Army resisting political control. It was divided by its own pattern of field army groups, and sometimes by personal allegiances; but there was no danger that its generals would reject the leadership of the Party in ideological and political matters. Defence issues were argued out within the Party, rather than between army and Party as such. The one respect in which developments in China during 1957 did seem to run parallel with changes in the Soviet Union was in the sphere of administrative reform. After a long debate over the question of state control, a series of state regulations in mid-November established a pattern of decentralisation which – like that in the USSR – tended to reduce the power of government ministries and to increase that of the Party at all levels.[5] Zhou Enlai appears to have been overruled, without being in any danger of losing his place in the top leadership. That was the starting-point for the ascendancy of Liu Shaoqi and Deng Xiaoping in the administration of the provinces: a pattern of control which Mao may have accepted in the beginning but which he eventually destroyed during the 'cultural revolution'.

The crisis of the autumn of 1957 was thus far more complex than a mere confrontation between Moscow and Peking; it involved not only international questions but also major differences *within* both the Soviet and Chinese leaderships. Internationally, one of the most important issues was that of military co-operation between socialist countries in an age of increasingly complex technology and continuing confrontation with the West. The Soviet Union provided a nuclear umbrella for the 'bloc' as a whole, whose effectiveness was vividly demonstrated on 4 October by the launching of the first *sputnik* – followed by a second on 3 November just as Mao arrived in Moscow for the Communist Conference. But responsibility for more conventional defence still lay with the armies of individual countries, which in Eastern Europe operated within the framework of the Warsaw Pact. The Chinese PLA remained outside that system; but its need for technological modernisation led some Chinese generals to urge close co-operation with the armed forces of Poland, East Germany and Czechoslovakia, and military missions from each of those countries visited China that autumn.

Yugoslavia's army was also outside the Warsaw Pact, But military co-operation with both Moscow and Peking (and also Hanoi) was possible in the event of a political *rapprochement* between Tito and the Soviet leaders. That possibility may have been discussed during the visit to China of the Yugoslav defence minister Vukmanovic-Tempo in September 1957. From an ideological point of view, however, there was a certain danger in extending the sphere of military collaboration beyond the group of countries that could be held together ideologically. The Russians may have been afraid of a situation where Yugoslavs and Chinese might collaborate with one another independently of the discipline of the Warsaw Pact, and that fear may explain Soviet willingness to enter into a technical co-operation agreement with Peking on 15 October, one of whose provisions was to provide the Chinese with their own nuclear weapons' technology.[6] But following the removal of Zhukov there seems to have been a retreat from the idea of using military ties to restore Soviet-Yugoslav relations, and a revival of ideological debate and discipline as the basis of international unity. The Yugoslavs immediately felt the effect of this change, which by the spring of 1958 had produced a new estrangement almost as severe as that of ten years before.

The Chinese on the other hand now found themselves with an opportunity to play a significant role in the ideological debate of the camp as a whole. Mao himself attended the November 1957 conference of world Communist leaders, which was principally concerned with redefining the international line in theoretical terms. He was accompanied to Moscow by a military delegation under General Peng Dehuai, whilst Zhou and Liu Shaoqi both stayed at home. The resulting Moscow Declaration put forward a much 'harder' revolutionary line than that enunciated by Khrushchev at the 22nd Congress of the CPSU, defining 'modern revisionism' as the main danger for the movement in present conditions. Whilst Tito was rebuffed, Mao's ideas gained acceptance – with a recognition too that Marxist–Leninist theory should be applied creatively to the conditions prevailing in each country. There was no question of a return to Stalinist notions of the Soviet Union as the only possible model for building socialism, despite a new Chinese willingness to 'learn from the USSR'.[7]

By the end of 1957 therefore the Soviet leadership had resolved its most pressing conflicts and Sino-Soviet unity was apparently restored. Within a year it would become evident that neither the military nor the ideological problems separating Moscow and Peking had been permanently settled: the issue of détente with the West would eventually drive them farther apart. But so long as their dispute remained ideological, with the Chinese becoming more (rather than less) anti-imperialist as time went on, any Chinese 'threat' to Soviet interests could easily be contained.


II


For much of 1957 North Vietnam was preoccupied with the campaign for the 'correction of errors' launched at the 10th and 11th Plenums of the VNWP Central Committee, whose purpose was to rectify mistakes made during land reform. A leading role in this movement was played by Nguyen Duy Trinh, who although originally a native of Nghe-Tinh had spent most of the time since 1945 in southern Vietnam and was not identified with previous decisions in the North. Frequent references in the Hanoi media to difficulties in Interzone IV suggest that the provinces of northern Central Vietnam were an area of special concern where acute conflicts still had to be resolved. But the course of the campaign cannot be reconstructed in detail from the very limited evidence so far available. It is important not to confuse the Vietnamese programme of 'correcting errors' with the *zheng-feng* campaign launched in China the same year; the purpose of the latter being to 'rectify' the working methods of the Party and government and to eliminate 'rightist' cadres. In April 1957 Truong Chinh (again playing an active role) did refer in a speech to the 'Maoist' theory of 'handling contradictions among the people'; but that did not imply either a new phase of mass mobilisation or another round of bourgeois criticism. Hanoi had no parallel to the climax of the Chinese 'hundred flowers' in May and June; nor was there a Vietnamese 'anti-rightist' campaign in the autumn of 1957.

North Vietnam's relations with the major Communist powers during 1957 centred upon the visit of Voroshilov to Hanoi from 20 to 24 May, and Ho Chi Minh's tour (with Hoang Van Hoan) of eight fraternal socialist countries in July and August.[8] Regarding Voroshilov, we know only that in speeches he was at pains to emphasise the 'peaceful' reunification of Vietnam and he gave no open support for a more violent strategy in the South. (His visit might, of course, have acquired a different significance later on, had Molotov succeeded in his attempt to remove Khrushchev from power in June; Voroshilov escaped identification with the 'anti-Party group' but subsequently was said to have supported it.) As for Ho's tour, the most remarkable thing was that whereas in 1955 he and Truong Chinh had visited only China and the USSR, on this occasion Ho was anxious to visit as many countries as possible – including North Korea and Yugoslavia. At that stage Zhukov was still influential, and military relations within the 'bloc' seem to have mattered more than ideology. Not inconceivably, Ho's aim was to prepare the way for closer military ties between Hanoi and its various Communist allies, including Belgrade, as well as to secure diplomatic and political support for an eventual resumption of the southern struggle. Ho may have shared Tito's suspicion of Moscow; at the same time he was anxious to avoid complete dependence on China.

North Vietnam was by then attempting to modernise its own armed forces, without losing touch completely with the tradition of 'people's war'. That was the purpose of a series of military conferences held during the spring and summer of 1957.[9] The Chinese PLA faced similar problems, on an even larger scale, but the Vietnamese were now interested in learning directly from the Soviet Union rather than imitating only the Chinese model. The issue of Party control over the armed forces may consequently have been as important in Hanoi as in Moscow. On 10 May – about the same time as Zhukov's virtual declaration of 'professional' independence – the Hanoi press reported the creation of a 'general directorate of cadres' under the command of an officer who had fought in the South before 1954, Nguyen Chanh. But four and a half months later on 25 September, it was suddenly announced that Nguyen Chanh had died the previous day and nothing more was heard of his department.[10] The eventual dismissal of Zhukov may explain why Vo Nguyen Giap himself ran into difficulties soon afterwards. Until that point, like Zhukov, Giap had been very prominent and had probably enjoyed comparable success in keeping the armed forces relatively independent of Party control. As a long-standing member of the top leadership of his own Party, it is unlikely that Giap was in danger of being 'purged'; but he probably had to accept some temporary loss of influence. When *Nhan-Dan* (5 November) published the Soviet Central Committee's resolution on the expulsion of Zhukov, a commentary drew attention to the importance of Party leadership in Vietnam too; it suggested that 'some comrades' had failed to understand that principle and had acted against the true spirit of Marxism–Leninism. Giap made no public appearances between then and 19 December 1957.

The question of the Party's role in relation to state organs may also have been at issue in Hanoi that autumn, as it had been in Moscow and Peking earlier in the year. A trend towards greater administrative power for the Party Secretariat would mean a greater burden of work, but also more power, for the secretary-general. When Truong Chinh was removed from that post at the VNWP 10th Plenum it was taken over by Ho Chi Minh himself. A little over a year later, however, there were signs that the actual work was being done by Le Duan, who appears to have been recalled to the Party Centre from his post in the South sometime in the summer or autumn of 1957. His first important public appearance in Hanoi – named third in order of precedence after Ho and Truong Chinh – occurred on 8 October during a visit by the Bulgarian premier Anton Yugov. Le Duan again appeared (in the role of a Party secretary) between 18 and 26 October, to meet a high-powered Soviet delegation led by one of the CPSU secretaries promoted after the crisis in June, A. B. Aristov. But perhaps the most remarkable aspect of Aristov's visit was the absence of any mention of either Vo Nguyen Giap or Ho Chi Minh. On one occasion the Soviet visitor drank the health of the North Vietnamese president, but at no point was Ho mentioned as either receiving the Soviet delegation or participating in formal talks.[11] (Nor has there been any report of his travelling abroad at that time, although one possible explanation is that he was not actually present in Hanoi.) The non-appearance of Giap can be linked to the dismissal of

Zhukov in Moscow, which coincided with Aristov's visit. The Soviet delegation may have been anxious to ensure that Hanoi followed the Soviet example in asserting Party supremacy over the armed forces. But Ho's absence at such a critical time implies a crisis of some magnitude in the Vietnamese leadership. Conversely, Le Duan's prominence suggests that he enjoyed the confidence of the new Soviet leadership. Many years later Hoang Van Hoan would refer to 1957 as the year in which Le Duan began to take control of the Party machine and to use it as the instrument of his own rise to power.[12]

Certainly there is reason to see Le Duan, at this and later stages, as a rival rather than as a close associate of Ho Chi Minh. Apart from differences of revolutionary experience, they also differed on the ideological issues which were again coming to the fore towards the end of 1957 and during 1958. Where Ho's background and ideas were in many respects similar to those of Tito, Le Duan was strongly 'anti-revisionist' and highly critical of the Yugoslavs. It is not necessary to pretend that Ho was essentially a 'nationalist' (as opposed to a Marxist–Leninist) in order to recognise this difference of views about the international line. Nor need one label Le Duan as 'pro-Soviet' (or Ho as 'pro-Chinese') in the context of 1957; the ideological debate in the Communist world cut across nationalities. The two men seem also to have held opposing views about strategy towards South Vietnam and the rest of Indochina. Le Duan seems continuously to have opposed the Geneva partition and would later emerge as the arch-proponent of a single Indochinese revolution, requiring the subservience of Laos and Cambodia to a reunified Communist Vietnam. Ho Chi Minh was more ready to accept Zhou Enlai's concept of Indochina.

Aristov's visit may have had a direct impact on Hanoi's strategy towards the South. Despite other differences, Vo Nguyen Giap and Le Duan were probably the most deeply committed among Vietnamese Communist leaders to an eventual resumption of armed struggle in the South. Before his temporary eclipse in October and November 1957, Giap had made a number of speeches emphasising Vietnamese unity and calling for more vigorous pursuit of the revolutionary line: notably for the Party anniversary on 3 March 1957, and for the twelfth anniversary of the start of anti-

French resistance on 23 September. Le Duan also made a militant speech in August 1957, before or soon after his recall to the North, urging Vietnamese patriots to 'hold aloft the banner of the leadership of the proletariat, advance to socialism, liberate the South, and achieve independence and democracy throughout the country'.[13] By the end of October, however, Hanoi appears to have adopted a more cautious line than that which seemed to be emerging earlier in the year, and Soviet restraint may have been one factor in the change.

The line that had been laid down in late 1956 (in Le Duan's 'Path of the Revolution in the South') had not necessarily precluded acts of violence as part of the predominantly political struggle. Several captured Communist documents referred to the existence of a 'Vietnam People's Liberation Movement' – thought to have come into existence in 1956 and to have replaced the southern branch of the Fatherland Front. But it remained a somewhat nebulous body and no documentary evidence so far available allows us to trace its precise relationship to the Party.[14] Around the middle of 1957, however, and especially after October, a campaign to 'exterminate traitors' began, which led to an increasing number of assassinations over the next two years. More spectacularly – perhaps to impress Aristov during his visit to Hanoi – bomb incidents against American targets occurred in Saigon on 22 October; and about the same time a small-scale guerrilla attack was made against a government post north of the city.[15] It is not impossible that Giap wanted to expand revolutionary violence to the point where armed struggle could be resumed during 1957–8; possibly, too, Nguyen Chanh's directorate had been intended to play some role in a new phase of the southern conflict. But after Aristov's visit, when Giap mysteriously disappeared, the Party adopted a line of political struggle supported by assassinations whose main purpose was to protect Party members against arrest or denunciation by Diem's agents. Le Duan was probably more concerned than Giap about ensuring the leading role of the Party at each stage of the developing struggle, and that may explain the difference between them at this point.

On 23 October a Saigon newspaper carried reports of discontent amongst the southern Viet-Minh units which had been regrouped in the North in 1955, and there may have been some truth in the story. More precise evidence of a retreat from immediate armed struggle in the South came a month later, in a Hanoi article by Tran Van Giau for the 17th anniversary of the abortive Nam-Ky rising of

TABLE 8.1 *Vietnam, the Communist powers and South-East Asia, October–November 1957*

| Soviet Union | China | Vietnam | South-East Asia |
|---|---|---|---|
| 4 Oct.: *Sputnik I* launched. | Early Oct.: Visits to China by delegations from USSR (A. B. Aristov), Hungary (Kadar), Bulgaria (Yugov), East Germany, Poland, Yugoslavia. | Early Oct.: Series of talks by Truong Chinh on October Revolution. | Oct.: *Laos*: Negotiations in progress between the two sides (from 25 Sept.). *Indonesia*: Negotiations in progress on Japanese reparations (completed 8 Dec. 1957). |
| 5–26 Oct.: Marshal Zhukov toured Albania and Yugoslavia. | 9 Oct.: Close of CCP Central Committee Third Plenum: radical speech by Mao Zedong. | 6–9 Oct.: Visit by Bulgarian premier Anton Yugov; first prominent appearance of Le Duan in Hanoi. | |
| | 13 Oct.: Mao again spoke at Supreme State Conference. | 9–12 Oct.: Army political conference to sum up re-education courses (held since spring). | |
| 15 Oct.: Yugoslavia recognised East Germany. | | 16 Oct.: Guerrilla attack on ARVN post in Binh Duong province. | |
| 16 Oct.: Sino-Soviet agreement on technical aid, including promise of nuclear weapons technology; Guo Moruo in Moscow. | | 18–26 Oct.: Visit to Hanoi by A. B. Aristov, with Supreme Soviet deleg'n. Note absence from view of Ho Chi Minh and Vo Nguyen Giap. | |

TABLE 8.1    *(Contd.)*

| Soviet Union | China | Vietnam | South-East Asia |
|---|---|---|---|
| 19 and 22 Oct.: *Kraznaya Zvezda* articles on role of Party leadership in armed forces; implied criticism of Zhukov.<br><br>26 Oct.: Zhukov returned home to be dismissed; replaced as defence minister by Malinovsky. | 19 Oct.: Publication of report to Third Plenum by Deng Xiaoping, which followed Mao's line on economy. | 22 Oct.: Bomb attacks against US targets in Saigon. | 2 Nov.: *Laos*: Joint communique of Souvanna Phouma, Souphanouvong, on agreement to integrate administration and armed forces, and to create coalition. |
| | 27 Oct.: *Renmin Ribao* on Mao's plan for agriculture.<br><br>31 Oct.: *Renmin Ribao* article by Liu Bocheng on learning from the Soviet Red Army. | 31 Oct.: Announcement that Ho Chi Minh, Le Duan and Pham Hung will visit Moscow for October Revolution anniversary.<br><br>1 Nov.–19 Dec.: No appearances by Vo Nguyen Giap. | |
| 2 Nov.: Announcement of expulsion of Zhukov from CPSU Central Committee. | 2 Nov.: Mao left for Moscow; Peng Dehuai also led military delegation to USSR for talks during November. | | |
| 3 Nov.: *Sputnik II* launched. | 3 Nov.: *Xue-xi* article on studying Soviet experience; criticising those who want to 'learn from all'. | | |

6 Nov.: Anniversary of October Revolution: Supreme Soviet speeches by Khrushchev and Mao.

14–16 Nov.: Moscow Meeting of Communist and Workers Parties of socialist countries. (Followed by meeting of 68 Parties throughout the world.) Attended by Mao; also by Ho Chi Minh, Le Duan, Pham Hung; but Tito did *not* attend.

18 Nov.: Mao's speech referring to the atom bomb as 'a paper tiger'.

14 Nov.: Series of State Regulations approved, on economic organisation; implying measure of decentralisation and increased role for Party (announced, 18 November).

5 Nov.: *Nhan Dan* on importance of Party control over the PAVN, and on learning from the CPSU.

6 Nov.: Meeting for anniversary of October Revolution: speech by Nguyan Duy Trinh. (Giap absent.)

19–20 Nov.: Visit to South Vietnam by Japanese premier Kishi.

4 Nov.: *Indonesia*: PKI leader D. N. Aidit urged stronger line against Dutch, over West Irian.

15 Nov.: *Pravda* came out in support for Indonesia's claim to West Irian.

19 Nov.: *Laos*: Inauguration of government of national union, with two Pathet Lao ministers.

Table 8.1 (*Contd.*)

| Soviet Union | China | Vietnam | South-East Asia |
|---|---|---|---|
| 22 Nov.: Moscow Declaration published. Condemnation of 'modern revisionism' as principal danger at present time; Tito refused to sign. | | 23 Nov.: Tran Van Gieu's article on Nam Ky uprising of 1940, with emphasis on need for preparation and strength.<br><br>28 Nov.: Le Duan and Pham Hung returned to Hanoi; Ho Chi Minh stayed away until 24 December. | 27 Nov.: *Indonesia*: Sukarno met Kishi in Jakarta; final stage of reparations negotiations. |

23 November 1940. He warned against the danger of premature revolt and insisted that the Party would only achieve final victory if it prepared the ground thoroughly, making sure of its own strength before taking action.[16] The 1940 rising had been a disaster and the historical analogy was obvious. During the next year or so the Party seems to have been consolidating its position in the South rather than attempting a direct challenge to Diem; but the change did not mean any weakening of Hanoi's perseverence in its long-term goals.

## III

Two days after Aristov's departure from Hanoi it was announced that the Vietnamese delegation to Moscow for the 40th anniversary of the October Revolution would comprise Ho Chi Minh, Le Duan and Pham Hung – the last-named perhaps secretly representing South Vietnam. The same group also attended the November meeting of world Communist leaders. In North Vietnam itself, however, Truong Chinh's plans for an elaborate celebration of the Soviet anniversary appear to have been set on one side. The meeting actually held in Hanoi on 6 November was addressed not by Truong Chinh but by Nguyen Duy Trinh, who carefully avoided commitment to a specific ideological line. China and the Soviet Union figured equally in his remarks about their great socialist achievements.[17] The Vietnamese leaders were probably anxious to postpone their own decisions on ideological and other questions until they knew the outcome of the Moscow meeting. It was not so much a case of waiting for 'orders from Moscow' as of inability to resolve internal difficulties until everyone had a clearer picture of the new international line. In the event the Moscow Declaration probably favoured the influence of Le Duan. On 28 November 1957 he and Pham Hung reappeared in Hanoi without Ho Chi Minh, who was said to have accepted an invitation to stay abroad a little longer, and it was they who reported on the Moscow meeting to a special session of the VNWP Central Committee early in December.[18]

In retrospect it is hardly possible to believe that either Ho or Giap could have been purged from the leadership as a result of this crisis. But the emergence of Le Duan almost certainly produced a new balance of forces within the Politburo, ensuring that Truong Chinh would not recover his position in the Party Secretariat even though he was to become a deputy premier in the government a few months later. By the time Ho Chi Minh reappeared in Hanoi towards the end of December, he and his close associates of the 1940s (Hoang Van Hoan, Vo Nguyen Giap and Pham Van Dong) had probably suffered a temporary loss of influence *vis-à-vis* both Le Duan and Truong Chinh. In the end, however, a new consensus was achieved which served as a basis for the next stage of the revolution. The Russians were probably content to encourage the promotion of Le Duan, if only because he was more independent of the Chinese than other top leaders in Hanoi. They presumably also welcomed the possibility of developing lines of communication with North Vietnam which did not depend wholly on Peking. From 8 to 24 January 1958 a delegation of French Communists visited Hanoi, effectively reviving a connection between the two Parties which had been strong in the colonial period. Not only did Le Duan play a prominent part in receiving the visitors on that occasion – for the first time his name appeared before Truong Chinh's in the published order of precedence.[19] From that point on, he was a power to be reckoned with in Vietnamese Communist decision-making. It would be wrong nevertheless to interpret the outcome of the crisis as the permanent victory of a 'pro-Soviet' faction in the Vietnamese Party. If anything, relations between the Soviet Union and China were closer at the beginning of 1958 than they had been six months earlier; what mattered was the more general 'swing to the left' in the Communist world as a whole.

## IV

The main barrier to renewal of the armed struggle in South Vietnam was still the international situation. Early in 1958 the Soviet premier Bulganin urged President Eisenhower to agree to another summit conference, similar to the one held in Geneva in 1955. For the next few months Russian diplomacy focused on the attempt to achieve some kind of détente, at least in the areas of East–West trade and suspension of nuclear weapons tests. The drive does not appear to have been affected by Khrushchev's own assumption of the premiership towards the end of March, when Bulganin was unceremoniously removed. But by April it was becoming clear that there was no real basis for Soviet–American agreement on issues of substance, and the initiative eventually stalled. Although the idea of détente was by no means dead, there were signs of a changing political mood in both Moscow and Peking: a further sharpening of the 'anti-revisionist' line, representing a significant 'swing to the left' by comparison with the years 1955–7.

By this time, following the Nagasaki incident, there was no longer any doubt about the failure of Chinese attempts to strengthen economic ties with Japan. Mao's 'great leap forward' implied a continuing desire for economic independence of the Soviet Union, but it was accompanied by a strengthening of the anti-imperialist line – leaving little room for Sino-American détente. Whilst military relations between the two major Communist powers ran into difficulties during the early months of 1958, their ideological positions appeared to converge as both the Soviet and Chinese media became increasingly critical of Tito's 'revisionism'. On 5 May 1958, the opening day of the second session of the Chinese 8th Party Congress, *Renmin Ribao* published a vigorous attack on Yugoslavia under the title 'Modern Revisionism must be Criticised', which *Pravda* immediately echoed. There may have been some doubt about how far Hanoi would be willing to join in criticism of Yugoslavia, in view of Ho's relationship with Tito. The Chinese attack of 5 May was not reprinted by *Nhan-Dan* until three days later, and even then not in full; on 12 May the Vietnam News Agency made a point of publishing an exchange of messages between Tito and Ho. But on 29 May a strong attack on 'revisionism' signed by Le Duan brought the Vietnamese firmly into line with other Parties.[20] By then too, North Vietnam was beginning to return to the political and economic line for which Truong Chinh had been criticised in 1956. At the National Assembly session of 16– 29 April 1958 Ho again spoke of the need to follow China's example, and at the end of the session Truong Chinh re-emerged in an official position when he and Pham Hung were both appointed deputy premiers.[21] Meanwhile, a series of articles in *Nhan-Dan* indicated the start of a new campaign against bourgeois intellectuals very similar to the 'anti-rightist' movement in China the previous autumn; several of those who had spoken out against land reform in 1956 were now forced to make their own 'self-criticism'.

Both Hanoi and Peking were by now becoming concerned about developments in Laos, where on 20 March 1958 the Vientiane government had made its first request to the International

TABLE 8.2 *Vietnam, the Communist powers and South-East Asia, March–May 1958*

| Soviet Union | China | Vietnam | South-East Asia |
| --- | --- | --- | --- |
| 3 Mar.: Soviet endorsement of Polish (Rapacki) Plan for disengagement in central Europe. | 5 Mar.: Fourth Sino-Japanese private trade agreement signed. | 7 Mar.: Letter from Pham Van Dong to Ngo Dinh Diem, proposing talks: start of major propaganda campaign against the South. | Early Mar.: *Indonesia*: Start of campaign by government forces loyal to Sukarno, to suppress Sumatra rebellion. |
| 13 Mar.: Yugoslav Communist League published its draft programme. | 16 Mar.: *Jiefang Junbao* on fighting war with inferior weapons; same day, Ye Jianying opened PLA academy of military science. | 12 Mar.: Series of DRVN–USSR aid agreements signed. | 11–13 Mar.: Manila Meeting of SEATO. |
| 15 Mar.: Soviet Union's Four-Point Peace Plan published. | | 16 Mar.: Congress of Vietnamese Buddhists opened in Hanoi. | 13 Mar.: *Indonesia*: Assembly ratified Japanese reparations agreement. |
| | | 18 Mar.: Le Duan talk to Fatherland Front meeting: calls for strong economy in North, intensification of revolutionary struggle in South. | |

20 Mar.: *Laos*: Souvanna Phouma's letter to International Commission seeking its withdrawal after 4 May.

19 Mar.: Series of anti-American demonstrations in Hanoi, etc.

23–7 Mar.: Visit to Hanoi by premier of Romania, Chivu Stoica; emphasis on full implementation of Geneva agreements.

27 Mar.: Letter by Vo Nguyen Giap to International Commission, complaining of US military activity in South Vietnam.

Mar. or Apr.: In Quang-Ngai province (South Vietnam), Communist leader Tran Nam Trung authorised preparations for local rising in Tra-Bong district.

20, 22 Mar.: Talks by Mao at Chengdu Conference of Party secretaries: 'great leap forward' in preparation.

24 Mar.: Soviet Memorandum again urging summit conference with Western leaders.

27 Mar.: Bulganin resigned as Soviet premier; succeeded by Khrushchev.

4 Apr.: Soviet proposal to suspend nuclear tests; Soviet tests were suspended unilaterally, 31 March.

5 Apr.: Soviet decision not to send delegation to Yugoslav Congress.

TABLE 8.2 (Contd.)

| Soviet Union | China | Vietnam | South-East Asia |
|---|---|---|---|
| | | | Mid Apr.: *Indonesia*: government forces took rebel centre of Padang, in Sumatra.<br>15 Apr.: Formal inauguration of Japan–Indonesian relations, and reparations agreement. |
| | 9 Apr.: Japanese premier Kishi's letter to Diet members indicated opposition to certain aspects of trade agreement with Peking. | 13 Apr.: *Nhan-Dan* article indicating start of campaign against counter-revolutionaries and rightists. | |
| | | 16–29 Apr.: National Assembly session: Truong Chinh and Pham Hung became deputy premiers; Hoang Van Hoan appointed vice-chairman of Assembly. | |
| 18 Apr.: Soviet Union raised issue of US nuclear-armed flights over Arctic.<br>19 Apr.: *Kommunist* criticised Yugoslav draft programme.<br>21–7 Apr.: Congress of Yugoslav Communist League, Belgrade. | 23 Apr.: Sino-Soviet Treaty on Trade and Navigation signed. | 23 Apr.: Ho Chi Minh's speech on need to follow China's example. | |

1 May: Hanoi Rally: Ho Chi Minh on people to unite in order to build the North and struggle for reunification.

2 May: Nagasaki 'flag incident' in Japan; no chance of trade agreement being implemented.

3 May: Western rejection of Rapacki plan marked end of Soviet hopes for an early summit meeting.

4 May: *Laos*: Supplementary elections held: Americans alarmed by relative success of Pathet Lao.

5 May: *Pravda* reprinted *Renmin Ribao* attack on revisionism; followed by attack of its own, 9 May.

5 May: *Renmin Ribao*: 'Modern revisionism must be criticised'; attack on Yugoslav programme.

5–23 May: CCP 8th Congress: second session. Strongly 'leftist' in tone, preparing way for 'great leap' policies.

8 May: *Nhan-Dan* commentary on Yugoslav programme; milder than Chinese.

12 May: VNA report of exchange of messages between Tito and Ho Chi Minh.

12 May: Chinese finally cancelled trade agreement with Japan.

Table 8.2  (*Contd.*)

| Soviet Union | China | Vietnam | South-East Asia |
|---|---|---|---|
| 15 May: *Sputnik III* launched. | 23 May: End of Chinese Party Congress. 25 May: Lin Biao promoted to top leadership within Politburo; also prominent at military conference, from 22 May to 22 July, emphasising self-reliance, role of militia. | 23 May: *Hoc Tap* article, criticising Yugoslav position more strongly. 29 May: Strong attack on 'revisionism' by Le Duan. | 14–15 May: Soviet and Chinese statements denouncing American involvement in Indonesian revolt. 18 May: Allen Pope incident. 22 May: US agreed to sell arms to Indonesia. 23 May: *Laos*: International Commission debated its own dissolution; no decision yet. |

Commission to bring its work to an end on the ground that after the supplementary elections of 4 May the Geneva settlement on Laos would have been fully implemented. Coincidentally the North Vietnamese stepped up their propaganda campaign for reunification, a new phase of which had begun with another much-publicised letter from Pham Van Dong to Ngo Dinh Diem dated 7 March. Large demonstrations were held in Hanoi and other northern cities on 19 March, a date originally designated as 'anti-America day' in the early 1950s; on 20 March, for good measure, a group of 'spies' from the South was tried in public and sentenced to death.[22] The question was whether it would be possible as time went on to transform the propaganda campaign in support of a low-level political struggle in the South into a fully-fledged revolutionary movement powerful enough to challenge and defeat the American presence in Saigon. In the changing global situation North Vietnam might at last find sufficient support in both Moscow and Peking for an intensification of its struggle against Diem. There was no longer any possibility of a single dramatic move leading to immediate reunification: Hanoi's aim now must be to step up the struggle year by year.

# Part III
## 1958–60

# 9 The Changing Pattern of World Tension

> The Iraqi Revolution signifies that the anti-colonial struggle has entered a new high tide. The greater the armed threats of the imperialists . . . the closer the unity between the national liberation movement and the socialist movement will grow.
>
> *Renmin Ribao*, Peking,
> 29 July 1958

> In the years of the gap, the Soviets may be expected to use their superior striking ability to achieve their objectives in ways which may not require launching an actual attack. Their missile power will be the shield behind which they will slowly but surely advance – through Sputnik diplomacy, limited brush-fire wars, indirect non-overt aggression, intimidation and subversion, internal revolution, increased prestige or influence, and the vicious blackmail of our allies. The periphery of the free world will slowly be nibbled away.
>
> John F. Kennedy, speech to Senate,
> 14 August 1958

## I

What can now be recognised as one of the critical turning-points in recent international history occurred during the summer and autumn of 1958. As a result, four years after the Geneva ceasefire, the world situation at last began to appear more favourable to the North Vietnamese aim of undermining American power in the South and bringing about national reunification. There were no illusions that victory would come quickly, but an intensification of the long-term struggle was beginning to seem feasible. As the global power struggle entered a new phase, both the United States and the Communist powers became more suspicious about one another's ultimate objectives and therefore more concerned about their own global security. The change can be attributed partly to the revival of 'leftist' ideology in the Communist world; but that was only one element in a complicated situation whose many cross-currents are not easily reduced to a single coherent picture. In this new situation Indochina would again become a focal point of East–West conflict, but events in Vietnam must still be understood against the wider international background.

Between May and October 1958 two consecutive crises brought the United States and the Communist powers once again to the brink of military confrontation. In retrospect they can be seen as marking the end of the period that had begun in 1955, and forming a prelude to the new period of tension which was about to begin. The first crisis erupted in the Middle East where a political conflict in Lebanon during May proved to be only one strand in a highly complicated sequence of manoeuvres, culminating in the Iraq revolution of 15 July. The outcome was not merely a setback for the American-sponsored Baghdad Pact. It was also the first time that a government which had chosen to ally itself positively with the United States was overthrown by an internal political upheaval. Although the Communist Party of Iraq was not directly responsible, the revolution provided the opportunity for it to expand its power – and perhaps eventually to lead the country into the Soviet camp. For that reason Khrushchev feared American retaliation, which in turn might have obliged the Russians themselves to become more deeply involved. The United States did send a unit of Marines to Lebanon, whilst the British reinforced their position in Jordan. But having secured those two areas the Western powers decided not to go farther, and after a series of proposals and counter-proposals for a summit meeting which never took place, London and Washington recognised the new regime in Baghdad in the first week of August. One result was to make the Americans increasingly dependent on their alliance with Iran – until the Shah also succumbed to a revolution two decades later. The crisis also served to demonstrate that there were limits to Washington's determination (or ability) to defend its interests by force in all parts of the world.

The Middle East crisis was important too in revealing – although not yet to the world at large – serious differences between Soviet and Chinese attitudes towards the United States, which seem to have surfaced during Khrushchev's unexpected visit to Peking between 31 July and 3 August 1958. The Soviet leader, anxious to avoid a confrontation over Iraq, had earlier made proposals for a summit meeting with the Western powers. By contrast, the Chinese had proclaimed themselves 'the faithful friend of nations striving for national liberation' and at one point even offered to send 'volunteers' to defend the Iraq revolution.[1] Mao was determined to pursue his own international line, rejecting the idea that Khrushchev was entitled to negotiate with the West on behalf of the socialist camp as a whole. Nor was he willing to heed Soviet criticisms of the 'great leap forward', although the Chinese leadership as a whole was almost certainly divided on that issue. The Sino-Soviet talks that summer allowed the two leaders to 'paper over' the differences between them, but as time went on Khrushchev would find the problem of China increasingly difficult to cope with.

The second crisis occurred soon afterwards in the Taiwan Straits, where Chiang Kaishek's forces still occupied the offshore islands of Quemoy and Matsu. On 23 August 1958 the PLA began to bombard Quemoy in what seemed like the first move of a campaign to invade the islands. The United States immediately reaffirmed its support for Chiang and provided the logistic support he needed to hold on to them. But Peking's motives were not at all clear and Soviet support for the bombardment was at best lukewarm, which led Western analysts to conclude that China was trying to hinder Soviet–American détente. Mao himself may have been less enthusiastic about the operation than some of his generals, who were still preoccupied with military modernisation, and he may have feared that an all-out attack on the islands would involve China becoming too dependent on Sino-Soviet military co-operation. Earlier the same year Mao is said to have rejected a proposal for joint naval defence which would have given the Russians permanent facilities on the China coast. He may also have had reservations about the military talks between Malinovsky and Peng Dehuai at the time of Khrushchev's visit to Peking.[2] By September the Chinese seem to have been ready to talk to the Americans again rather than accept Soviet conditions for military aid; but that did not mean they were willing to back down on the Taiwan issue altogether.

On 6 September Zhou Enlai indicated that the Chinese would like to resume ambassadorial talks with the Americans, and a new series of meetings began in Warsaw ten days later. The fighting nevertheless continued, with a critical engagement on 27–8 September in which the Communist side suffered a serious reverse. A week later, on 6 October, the PLA suddenly announced a unilateral ceasefire. Despite further shelling later in the month, coinciding with a visit by Dulles to Taipei, it was now clear that the conflict would not escalate. Soon afterwards a Communist decision to shell the islands only on alternate dates made it possible for Chiang to reinforce them without difficulty. Meanwhile the Americans seemed to adopt a more conciliatory line towards Peking at the end of September, which may have alarmed the Russians a little; but there was no Chinese response. During October the Chinese reiterated their demand for a total United States withdrawal from Taiwan, leaving no room for compromise on smaller issues, and on 27 October *Renmin Ribao* published a series of quotations from Mao's writings under the title 'Imperialism and all Reactionaries are Paper Tigers' – which again signalled a hardening of the anti-imperialist line.[3]

It is not impossible that Mao endorsed the Quemoy operation precisely in order to demonstrate the ineffectiveness of conventional warfare against the United States – without, that is, an unacceptable degree of military dependence on the Soviet Union. Many years earlier, during the anti-Japanese war, Mao is thought to have adopted a similar attitude to conventional strategy when he authorised Peng Dehuai to proceed with the 'hundred regiments' offensive of 1940; there too, Communist forces ignored his ideas of revolutionary warfare and suffered a major defeat. In 1958 the first casualty of the Quemoy failure was the army chief-of-staff, Su Yu, a leading 'moderniser', who was dismissed in October. But Mao may already have set his sights on removing Peng Dehuai as defence minister and promoting Lin Biao in his place, which he finally succeeded in doing in August 1959.

Taiwan itself ceased to be the principal focus of Chinese anti-imperialism in the period which followed – and Chiang Kaishek virtually abandoned any ideas he may have had about returning to the mainland in the foreseeable future. By the end of the year Peking was concentrating much more on two other areas where its security seemed to be threatened: Tibet and Laos. The 'autonomous' Tibetan government was facing an increasingly effective anti-Communist revolt, which by the end of 1958 was receiving secret assistance from the American CIA.[4] By that time too, there were signs of potential conflict between China and India over disputed sections of their common border. The latter had not previously caused trouble, but New Delhi now became concerned about a Chinese road linking Sinjiang and Tibet across an area it still claimed as Indian territory. On 18 October, after the disappearance of an Indian patrol sent out to investigate the road, the Indian government made a formal protest to Peking: the first in a long series of diplomatic exchanges which became increasingly bitter as the Tibetan crisis reached its climax in the early months of 1959.

In Laos too the Chinese were worried about the growing American presence close to their southern borders, following the collapse of Souvanna Phouma's coalition and the appointment of Phoui Sananikone as prime minister in July–August 1958. The change represented a threat to Zhou Enlai's strategy of building separate relations with Laos and Cambodia, and if the Americans persisted with their plan to draw Laos into the SEATO alliance there was a danger that Zhou himself would be unable to sustain China's hitherto moderate line in Indochina. But there was no indication of any serious Chinese concern about Vietnam at this stage, or of Chinese support for an intensification of the struggle against Diem.

In the aftermath of the crises over Iraq and the Taiwan Straits, there appeared to be a return to something like global stability towards the end of 1958. Moscow's strategy was still based on a belief that its increasing military strength, symbolised by the *sputnik*, had opened the way to a more serious dialogue with the West – which might result in long-term agreements in such areas as arms control, disengagement in Europe, and East–West trade. Khrushchev's proposals for a new summit meeting along the lines of that held in 1955 were rebuffed by the West, as were his suggestions for formal trade treaties. Nevertheless on 14 August 1958 the United States and its allies agreed to relax previous restrictions on private trade with the Soviet 'bloc' (excluding China), and at the end of October three-power talks opened in Geneva on the technical aspects of limiting or banning nuclear weapons tests.

But whilst both sides recognised the need to avoid actual armed conflict, they did not cease to prepare for the ultimate possibility of war. Soviet progress in rocket technology led the Americans to fear the emergence of a 'missile gap' between the two superpowers in the early 1960s, to which they responded by strengthening their own strategic capabilities in Europe and by accelerating the rearmament of West Germany and Japan. The resulting escalation of the arms race made Europe once again a focal point of international tension in a way it had not been since 1955, and also brought Japan into Soviet–American global calculations. East–West negotiations on certain issues were thus accompanied by underlying anxieties which would generate periods of acute tension during the next three or four years.

In the case of Japan conflict centred upon the revision of the bilateral security treaty with the United States, originally signed in 1951. Although full-scale rearmament was prohibited by the Japanese constitution, the Kishi government was willing to expand its 'self-defence' forces and in September 1958 foreign minister Fujiyama visited Washington to initiate negotiations for a revised treaty. The Chinese (as well as the Russians) felt threatened by this move, which was denounced by Chen Yi, on 19 November 1958.[5] In Japan itself the Communist Party took the lead in organising a campaign to mobilise public opinion against it, which culminated in the Tokyo riots of Summer 1960. Meanwhile in Western Europe the 'left', with some encouragement from Moscow, sponsored a campaign for nuclear disarmament in an attempt to mobilise opinion against the deployment of American intermediate range missiles; but the movement never acquired the same political momentum as its counterpart in Japan.

More significant was the diplomatic offensive on which the Soviet Union and its allies embarked in the autumn of 1958, with the ostensible aim of securing a German peace treaty and so changing the status of Berlin – and also in the hope of creating differences between the United States and its European allies. The demand for a German peace settlement, which earlier negotiations in 1946–7 and again in 1954 had failed to achieve, was revived by East Germany on 5 September 1958. Two months later, on 12 November, the Soviet Union called specifically for a change in the status of Berlin: a challenge which the United States, Britain and France were bound to resist but which they could only meet effectively if the NATO alliance remained firm. The ensuing crisis over Berlin lasted until 1961. The issue had special relevance for Vietnam in that the Russians and their allies were now questioning the post-war military arrangements which had governed all practical relations between the great powers in Germany since 1945, despite the absence of any political settlement. The North Vietnamese, determined to reverse the partition of their own country under the military agreement of 1954, may have taken comfort from the Soviet Union's support of East German demands at this stage.

There were signs too of a new challenge to the partition of Korea, which had remained undisturbed since 1953. The Chinese completed the withdrawal of their 'volunteers' from North Korea towards the end of October and on 10 November 1958 called on the United Nations (in effect the United States) to withdraw from the South. Although no major crisis ensued, the move emphasised the essentially temporary nature of the Korean armistice in Communist eyes. The common experience of the Communist Parties of the three divided countries was highlighted by visits of the East German and North Korean leaders to Hanoi (as well as to Peking) in late 1958 and early 1959: Kim Ilsung at the end of November, followed by Grotewohl the following January.[6] The analogy between Vietnam and Berlin was to become increasingly important over the next few years; but these diplomatic moves did not mean that Hanoi was free to resume armed struggle immediately without more explicit encouragement from Moscow and Peking.

## II

The Vietnam question must also be seen against the background of other developments during 1958, which was a significant year in the evolution of what was to become known as the 'national liberation movement' in the third world. The most dramatic events occurred in Cuba, where Castro had been engaged in building up a small guerrilla force since his return to the island late in 1956. His campaign at last began to make significant progress from about the middle of 1958, when he secured (or agreed to accept) the support of the Cuban Popular Socialist Party – that is, the Communists – and was joined in the Sierra Maestra by Carlos Rafael Rodriguez. During 1957 the Communists had criticised Castro's plans for armed struggle, and even as late as April 1958 their refusal to respond to his call for a general strike in Havana had guaranteed its failure. But some time between June and the middle of August that year they committed themselves to his cause, helping to create a Front which could unite all anti-Batista forces behind a single revolt. Whether Castro himself was secretly a Marxist–Leninist is irrelevant to the question of the Communists' own attitude, which underwent a significant change at that time. Nor is it necessary here to consider the extent to which Castro's charismatic victory depended on their practical support. The result of the alliance is not in doubt: from about the end of August, Castro and Guevara launched a guerrilla campaign across the island which gave them sufficient strength to take Havana itself at the beginning of 1959.[7]

In Algeria too the nationalist struggle against the French which had begun in 1954 was by this time gaining momentum. It occasioned the political crisis which brought De Gaulle to power in France at the end of May 1958; and in September a Cairo meeting of the 'Front de Libération Nationale' (FLN) established a provisional government. The FLN, however, did not depend at all on Communist participation. The one leader who might have emerged as a serious Marxist–Leninist, Abane, had been eliminated towards the end of 1957. The absence of a Communist element in the top leadership may explain why, at least until late 1960, the Soviet Union remained fairly cool towards Algerian visitors to Moscow. The Chinese, however, immediately recognised the provisional government and in December 1958 gave a warm welcome to its delegation in Peking.[8]

We have already seen how the Chinese also showed more enthusiasm than Khrushchev for the July revolution in Iraq, which they would have liked to see develop as a liberation movement if the United States had decided to intervene. In Iraq, moreover, the Communist Party did emerge as a staunch ally of the revolutionary regime. Elsewhere in the Middle East the struggle against British rule in Aden (South Yemen) was likewise entering a new phase, with a series of strikes and bomb attacks in March 1958, followed by a more persistent strike movement during 1959. The fact that South Yemen later became a full member of the 'socialist camp' does not in itself prove a Communist role from the start; but there is nothing to suggest that the Party there opposed the struggle at this stage. Another area where the first stirrings of revolutionary nationalism could be discerned in 1958 was the Belgian Congo, where the colonial authorities announced plans for gradual political evolution in July, and where the first serious nationalist riots occurred at the beginning of 1959. The question of possible Marxist–Leninist involvement there too in the initial phase has never been resolved. But again the Chinese certainly took notice of what was happening: on 25 January 1959 rallies were held in Peking in support of both the Cuban and the Congolese people, with Peng Zhen as principal speaker.[9]

It is not necessary to regard these developments in widely scattered parts of the world as emanating from some single all-embracing 'Communist conspiracy'. But collectively they represented a significant change of mood in key areas of the third world. Neither 'local' Communist Parties nor the leaders in Moscow and Peking could afford to ignore the changing pattern of revolutionary opportunity in the third world. Even if they had no part at all in creating the initial impulse towards 'national liberation', it was a historical trend with which they must come to terms and was bound to be the subject of a major international Communist debate.

Vietnam differed from Cuba and these other countries in several respects, not least because the American military presence in the South made armed struggle there a much more formidable task. It would require far more than a Castro-style 'march from the Sierra' to achieve final victory; fraternal military assistance would be required sooner or later. In addition Vietnam's position was, as we have seen, comparable in principle with those of Korea and Germany. Any attempt to use military means to upset the *de facto* partition would have serious international repercussions. For precisely that reason, however, Hanoi's only hope of eventual reunification lay in developing the revolutionary struggle within the South to a point where it could be presented as a 'national liberation' movement against the United States. Towards the end of 1958 Hanoi was at last beginning to move in that direction. The decision to intensify the southern struggle was finally taken at the 15th Plenum of the VNWP Central Committee sometime in January 1959, although it was not made public until the following May.

### III

Despite the critical significance of this period, both for East–West and for Sino–Soviet relations, relatively little attempt has been made to analyse the internal politics of the Soviet and Chinese leaderships during the second half of 1958. However, enough has been said in previous chapters to demonstrate that decision-making in Hanoi is intelligible only in the light of what was happening in the major Communist capitals; and since this period was perhaps the most crucial of all for the Vietnamese, events in Moscow and Peking cannot be ignored.

In Western studies of Soviet politics, the crisis of 1957 has been examined much more fully than the apparently inconclusive debates and manoeuvres of 1958. In the latter much appears to have hinged on the attitude of different leaders towards Bulganin, who had been replaced by Khrushchev as premier in March 1958 and was removed from the Party Presidium on 5 September the same year. At a Plenum of the CPSU Central Committee from 15 to 19 December he was subjected to formal criticism and obliged to make a 'confession', and his future was again an issue at the 21st Congress of the CPSU from 27 January to 5 February 1959. Although he had lost power himself, his cause was still supported by a significant minority in the leadership and neither he nor any other 'silent member' of the earlier 'anti-Party group' was expelled from the Central Committee.[10] The debate may have gone much deeper than the agricultural issues on which Khrushchev concentrated in public; but if so, we have no means of knowing what its real focal point was.

Nor is it easy to assess the consequences, if any, of the promotion of A. N. Shelepin to replace General Serov as head of the KGB towards the end of 1958. Possibly that was a further gain for the Party as opposed to other organs within the Soviet system, Shelepin having previously been head of the Communist Youth League. But it was not necessarily a gain for Khrushchev himself or for the line of 'peaceful co-existence'. The one small indication of Shelepin's international thinking that has emerged from later Western research would suggest that, a decade or so later, he favoured the strategy of supporting Communist revolutions in Asia rather than nationalist regimes whose 'bourgeois' character made them inherently unreliable.[11] It would be absurd to pretend that Shelepin's promotion was enough to change the whole shape of Soviet global strategy; but it may have been in keeping with a general trend towards greater emphasis on revolution in the third world.

The CPSU 21st Congress, which approved a new seven-year plan, may have represented the highest point of Khrushchev's personal power as Party first secretary; even so, he could not get his way on all issues. The Congress was also important in the evolution of Sino-Soviet relations, since Khrushchev (for the first time) aired his criticisms of Mao's 'great leap forward' in an indirect – but unmistakable – attack on the Chinese economic model. The Soviet leader was probably encouraged by the fact that Mao himself had been obliged to 'retire from the front line' at the CCP Central Committee's 6th Plenum (28 November–10 December 1958) and was about to be replaced as head of state. The Chinese delegates to the CPSU Congress, Zhou Enlai and Kang Sheng, may have been willing to move back towards closer relations with Moscow so long as the socialist camp as a whole continued to maintain the anti-imperialist line.

Probably the most burning question for the Chinese leaders at the beginning of 1959 was whether to revert to a policy of 'learning from the Soviet Union' and to accept Moscow's conditions for increased material support. On at least two occasions (1 January and 1 March) *Renmin Ribao* carried articles calling for greater reliance on Soviet aid, signed by Chen Yun – a leader who had not been heard from for some time and who after early March would again disappear from the limelight without actually being purged. Meanwhile the Chinese media had nothing but praise for Khrushchev's seven-year plan. But Mao himself seems to have fought a rearguard action against any return to dependence on the USSR, and we know from a speech he made on 23 July 1959 that he strongly disapproved of the line followed by the Party during the first two months of that year.[12] Some time in March or April, it would appear that Mao succeeded at least in preventing a major reversal of his fundamental principle of 'self-reliance'; but he was obliged to allow Liu Shaoqi to succeed him as head of state.

In all this, the Vietnamese Party leaders could merely watch and wait. Following their own 15th Plenum, Ho Chi Minh and Hoang Van Hoan attended the CPSU 21st Congress in Moscow and no doubt had talks in Peking on the way. Until Sino-Soviet relations were clarified, they and their colleagues decided not to take up a clear position of their own, and to delay publication of the 'hard line' 15th Plenum resolution. But Hanoi may have had some reason to hope that, even if Khrushchev succeeded in initiating another attempt at détente in Europe, the 'hardliners' in Moscow would be sufficiently powerful to ensure support for the new struggle in South Vietnam. And even if the Sino-Soviet *rapprochement* did not materialise after all, there was a possibility that in the long run the Russians and Chinese would begin to compete with one another in encouraging third world national liberation movements – including the revolution in South Vietnam.

## IV

Soviet and Chinese policies towards the West in fact began to diverge fundamentally in March 1959; the turning-point being the visit to Moscow of British prime minister Harold Macmillan from 21 February to 3 March, which opened the way to serious negotiations on the German question. By 19 March Khrushchev agreed to a meeting of the 'big four' foreign ministers, to begin in Geneva on 11 May. Although it fell short of the summit conference for which the Soviet leader had been pressing a year earlier, this marked the beginning of a new sequence of East–West exchanges which would culminate in the Khrushchev–Eisenhower meeting at Camp David the following September. The Chinese disapproved of talks of any kind with the Western powers so long as the Taiwan issue remained unresolved; and the easing of tension in Europe after the Khrushchev–Macmillan statement contrasted sharply with the harsh tone of Chinese commentaries on Laos and Tibet. On 11 March *Renmin Ribao* denounced the claim of the Vientiane government to be no longer bound by the Geneva Agreement. Further articles in the next few days attacked the Americans for encouraging fugitive KMT forces to violate the frontier between Laos and Yunnan. The situation was even more serious in Tibet, where the anti-Chinese rebellion spread to Lhasa on 10 March and could only be suppressed by military action. By the end of the month the Chinese authorities were obliged to dissolve the regional government and place the whole of Tibet under direct rule from Peking, leaving the Dalai Lama to make a dramatic escape across the mountains to India with the help of the CIA.[13] Mao and his colleagues may already have felt they were not receiving sufficient support from their Soviet allies against American actions along their southern borders.

North Vietnamese leaders must now have been placed in a difficult position. They had reason to fear Soviet–American détente, which might jeopardise their hope of developing the revolutionary movement in the South and achieving eventual reunification. On the other hand they were aware that any long-term challenge to the Americans would require Soviet as well as Chinese support, and they had no wish to side openly with Peking against Moscow. On 5 March, *Nhan-Dan* expressed full support for the Khrushchev–Macmillan statement and for the view that international disputes should be settled by peaceful negotiation. It would have been impolitic for Hanoi to do otherwise when a Vietnamese delegation was currently negotiating long-term aid agreements in Moscow, which were signed a few days later. At the same time, North Vietnam sought to cultivate friendly relations with other East European countries, sending Vo Nguyen Giap to attend the Polish and Hungarian Party Congresses in the latter part of March, and welcoming the Hungarian premier to Hanoi in April.[14]

Meanwhile, between 26 February and 8 March 1959 Ho Chi Minh visited Jakarta where he and Sukarno issued a joint communiqué attempting to recapture the 'spirit of Bandung'. Indonesian sympathy was vital to any effort to create an 'international united front' in support of a new phase of the struggle in Vietnam. Ho was probably also anxious to maintain close ties with the PKI, whose leader D. N. Aidit visited Hanoi at the beginning of April on his way home from talks in Moscow and Peking. It was natural for Indonesian and Vietnamese Communists to make common cause in face of a possible Sino-Soviet rift, since both were anxious to follow an anti-imperialist line without losing the support of Moscow. The Russians were no doubt equally keen to avoid quarrelling with the two most important Communist Parties in South-East Asia, but at a time when they were trying to negotiate solutions to European and bilateral Soviet–American problems it was not clear how far they would go in encouraging revolutionary activities whose ultimate target was the United States. The situation was very different from that of 1955, when détente had been world-wide and when Afro-Asian solidarity had not implied military confrontation with the West. In the new revolutionary phase now beginning, the Russians could not afford to abandon completely to Peking the leadership of the anti-imperialist struggle in South-East Asia; nor did they wish to drive the Chinese back towards independent conciliation with Japan and the West.

On 18 April 1959, in an important statement to the National People's Congress, Zhou Enlai rejected the idea that anything could ever breach the 'steel bulwark' of Sino-Soviet unity. At the same time he praised Chinese diplomatic success in developing relations with many Afro-Asian states, and emphasised the significance of the 'national independence' movement throughout the world. He denounced American attempts to create 'two Chinas'; also their encouragement of both German and Japanese 'militarism', and the strengthening of the SEATO alliance. Washington nevertheless believed it could detect the opportunity for a new Sino-American initiative, and a week later revived the idea of an exchange of newsmen. Once again however, the move was rebuffed by Peking: at the 89th ambassadorial meeting on 19 May the Chinese representative reiterated his demand for a withdrawal from Taiwan before other issues could be discussed.[15] By 11 May, when the Soviet and Western foreign ministers finally sat down together in Geneva, it was abundantly clear that whatever the prospects might be for negotiations on Germany, no comparable opportunity existed in relation to South-East Asia.

Precisely at that moment a new crisis began to develop in Laos when a unit of Pathet Lao forces suddenly rebelled against integration into the Royal Army. Two days later, on 13 May, Hanoi published the strongly worded communiqué of the VNWP Central Committee's 15th Plenum calling for the overthrow of Ngo Dinh Diem. The North Vietnamese were now in a position to force the pace, leaving both the Chinese and the Russians with little choice but to support them. Whether they acted with full Soviet support is impossible to say, but the move was certainly in keeping with the logic of the international situation – and also that of the changing situation in Indochina, to which we must now turn.

# 10 The Return to Armed Struggle

Our whole people, uniting and struggling with heroism and perseverance, will certainly smash the American imperialists' scheme to seize our land, and the plot of their lackeys to sell our country. On the basis of the consolidation of North Vietnam and its steady development in all fields, and of the broad and powerful development of the patriotic movement in the South – and with the approval and support of peace-loving people all over the world – our struggle for national reunificaction will certainly be successful.

Communiqué of 15th Plenum of VNWP Central Committee,
published 13 May 1959

The enemy would not allow us any peace. In the face of enemy operations and destructive pursuit, the armed propaganda teams – even if they wished to avoid losses – would never be able to engage the enemy in warfare and would never be able to become an actual revolutionary army . . . Therefore at the end of 1959 when we launched an additional armed struggle in coordination with the political struggle against the enemy, it immediately took the form in South Vietnam of revolutionary warfare: a long-range revolutionary warfare.

Internal Communist account (the 'Crimp' Document,
captured by American forces in
January 1966

I

During the second half of 1958 and the early months of 1959 the Indochinese Peninsula once again began to emerge as a focal point of conflict between the United States and the Communist Powers. From Washington's point of view the gravity of the situation arose not so much from actual events in Vietnam – although a perceptible change was taking place there – but from a general apprehension that in the changing international situation the American position in mainland South-East Asia was likely to be challenged. The Americans were conscious of having lost ground in Indonesia, following the collapse of the outer islands revolt, and as a result attached greater importance to their bilateral ties with South Vietnam, Thailand and Laos. In this there was a curious irony. Both in 1954 and again ten years later the Pentagon hawks invoked the so-called 'domino theory' to justify proposals for military action in Indochina, arguing that if South Vietnam came under Communist control the rest of South-East Asia would be in danger. But in 1958 the reality was that the most important single country of the region had already refused to ally itself with the United States. The 'loss' of Indonesia was not yet complete, in that some elements loyal to Sukarno were still anti-Communist; and American oil investments had not been affected by the campaign against the Dutch. But the United States desire for a stronger military presence in mainland South-East Asia was partly a result of what had already happened in the maritime half of the region.

The fact that Indochina was becoming more vital to American global strategy made it also more important in the calculations of the Soviet Union and China. In these circumstances the North Vietnamese, as we have seen, began to find their allies more willing to countenance an intensification of the struggle against Diem. It is impossible to pinpoint one specific decision as the starting point of the conflict which ensued. Nor is it easy to say that the decision for war was taken exclusively by one side or the other, representing a clearly definable act of 'aggression'. The conflict grew out of a series of moves and counter-moves in which each side attempted to strengthen its own position *vis-à-vis* its potential adversary. All that is certain is that the period from October 1958 to July 1959 contains the actual 'origins' of what became the Vietnam War.

A turning-point of some significance for Indochina was the coup in Thailand on 20 October 1958, when Sarit Thannarat proclaimed military rule in place of the constitutional system instituted in 1932. Although his faction had dominated the assembly and government since the earlier coup of September 1957, it was only now that he secured sufficiently firm control to commit Thailand unequivocally to the American alliance. Whereas Phibun's government had been willing to improve its relations with Peking, Sarit was now strong enough to turn his back on China's 'Bandung' strategy, in so far as it still survived. A sign of the change was the banning of trade with China (except Taiwan) in January 1959.[1] Another consequence of military rule was to strengthen Thailand's determination to play an active role in Laos – and if possible Cambodia – thus reviving the close relationship between these countries and Bangkok that had existed before the coming of the French in the nineteenth century.

In Cambodia Sihanouk remained unreceptive to American suggestions that he needed more protection against the Communist 'threat'. According to his own account, the Americans and South Vietnamese began plotting to overthrow him towards the end of 1958. He later accused them of planning a military coup, with the tacit support of his chief of staff Lon Nol, in which the key role would have been played by the general in charge of Siem Reap province, Dap Chhuon. By 21 February 1959 the prince had collected enough evidence to order the latter's arrest and to denounce the whole affair.[2] (He escaped a further plot against his life the following August.) Sihanouk was thus able to preserve his neutrality and maintain relations with the Communist world, despite the presence of a relatively impotent 'pro-American' element within the army. In any case Cambodia was not yet the principal target of either side in the conflict then taking shape: its turn would come a decade later.

In Laos, on the other hand, the collapse of the coalition government in July 1958, and the appointment of Phoui Sananikone as prime minister a month later, opened the way to closer relations with both Thailand and the United States and permitted an expansion of Western economic and military aid. Monetary reforms, which the Americans regarded as a necessary prelude to increased aid, were carried out by mid-October – drawing Laos more effectively into the 'imperialist' system. There was no longer any question of Vientiane developing closer ties with Peking. The next stage came when right-wing officers of the Royal Laotian Army demanded a greater voice in the government, with the result that on 24 January 1959 Phoui was obliged to reshuffle his cabinet to make room for a number of military leaders – including Sarit's cousin Colonel Phoumi Nosavan.

It might be possible to represent Hanoi's moves in 1958 as a direct response to this strengthening of United States influence in Thailand and Laos. But North Vietnamese strategy also had its own logic, and the growing determination to step up the revolution in the South was now in accord with the changing international Communist line. There is little to support later claims by Hanoi that what happened in South Vietnam in late 1958 and early 1959 was a purely spontaneous popular revolt against the repression of the Diem regime, in which the Communists merely seized an opportunity not of their own making. It is possible, as captured cadres sometimes claimed later under interrogation, that the decision to intensify the struggle was taken as a result of pressure from the southern rank and file of the Party. Certainly the South Vietnamese authorities had scored a number of successes against the revolutionary movement during 1958 and the Party's strength was being sapped by frequent arrests under the anti-Communist 'denunciation campaign'. But there was still only one Party Centre (in Hanoi) and Vietnamese Communist publications of the 1970s leave little reason to suppose that vital decisions affecting the southern struggle were ever made anywhere else.

We have already seen that Hanoi had stepped up its propaganda against Saigon as early as March 1958, with mass demonstrations in support of Pham Van Dong's latest letter to Diem and a public trial of captured 'spies' from the South. Inside South Vietnam, moves were made around the middle of the year to promote the formation of anti-government organisations amongst the 'montagnard' people in upland areas. A conference to mobilise the minority people of Tra-Bong district (Quang-Ngai province) in June or July was followed by small-scale revolts in that area before the end of 1958, whilst the campaign to assassinate government officials was already under way in some lowland areas. An American embassy report of 7 January 1959 came to the conclusion that increasing violence in districts remote from Saigon implied a 'carefully planned campaign aimed at undermining the stability of the Diem government'.[3] A later Communist account indicated that at the end of 1958 the Party ordered the creation of a 'people's armed forces command' to bring various elements of the southern 'liberation forces' more firmly under its own control.[4] Defectors in the later stages of the war also referred to that as the point at which the leadership judged the situation was becoming 'ripe' for a new struggle.

An incident destined to figure prominently in Communist propaganda was the so-called 'Phu-Loi Massacre' of 1 December 1958. Substantial numbers of Communist cadres and sympathisers, along with many who may have been no more than suspects, were by that time languishing in Diem's 'political re-education' centres. The incident in question occurred at one such centre where, according to Hanoi's version, about 1000 of 6000 inmates were deliberately poisoned by their guards and many more killed in the suppression of the ensuing revolt. On 18 January Vo Nguyen Giap brought the affair to the attention of the international Commission, and in Hanoi a special committee was formed by the Fatherland Front to 'investigate' it.[5] But the propaganda treatment of the incident makes it impossible for historians to get at the truth of what actually happened. One possibility is that a relatively minor incident at the Phu-Loi camp was magnified because it happened to coincide with Hanoi's decision to expand the struggle.

In retrospect it would appear that key decisions on the revolution in the south were taken at the 14th and 15th Plenums of the VNWP Central Committee, held respectively in November 1958 and early January 1959. The published communiqué of the 14th Plenum, which appeared in *Nhan-Dan* on 8 December, made no mention of the South. It merely recorded that the meeting heard three important statements: by Truong Chinh on the co-operativisation of agriculture, by Nguyen Duy Trinh on the three-year plan for 1958–60, and by Le Duan on the international situation.[6] That division of responsibility reflected the new balance of personalities within the leadership which had emerged towards the end of 1957. It also provides a further reason for supposing that Vo Nguyen Giap continued to be less prominent than before. Two weeks later, on 22 December 1958, the usual article for army day was signed jointly by Giap and Nguyen Chi Thanh and the emphasis was again on political work in the PAVN.

Le Duan's report was probably directly relevant to the southern struggle, which could never be divorced from international considerations. Whilst there may have been signs that the international line was gradually changing, North Vietnamese leaders were still obliged to devise a strategy in the South that did not conflict directly with Moscow's interest in détente. Nor were they likely to remain united if they adopted a line which had the support only of Peking. At the same time it was necessary to take account of the actual situation on the ground, and information from later defectors indicates that immediately after the 14th Plenum Le Duan paid a secret visit to the South to make his own assessment. As an advocate of intensifying the revolutionary struggle, he himself (rather than discontented southern cadres) may now have been trying to convince his colleagues in the Politburo that the time had come for stronger action. His assessment was presumably considered at the 15th Plenum, which must have met sometime before Ho Chi Minh and Hoang Van Hoan left for Moscow in mid-January to attend the CPSU 21st Congress. It was then that the Central Committee decided on what can now be recognised as a fundamental change in southern policy. The communiqué, not published until 13 May 1959, called on the people of Vietnam as a whole to unite in order to 'smash the schemes of the American imperialists to seize our land'.[7] It made no direct reference to an armed struggle; but a decision to increase the level of violence does seem to have been made by the middle of May.

Meanwhile one other North Vietnamese action at that time must be taken into account. In December 1958 there occurred the 'Huong-Lap Incident', at a point near the Vietnamese–Laotian border just west of the demilitarised zone between North and South Vietnam where Hanoi suddenly laid claim to a number of mountain villages which had always appeared on French maps as part of Laos. There were grounds for supposing that the border had indeed not been properly defined at that point during the colonial period, so that North Vietnam may have had a legal case. But no such claim had been made at the time when Vietnam was partitioned in 1954, and the demilitarised zone did not extend into the disputed territory; therein lay its real value to the Communist side. In the second half of December, according to American sources, a North Vietnamese unit crossed the border in the direction of Tchepone and occupied the disputed villages. Hanoi then protested against Laotian air raids on what it now claimed as the Vietnamese 'district of Huong-Lap'. Laotian ground forces were not strong enough to retake the area, with the result that North Vietnam now controlled a small corridor of land on either side of the 17th parallel, lying beyond the range of South Vietnamese defences along the demilitarised zone, through which they could infiltrate men and supplies southwards: in effect the forerunner of the 'Ho Chi Minh trail' of the 1960s.[8]

## II

The Huong-Lap incident had an immediate impact on politics in Laos where it was used by Phoumi Nosavan as an additional reason for strengthening the right-wing element in the government. If North Vietnam eventually decided to resume armed struggle on a significant scale, requiring the infiltration of men and supplies into the southern zone, control of at least the border areas of Laos would become a factor in the Vietnam conflict. The mere possibility of that development must have increased Washington's determination to establish its own friends firmly in power in Vientiane. On 11 February 1959 Phoui Sananikone repeated the claim, originally made by his predecessor the previous March, that the Geneva agreement on Laos had already been fully implemented. He went a step farther than Souvanna Phouma to draw the logical conclusion that Vientiane was no longer bound by the Geneva restrictions on foreign military aid. Hanoi reacted immediately by denouncing the claim as itself a breach of the Geneva Agreement on Laos, which it continued to insist must be treated as one component of a single settlement. That was the background to the Chinese outburst of 11 March which we have already noticed as one feature of the general reaffirmation of the anti-imperialist line in Peking.[9] Whereas in 1956–7 there had been signs of potential (if not actual) Sino-Vietnamese rivalry in relation to Laos and Cambodia, the two countries were now united in their opposition to an American policy apparently designed to bring Laos into full membership of the SEATO alliance.

The Laos situation came to a head in May 1959, at precisely the same moment as a Politburo meeting in Hanoi decided to publish the 15th Plenum communiqué: a coincidence which can hardly have been accidental, even though the connection cannot be traced explicitly. The Pathet Lao had been aware since March of the government's intention to integrate their two remaining battalions into the command structure of the Royal Laotian Army, and that the date fixed for the final transfer was 11 May. Dissatisfied with the new arrangements, the battalion stationed in the Plaine des Jarres decided to resist integration – whereupon the government issued an ultimatum for it to accept new officers or surrender its weapons. By 17 May this had led to an armed confrontation, in which the Pathet Lao unit succeeded in avoiding encirclement and escaped towards the North Vietnamese border.[10] Meanwhile, also on 11 May, the authorities in Vientiane arrested the Pathet Lao leaders still in the capital, including Prince Souphanouvong, Phoumi Vongvichit and Colonel Singkapo. The effective leadership of the movement consequently passed to leaders who had stayed in the maquis, among whom was the strongly pro-Vietnamese Kaysone Phomvihane. Later the same year, when the Neo Lao Hak Sat ('Patriotic Front') held its third national congress, Kaysone was elected vice-president and so became the most senior figure still at large. The likelihood that this amounted to a significant change in the Pathet Lao leadership seems to be confirmed by evidence of a diary found ten years later on a captured Vietnamese cadre in Laos, which mentioned May 1959 as the date when the VNWP Central Committee began to reassert its influence over the clandestine Lao people's Party.[11]

In Vietnam itself, publication of the official communiqué of the 15th Plenum on 13 May coincided with various secret military moves whose details are now known from information supplied later in the war by captives and defectors. They included the formation of the 559th transportation group directly under the command of the Party Centre, which was given the task of developing an infiltration route through southern Laos; and (in June) the creation of a new special battalion which was based at the naval headquarters of Quang-Khe and given responsibility for infiltration by sea.[12] It took some time before these decisions bore fruit; but according to an account probably derived ultimately from American intelligence sources, the actual movement of cadres from North to South Vietnam was observed from July onwards – albeit on a modest scale by comparison with what would follow during the 1960s.

In South Vietnam, May 1959 also saw two important government moves. The notorious 'Law 10/59' of 6 May, which established special military tribunals to deal with anyone suspected of pro-Communist activities, would later become a major target of North Vietnamese propaganda. Although its actual effects are difficult to assess, it probably played some part in making the rest of 1959 one of the 'darkest periods' in Southern Communist experience. A less dramatic event, but one of considerable economic importance, was the signature on 13 May of the long-discussed reparations agreement between South Vietnam and Japan. Although not so generous as the earlier agreements with Indonesia and the Philippines, it provided Saigon with additional moral and financial support at a time when both were needed.[13]

The conflict in Laos entered a new phase in the second half of July 1959, when Pathet Lao forces initiated guerrilla attacks in the province of Sam Neua bordering on North Vietnam. Their principal objective was probably to recover control of rural areas in that province, as a base for future operations, rather than to threaten the government in Vientiane. The latter, however, supported by the Americans, immediately accused Hanoi's forces of invading Laos. A United Nations team subsequently found evidence of North Vietnamese 'Intervention', but not 'aggression'; but the investigators were not allowed to enter Communist areas, and their negative report did not completely refute the claim by Laotian government officers that Pathet Lao forces alone were too weak to have made significant gains without substantial assistance from Hanoi. Although North Vietnamese regular units were not involved, it is quite likely that Vietnamese 'advisers' played a decisive role in the guerrilla operations.[14] The question of North Vietnamese motives for action at this point is therefore a legitimate one to ask, although not easily answered. These developments in Laos, moreover, coincided with the start of serious infiltration into South Vietnam, which depended on Communist control of eastern Laos and the 'Ho Chi Minh trail'.

## III

Ho Chi Minh himself was away from Hanoi when the conflict in Laos began to escalate, spending almost the whole of July 1959 in the Soviet Union, and most of August in China.[15]

His tour on this occasion took place during what appears to have been the most serious crisis so far in the evolution of Sino-Soviet relations, and his arrival in China coincided with the dramatic fall of Peng Dehuai. Between late April and early June the Chinese defence minister had visited Eastern Europe and the Soviet Union, perhaps in the hope of finding some basis for continuing Sino-Soviet collaboration at least in the military sphere. The Russians, however, regarded the issue of conformity with the Soviet line as still important. Further Soviet aid to China may have been conditional on Mao's abandonment of the 'great leap forward', to which Peng himself was in any case strongly opposed. There was also the question of Peking's ideological line on imperialism. Some progress towards improving Sino-Soviet relations may have been reflected in the signing of a new consular agreement on 23 June, and in discussions about new long-term trade arrangements. But at this point the Chinese apparently decided to test Moscow's good faith by demanding delivery of a sample atomic bomb, supposedly promised to them under the scientific agreement of October 1957. Khrushchev's refusal in late June brought matters to a head, and during July, there was a major confrontation between Peng and Mao at a meeting on Mount Lushan. By 23 July it would seem that Peng had all but lost.[16]

Meanwhile the Russians were moving step by step towards détente with the United States. The 'hardliner' Kozlov visited North America during the first half of July. Later the same month his visit was returned by Vice-President Nixon, and the outcome was an invitation to Khrushchev to tour the United States in September. In the interval (14–23 July) the Soviet leader made a trip to Poland, where he may have needed to strengthen international unity before negotiating with the West. It was also necessary for the Russians to define a new line on imperialism, and it was there that they clashed most forcefully with the Chinese. This was the context of a new crisis in Iraq, where on 9 July 1959 the militant wing of the Communist Party suddenly gained majority support for a 'Maoist' armed rebellion against the nationalist regime in Baghdad. The revolt was speedily crushed and by the end of the month the Iraq Party was obliged by Moscow to conduct a self-criticism.[17] But it was less easy for Soviet leaders to restrain the revolution in Indochina. To support Hanoi's latest moves might jeopardise the bid for détente with the United States; but not to do so meant allowing the Chinese a free hand in the area, perhaps even in Asia as a whole.

The meeting of the Chinese leadership on Mount Lushan culminated in a formal plenum of the CCP Central Committee from 2 to 16 August, at which Peng Dehuai was removed from office and became the (unnamed) target of a new campaign against 'right deviationism'. His fall, accompanied by the removal of China's ambassador to Moscow (Zhang Wentian), put an end to the possibility of a full-scale Sino-Soviet economic *rapprochement*: Soviet analysts later identified 1959 as the year in which economic, technical and cultural co-operation between the two Communist powers virtually ceased. But other issues had still to be settled and the situation probably remained fluid during the second half of

August. Liu Shaoqi, now Chairman of the People's Republic, seems to have strengthened his position; at the same time Zhou Enlai, who had been absent from public view since late June, reappeared in Peking on 22 August and was able to reassert the role of government (as opposed to Party) organs in criticising the statistical failures of the 'great leap forward'. But from our point of view the main outcome of the crisis was that the Chinese line became more anti-imperialist than ever.

That did not necessarily mean, however, that Peking would immediately endorse the North Vietnamese line of expanding the struggle in South Vietnam. Ho Chi Minh, arriving in north-western China in early August while the Lushan Plenum was still in session, was obliged to make his way slowly overland by way of Urumchi and Xian and did not arrive in the capital until 13 August. He had formal meetings with Liu Shaoqi on 20–1 August and presumably also met Zhou Enlai; but Mao himself was still in the South. The Vietnamese leader cannot have been much encouraged by the deterioration in Sino-Soviet relations. He had no choice but to wait upon the outcome of further Chinese debate, and it is highly unlikely that he secured any firm Chinese commitment to support an immediate return to armed struggle in Vietnam before he left for Hanoi on 26 August. For the time being Peking continued to regard Laos, and also the situation on the Sino-Indian border, as more important than Vietnam. A new intensification of guerrilla activity in Laos at this time led the Americans to increase their military assistance to Vientiane; a decision whose long-term significance was probably much greater than was implied by the public announcement on 26 August.[18] Almost simultaneously violence erupted on the border between China and India, where small clashes from late July onwards culminated in a more serious incident at Longju on 25 August 1959. About the same time, Nehru dismissed the Communist state government in Kerala which had taken on a pro-Chinese stand. These developments ought logically to have evoked a strong protest from Moscow in support of the Chinese; but on 10 September a TASS statement calling for a peaceful settlement of the border dispute failed conspicuously to take Peking's side.[19] Nor did the Russians veto a resolution in the United Nations Security Council on 7 September appointing a four-man team to investigate the situation in Laos, despite the protests of Peking and Hanoi. In both areas tension began to ease by the middle of that month, and the end of the immediate political crisis in China itself appeared to

TABLE 10.1   *Indochina and the Sino-Soviet Crisis, July–September 1959*

| Soviet–American détente | China | North Vietnam | Laos |
|---|---|---|---|
| 28 June–13 July: F. R. Kozlov visited United States. | | 2 July: Ho Chi Minh arrived in Moscow for talks with Khrushchev. (In Baku, 23 July) | |
| 13 July: Resumption of Geneva Foreign Ministers' Conference (until 5 August). | | July: Start of significant infiltration from North to South Vietnam, via 'Ho Chi Minh trail'. | Mid-July: Start of guerrilla warfare in Sam Neua province. |
| 14–23 July: Khrushchev in Poland. USSR accepted Oder–Neisse line. | 14 July: Peng Dehuai's letter to Mao, at Lushan meeting, criticising 'great leap forward'. | | |
| | 18 July: *Pravda* criticised 'people's communes' in China. | | 23 July: Phoui Sananikone appealed for more US aid to counter Pathet Lao revolt. |
| | 23 July: Mao's speech at Lushan, indirectly attacking Peng Dehuai. | | |
| 25 July–2 Aug.: Vice-president Nixon visited Moscow. | | 1–12 Aug.: Ho Chi Minh toured north-western China before reaching Peking. | 2 Aug.: Pathet Lao appealed for anti-US struggle in Laos. |
| | 2–16 Aug.: CCP Central Committee held 8th Plenum at Lushan: fall of Peng. | | |
| | 24 Aug.: Liu Shaoqi convened Supreme State Conference. Reemergence of Zhou Enlai | 21 Aug.: Ho had talks in Peking with Liu Shaoqi. | |

after disappearance for two months.

25 Aug.: Longju Incident on Sino-Indian border: serious tension.

26–28 Aug.: Tacit US–Soviet agreement not to resume nuclear tests.

26 Aug.: Ho returned to Hanoi

26 Aug.: US announced expansion of aid to Vientiane.

1 Sept.: Promotion of Nguyen Chi Thanh and other generals.

4 Sept.: Phoui Sananikone appealed to United Nations against alleged North Vietnamese 'aggression'.

7 Sept.: Pham Van Dong's letter opposing any action by UN in relation to Laos.

7 Sept.: United Nations resolution appointing team to investigate situation in Laos.

7 Sept.: Agreement at UN to set up Ten-Power Disarmament Committee.

8 Sept.: Zhou Enlai's letter to Nehru on border question.

9–20 Sept.: Tanzan Ishibashi visited Peking; talks with Zhou.

10 Sept.: Soviet statement urging peaceful settlement of Sino-Indian dispute; did not take sides.

11 Sept.: Fighting in Laos began to subside.

12 Sept.: Pham Van Dong's remark to French consul: 'We will be in Saigon tomorrow'.

15–28 Sept.: Khrushchev's visit to the United States.

be signalled by an announcement on 17 September that Lin Biao had officially succeeded Peng Dehuai as defence minister. As in the case of the Taiwan Straits crisis a year earlier, the Chinese were not willing to push confrontation beyond a certain point. There was even some possibility of an improvement of relations with Japan, and even the United States, in the weeks that followed. But as we shall see, Zhou Enlai's attempts to reverse the trend and restore the 'Bandung' strategy in all its aspects did not succeed.

The long-term consequences of the Lushan Crisis were of the greatest significance for South-East Asia. Whether Lin Biao, as was alleged after his death in 1971, really had some long-standing allegiance to Moscow is a question which outsiders can never hope to answer with any confidence. But there seems little doubt that he was dedicated to preventing any *rapprochement* or détente between China and the West, or with Japan. The attack on India symbolised an anti-imperialist line, and served to focus the conflict between Moscow and Peking on imperialism as an ideological issue. Whilst Khrushchev was left to pursue 'peaceful co-existence' with Western Europe and the United States, China would become increasingly identified with the encouragement of anti-American opposition movements throughout Asia, Africa and Latin America. It was too early to regard the promotion of Lin Biao as a final victory for the 'Maoist' line that would emerge in the mid-1960s. For one thing it was balanced by the appointment of Luo Ruiqing to be chief-of-staff of the PLA: a man whose military thinking was much more conventional than that of Lin Biao. But Luo too was strongly anti-imperialist, and his speeches of 1965 suggest that he favoured an even more vigorous anti-American policy in Indochina.

The consequences of the crisis for North Vietnam itself are not easily gauged, but a significant change does seem to have occurred within the Hanoi leadership shortly after Ho Chi Minh's return home at the end of August. A series of promotions in the armed forces, announced on 1 September, included the elevation of Nguyen Chi Thanh to a rank equal to that of Vo Nguyen Giap – making them the only two full generals in the PAVN.[20] Thanh appears to have had close Chinese links at one stage, and was later to play an important role in the escalation of the armed struggle in South Vietnam. Giap also became more active again during the latter part of the year. Truong Chinh also remained influential. But the 'pro-Soviet' Le Duan was considerably less prominent between autumn 1959 and about March 1960. It seems not unreasonable to conclude that, for the time being, Hanoi found the Peking line more congenial than Khrushchev's conciliatory attitude towards the United States – even though the Chinese were still unwilling to abandon completely their strategy of restraint in Indochina.

IV

In the second half of September the international situation was dominated by Khrushchev's visit to the United States, which began with an address to the United Nations on the 18th and ended with a bilateral summit meeting at Camp David on 26–7 September 1959. This marked the beginning of a dialogue between the superpowers which in one form or another would last for twenty years and would involve continual efforts to achieve mutual restraint in same spheres. Unfortunately the dialogue was punctuated by the failure to prevent certain specific crises from leading to armed conflict – Vietnam being in the end the most spectacular failure of all. Then and later it always proved easier to reach agreement (or to avoid conflict) in Europe and on bilateral issues than it was in Asia.

The Americans – particularly some members of Congress – were now looking for a parallel improvement in Sino-American relations. In September 1959 Senator Wiley launched a Congressional study with the observation that the United States could not ignore forever the fact that 'China may in a few years rank as one of the great powers'. The same month the Senate Foreign Relations Committee received another report (by Conlon Associates, Inc.), arguing that the strategy of 'containment through isolation' should eventually be replaced by one of 'exploration and negotiation'. This new optimism about China may have found encouragement in the visit to Peking, from 9 to 20 September, of the senior Japanese politician Ishibashi who had been Kishi's predecessor as prime minister; and two months later that of another leading figure of the Japanese ruling party, Matsumura Kenzo.[21] But in the event these initiatives led nowhere; there was to be no new breakthrough in Sino-Japanese or Sino-American relations.

Immediately after his talks in the United States, Khrushchev flew to Peking in the hope of restoring a measure of unity in the socialist camp. China's national day celebrations on 1 October that year became the occasion for what amounted to an Asian Communist summit: Ho Chi Minh, Kim Ilsung, the Mongolian leader Tsedenbal, the Japanese Nosaka Sanzo and the Indonesian Njoto– as well as Khrushchev, Suslov, Gromyko and a number of representatives of East European Parties – all appeared with Mao and his colleagues on the rostrum at Tian An Men Square.[22] The Soviet leaders had probably not given up hope of eventually reimposing their own discipline over the international Communist movement, even though for the time being they were obliged to accept that the Chinese would go their own way. On their own side neither the Chinese nor any other Asian Party was in a position to prevent the Soviet Union pursuing détente with the West. But they may have secured Khrushchev's tacit acceptance of the principle that easing tension in Europe did not necessitate a total abandonment of anti-imperialist revolutionary activity elsewhere. The North Vietnamese would be the chief beneficiaries of any such understanding.

The question now was not whether there would be an escalation of the struggle in South Vietnam, but what form it would take. It was ironical – if it was not deliberately planned – that the Camp David meeting coincided with the first significant attack on South Vietnamese forces by a 'liberation battalion' of guerrillas in the Plaine des Joncs (south west of Saigon) on 26 September 1959. The second half of that month also saw a marked increase in the rate of assassinations of government officials in rural areas, which would continue during the rest of the year. The mood in Hanoi was illustrated in a remark reportedly made by Pham Van Dong to the French consul in Hanoi on 12 September: 'You must remember, we shall be in Saigon tomorrow . . . .'[23] In early October Ho Chi Minh's further talks in Peking, with both Khrushchev and the Chinese leaders, appear to have sanctioned a policy of limited armed struggle; which (as we shall see) was reflected on the ground in South Vietnam towards the end of 1959. The agreement on long-term co-operation between the Soviet Union and the DRVN, signed in Moscow on 17 November, seems to have amounted to a decision to assist Hanoi's three-year economic plan without demanding total restraint in its policy towards the South.

Khrushchev did not succeed in reversing the Chinese decision against a return to economic dependence on the Soviet Union. But by November it would seem that the Russians did persuade the

Chinese to abandon the idea of improved relations with Japan, or with the West. The day after Matsumura ended his visit to Peking, on 11 November, the American secretary of state reaffirmed Washington's interest in an exchange of Chinese and American journalists; but to no avail.[24]

By that time, too, it was becoming evident that neither Soviet nor Chinese leaders were interested in a return to the strategy of total restraint in Indochina. Whilst they might still pursue their rivalry in other parts of Asia by following a pragmatic policy towards 'genuinely independent' regimes, there was no longer any basis for 'moderation' towards right wing governments in Laos, Thailand and South Vietnam, which had become militarily as well as politically committed to the United States. Saigon, in particular, was becoming a natural target for an international anti-imperialist struggle. The one element of Zhou Enlai's 'Bandung' strategy which was allowed to survive was his attempt to make peace with at least some nationalist regimes in other parts of Asia. The response was not always satisfactory from Peking's point of view. Chinese notes to New Delhi on 7 November and 17 November 1959 failed to achieve any reconciliation and Nehru's rebuff was probably encouraged by the Americans during a visit to India by President Eisenhower in December. But the Chinese had more success in their approach to Indonesia and Burma. Relations with Jakarta had deteriorated badly between July and November, over the issue of Chinese residents in Indonesia; but an exchange of letters towards the end of the year succeeded in reversing the trend, and on 20 January 1960 the two governments formally ratified their earlier 'dual nationality' treaty. Also in January, the Burmese premier Ne Win visited Peking to sign a friendship treaty and to initiate a resolution of the border issue between the two countries. It is not necessary to see any contradiction between Zhou's action in these cases and the Chinese view of Indochina. What China sought was an international united front, directed ultimately against American imperialism, with Laos and Vietnam as the focal area of conflict.

The Americans were now becoming seriously alarmed by the situation in East Asia. Few internal documents have been released for this critical period, but a declassified staff report to the National Security Council on 23 November 1959 seems to indicate a significant change of mood: it noted the fears of CINCPAC (Admiral Felt) that United States forces in the Pacific might not be adequate to counter an increasingly aggressive Chinese Communist

stance.[25] Two days later, in a move which may have been calculated
to put a break on détente with Moscow, the American delegation at
the continuing talks in Geneva on limiting nuclear tests raised the
objection that underground tests might still escape detection – and
that further technical negotiations were necessary before an
agreement could be signed. There followed a slow retreat from the
'Camp David spirit'. American caution in face of a general 'hardening' of Sino-Soviet actions in Asia would make the year 1960 one
of crisis, instead of a triumph for Eisenhower's 'crusade for peace'.

## V

In Hanoi, despite the promotion of Nguyen Chi Thanh in
September, Vo Nguyen Giap seemed now to have regained his
former prominence. Army day in 1959 (22 December) was the
occasion for which the veteran commander of Dien-Bien-Phu
produced his celebrated essay, *People's War, People's Army*.[26] The
'pro-Chinese' Hoang Van Hoan also continued to be influential,
especially in the constitutional sphere: as the Politburo representative on the National Assembly Standing Committee he was
closely involved in preparing a new constitution for the DRVN,
which after many years' delay was finally ready for approval by the
full Assembly at the end of the year. But it was Truong Chinh who
delivered the keynote speech for the 30th anniversary of the
foundation of the VNWP early in January 1960. What was equally
remarkable was the decision (announced on 11 November 1959)
that in 1960 the 30th anniversary would be commemorated on
6 January: a date which had been recognised as that of the Party's
foundation throughout the 1930s but which would later be
'corrected' (to 3 February) by the Third Party Congress the
following September. Truong Chinh was probably asserting his
own version of Party history, whilst the subsequent 'correction'
almost certainly reflected his loss of power for a second time in mid-
1960. In the anniversary speech he sought to define the Party's
strategy for a new stage of the Vietnamese revolution, which was to
include more vigorous action in the South as well as the continuation of agricultural transformation in the North.[27]

Sometime during November 1959 an order to create small armed
units reached village level in Long-An province. An internal

Communist document, captured by the Americans more than six years later, also referred to the Party's decision to 'launch an additional armed struggle' at the end of 1959.[28] The decision was probably taken, or rather transmitted from the VNWP Central Committee, at the 4th Plenum of the Nam-Bo Party Committee sometime in October. But the armed struggle was primarily intended to reinforce an expansion of political struggle, and the same plenum called for enlargement of the 'struggle movement of the masses'. That decision too was passed down to the districts and villages of Long-An province in November. The first results emerged during the week from 17 to 25 January, which saw a sharp increase in anti-government activity in that province. In Ben-Tre, long known as an area of strong Viet-Minh support, a 'mass uprising' occurred during the same week, which has been described in some detail in a published memoir by the famous woman guerrilla leader Nguyen Thi Dinh.[29] The culmination of this new upsurge of activity was the attack by a 500-strong guerrilla force on an ARVN ammunition base in Tay-Ninh province on 25 January 1960.

There was thus every reason for the government in Saigon and its American allies to see in the decisions of the Communist side during 1959 a serious threat to their own position and to the Geneva settlement as they understood it. It might reasonably be asked whether the International Commission for Vietnam, which still met regularly and maintained teams around the country, could not have done more to prevent the revival of armed struggle in the South. It did, of course, receive a number of complaints from both sides and did its best to investigate them. But its terms of reference, designed to meet the circumstances of 1954–5, were not appropriate for the situation that had arisen by late 1959. Having been created to supervise the implementation of the ceasefire Agreement, rather than the Geneva Final Declaration, the Commission had not been given political responsibilities. Once the regroupment into military zones had been completed, it was left with only three specific tasks: to report any violation of the demilitarised zone; to prevent the introduction of weapons and military personnel beyond the level authorised by the Agreement; and to investigate charges of reprisal against individuals for their actions before the ceasefire. The Commission was fairly successful in ensuring that neither side made more than minor incursions into the demilitarised zone; but its interim reports suggest that by 1959 it was not always getting satisfactory answers – or being allowed to make thorough inspections – regarding possible increases in external military assistance to either North or South Vietnam. The effectiveness of the Commission was also being hampered by the inability of the Polish and Canadian delegates to agree on controversial issues. In relation to its third task, the Commission's reports were careful to point out that the duty to prevent 'reprisals' did not extend to an over-all responsibility for maintenance of human rights in either North or South, *after 1954*. Thus it was beyond the competence of the Commission to investigate complaints against 'Law 10/59'; nor for that matter was it entitled to inspect security procedures in the Democratic Republic.[30]

This lack of any authority to interfere in the politics of North or South Vietnam meant that the International Commission was powerless to prevent the growth of a political struggle movement against the Diem regime even when it began to include terrorist violence against Saigon officials and village headmen. By proceeding very gradually – from a revolutionary struggle that was entirely political, first to the stage of 'armed propaganda' and then to the point where an essentially southern-based movement could launch guerrilla attacks – the Communist side was able to bypass the Geneva Agreement altogether. No one has been able to define the precise moment when the Communists first violated the ceasefire in a way that could have been legitimately investigated by the Commission.

# 11 The American Response: from Aid to Counterinsurgency

Now that the United States no longer has a monopoly of long-range nuclear weapons, any weakening of our support to outlying allied positions makes the danger of local aggression even greater, and accordingly the military assistance programme becomes even more essential to our security.

> Draper Report, Preliminary Conclusions,
> March 1959

The United States is likely to remain the only major outside source of power to counteract the Russian–Chinese Communist thrust into Southeast Asia. Thus the retention of this area in the free world will continue to depend on the extent and effectiveness of US support, as well as on the local efforts of the countries themselves. . . . The underlying purpose of US assistance in the area is to help the non-Communist countries to develop more effective political organisations, strengthen their internal administration and enlist greater allegiance in urban and rural districts. In part this purpose will be served by programs of military and economic aid.

> US National Security Council
> Policy document, July 1960

We believe U.S. should at this time support Diem as best available Vietnamese leader but should recognise that overriding U.S. objective is strongly anti-Communist Vietnamese government which can command loyal and enthusiastic support of widest possible segments of Vietnamese people, and is able to carry on effective fight against Communist guerrillas. If Diem's position in country continues [to] deteriorate . . . it may become necessary for U.S. government to begin consideration [of] alternative courses of action and leaders to achieve our objective.

> Ambassador Durbrow
> in cable from Saigon to State Department,
> 16 September 1960

I

The Communist decision to intensify the revolutionary struggle in South Vietnam and Laos presented a serious challenge to the fundamental principles on which the United States had based its Asian defence system. The global network which the Marxist–Leninists dubbed 'American imperialism' depended on the concept of mutual assistance, which since 1950 had generated an expanding programme of United States military and economic aid across Asia. Whereas the European powers had openly conquered traditional Asian states in the nineteenth century, subjecting them to one form or another of colonial rule, American policy was directed towards encouraging independent Asian nations to modernise themselves with Western aid. In principle therefore, it was the independence and stability of Asian countries rather than American power as such which had to be defended. The concept of mutual assistance had worked well in Europe after 1945, and also in the case of Japan; but when it came to America's allies in the 'third world', which lacked their own industrial base and were unable to support either modern armed forces or advanced military production, a somewhat different set of problems arose. In those areas 'defence support' required a close relationship between military assistance and economic aid, and a continuing commitment on the part of the Asian governments themselves which might prove politically difficult to sustain.

A significant landmark in American thinking about military assistance was the series of reports produced between November 1958 and August 1959 by a presidential committee under the chairmanship of William Draper. It coincided precisely with the period during which Hanoi was making up its mind to resume armed struggle in South Vietnam. The terms of reference of the committee were 'to assess the extent to which future military assistance can, by strengthening our friends and allies, advance US national security and foreign policy interests'.[1] One purpose was to develop arguments strong enough to convince Congress of the necessity for larger foreign aid programmes at a time of economic recession. The need for such arguments became clear that same summer when a series of widely read newspaper articles, published in July 1959, criticised the appalling waste and corruption in the administration of aid to South Vietnam.[2] Both Houses of Congress immediately began hearings on the issue, so that by the time the

Draper Committee submitted its final recommendations the subject was receiving national attention. Nevertheless, provided the efficiency of aid administration could be improved, there seems to have been general agreement both in Washington and amongst the New York financial community that military assistance must be expanded – not merely for the benefit of recipient countries, but as an integral part of the United States' own global defence arrangements. Memories of Korea were still strong: the American objective was to develop a system in which other countries in East and South-East Asia would be able to defend themselves without the deployment of American combat troops.

One notable feature of the Draper Reports was their emphasis (except in the case of NATO) on bilateral relations with individual countries rather than on the regional military pacts which Dulles had been so eager to create five years before. SEATO remained a framework for developing and testing the military preparedness of Western and Asian forces in the region, and to that end continued to hold exercises in Thailand and elsewhere. But in a situation where identity of interests between the United States and its European allies could not always be guaranteed, especially where France was concerned, Washington was anxious to establish its own separate commitment to key South-East Asian allies: in particular South Vietnam, Laos and Thailand. It also sought greater co-ordination of its aid programmes towards various Asian countries, outside the multilateral framework. In April 1959 Under-secretary Douglas Dillon convened a meeting at Baguio (in the Philippines) of all United States ambassadors and military commanders in Asia. Its proceedings have remained secret, like those of many similar conferences in later years, but they may have been of greater consequence than the more publicised deliberations of the SEATO Council whose meeting in New Zealand preceded it.[3]

A second notable aspect of the Draper enquiry was its assumption of a close connection between security and economic development. Economic assistance was essential if 'underdeveloped' countries were to support significant military establishments capable of handling modern weapons. At the same time military units might themselves play a creative role in 'civic action' programmes, and an educated officer corps could contribute to economic and political modernisation. In South Vietnam, for example, during 1959 as many as 4000 Vietnamese soldiers were said to be engaged in building 152 bridges and 274 kilometres of forest highway which would in future have economic as well as military value. Lest it be feared that such thinking might imply some kind of Asian or Latin American inferiority, the authors pointed out that in North America itself the US Army had contributed to the opening up of the West in the early nineteenth century.[4] One of the staff papers accompanying the final Report discussed American military training and educational programmes as a means of influencing the political and cultural values of 'new nations'. Nor was this idea relevant only for countries already committed to a close alliance with the United States. Even in neutral countries like Cambodia or Indonesia the Americans might win support and encourage non-Communist elements by offering military aid and training – without demanding an exclusively pro-Western orientation in return. In this respect the new philosophy was potentially more flexible than that of the mid-1950s.

The Draper Committee was more concerned with the modalities of aid than with strategic questions. Its staff, however, included a number of military officers (among them Colonel Lansdale, now in the Pentagon after his service in Vietnam) who believed that decisions on aid should be geared to a more precise assessment of the 'threat' which it was supposed to meet. An analysis of this problem published later by a member of Draper's staff, Colonel Amos Jordan, provides a glimpse of the type of thinking which must have influenced Pentagon debates during the critical period of 1959–60.[5] By then it seemed unlikely that Communist military forces would embark on a conventional war in South-East Asia so long as the American commitment to its allies remained firm. The essential problem, already emerging in South Vietnam and in Laos, was how to deal with a revolutionary movement operating from political bases inside a 'threatened' country and gradually acquiring a capability for anti-government violence. Even when the Americans could demonstrate that such a movement was aided and abetted from outside, they could not counter it by immediately invoking the concept of aggression. Quite apart from the supposed 'missile gap' (and the possibility of 'mutually assured destruction') it was unthinkable that they would respond to revolutionary violence in one small area of the world by launching a nuclear attack against China or the Soviet Union – or even against a country like North Vietnam. The challenge must be met on its own level.

Out of this realisation grew the doctrine of counterinsurgency, which embraced two essential ideas. On the one hand it was necessary to guarantee the political and economic stability of the threatened government by means of increased aid, enabling an improvement of administrative efficiency at grassroots level. (In that context it might also be necessary to inaugurate specific new security programmes.) On the other hand it was also important to provide counter-guerrilla assistance, to enable the armed forces of the threatened country to defeat rebel terrorist and guerrilla units in the field. An American capability in this sphere was slowly being developed by the US Army's Special Forces, and by corresponding units in the Air Force, working closely with the CIA. Such units could be sent in to advise and train the special forces of an Asian country without risking the international repercussions of an overt military intervention. They were also equipped to provide logistic and other forms of support for paramilitary operations, and we have already seen the role played by forces of this kind in the unsuccessful campaign against Sukarno in Indonesia in 1957–8. In Indochina the Pentagon Papers offer occasional glimpses of the presence from the mid-1950s of both American special forces and also Filipino groups of various kinds. Their task was to pass on expertise in unconventional warfare to newly-formed South Vietnamese and Laotian units.[6] Also important in this area was a Taiwan-based airline (effectively controlled by the CIA) which had been established some years earlier as Civil Air Transport but which in March 1959 was renamed Air America, Inc. Although it is not yet possible to attempt a detailed history of these forces during the late 1950s, there can be little doubt of their importance in the evolution of counterinsurgency as a special form of military assistance; and of United States thinking about Vietnam.

## II

The application of the new philosophy of 'defence support' to Laos and South Vietnam can be traced in a series of American decisions taken during 1959–60. It was a common but erroneous assumption in later years that counterinsurgency was invented by the Kennedy Administration. A more careful examination of the record suggests that the new president merely gave final shape to a doctrine which had gradually evolved during the eighteen months or so before he took office. The starting point was the crisis of 1959 in Laos, where the Americans responded quickly to the Pathet Lao resumption of armed activity in July and August. Military assistance to Phoui Sananikone had been growing since the economic reforms of the previous October, which had coincided with Sarit's military coup in Thailand. From February 1959, moreover, the Laotian premier refused to be bound by the Geneva restrictions against introducing new weapons, which left the way open for the United States to replace France as the principal Western military power in Laos. The outbreak of fighting in Sam Neua province forced Phoui to appeal for additional American support towards the end of July; and on 26 August the State Department announced an immediate grant of sufficient aid to permit a 'temporary' expansion of the Laotian armed forces and local militia, various improvements in their logistic capabilities, and an emergency military training programme.[7]

The Vientiane government sought to present the Laotian crisis as the product of North Vietnamese 'aggression', but a United Nations team sent to investigate the situation in September and October submitted an inconclusive report. There was thus no easy way to invoke the deterrent principle against the activities of the Pathet Lao. The Americans recognised that their only hope of strengthening the pro-Western regime lay in an expansion of aid, combined with covert operations, which would involve American 'advisers' as an adjunct to the still legal French mission in Vientiane. (A US MAAG was not formally established until 1961.) Air America's unmarked planes began flying into Vientiane around 23 August; about the same time, the Americans began to send in special forces teams disguised as civilians, with the aim of recruiting unconventional forces amongst the minority Meo population. Thus began a clandestine CIA involvement in Laos whose very existence would be denied by Washington until as late as 1970. There was close collaboration, too, between the Laotian government and Taiwan, following a visit to Taipei by Colonel Ngon Sananikone in the second half of August: a development which must have increased the sense of outrage in Peking.[8]

The United States still needed the support of its Western allies for its policy in Laos, and neither the British nor the French were willing to abandon the spirit of the Geneva settlement altogether. That factor may have played some part in the political crisis which arose at the end of 1959, after the removal of Phoui Sananikone's government in what amounted to a military coup. On 4 January

1960 the French and British ambassadors, together with the Australian chargé d'affaires, accompanied the American ambassador to Luang Prabang to impress upon the king that a military regime was unacceptable. The latter thereupon appointed a new civilian cabinet under Kou Abhay, but it was clear that Phoumi Nosavan (now a general) wielded even more power than before.[9] The national assembly having been dissolved in December, new elections were held in April 1960 and this time were easily rigged to produce a result favourable to the rightists. By then it looked as though the Americans had finally succeeded in establishing in Laos the kind of regime most suitable to become a recipient of their expanding aid programmes, with military officers playing an important but internationally unobtrusive role.

In South Vietnam, United States aid had been essential to the survival of a separate state from the beginning; by 1959 the Americans were contributing over US $250 million a year in military and economic support for the Diem regime. By way of comparison, aid to Thailand totalled only US $76 million that year – and was untypically high owing to the inclusion of special additional loans for economic development.[10] Given that the respective populations of the two countries were 12.5 million (South Vietnam) and 22 million (Thailand), it is clear that South Vietnam was in proportion even more dependent on American aid. It is hardly surprising that this massive support for Saigon became a subject of public controversy by the summer of 1959. If at some stage even more aid became necessary, to meet an active military threat to the Diem regime, the kinds of question raised by the Draper Reports about the direction and organisation of military assistance would become highly relevant. So too would the demand for some kind of accountability on the part of the Diem regime.

The actual American military presence in South Vietnam between 1955 and 1959 consisted of 342 men attached to MAAG and an additional 350 men belonging to TERM, due to be dissolved at the end of 1960. The United States claimed the right to have as many as 888 men there, since that was the combined total of French and American advisers and instructors assigned to Bao-Dai's 'national' armed forces at the time of the Geneva ceasefire. They did not openly exceed that level (or even reach it) before Kennedy's

TABLE 11.1   _United States aid to Indochina, 1958–9_

|               | Economic aid (US $) | Military aid (US $) | Total (US $) | Population (million) |
|---------------|--------------------:|--------------------:|-------------:|---------------------:|
| Cambodia      | 24,600,000          | 4,435,000           | 29,035,000   | 5·5                  |
| Laos          | 25,400,000          | 7,600,000           | 33,000,000   | 2·5                  |
| South Vietnam | 206,900,000         | 45,855,000          | 252,755,000  | 12·5                 |
| Total         | 256,900,000         | 57,890,000          | 314,790,000  | 20.5                 |

SOURCE   Based on data given in Jordan (1962) p. 10, from official US sources; the figures relate to financial year 1959, ending on 30 June 1959.

decisions of late 1961 – by which time the ceasefire had virtually broken down. American military assistance, therefore, was directed mainly towards financing, training and equipping the armed forces of the Republic of Vietnam (usually known as ARVN), which by 1960 numbered 150,000 men. The Geneva Agreement had placed tight restrictions on the extent to which new military supplies and personnel could be introduced into the country from outside, and there were frequent allegations by Hanoi during the late 1950s that the Americans were going beyond those limits and so were in breach of the agreement. It could be argued indeed that any attempt to improve the capabilities of ARVN amounted to an unacceptable change in the situation that had prevailed in August 1954. But North Vietnam was also making every effort to modernise and strengthen its armed forces during the same period.

Until 1959, or perhaps early 1960, the principal concern of the MAAG commander General Williams was to improve Diem's ability to meet a conventional attack from the North – or at least to hold the line long enough to allow SEATO or American intervention. The 'special forces' element in Saigon military planning was at that stage quite small. A 'first observation group' (formed early in 1956) was supposed to operate just south of the demilitarised zone, ready to carry out guerrilla operations behind the lines in the event of a Communist invasion. At some point it also began to undertake its own covert operations into North Vietnam; but until 1961 it had fewer than 300 men. Another early development was the establishment of a commando training centre at Nha-Trang, at which a small detachment of US Special Forces from Okinawa spent several months during 1957–8 training about 60 Vietnamese to become instructors for ARVN's special forces.[11]

But there was no general appreciation that Communist guerrilla warfare would soon emerge as a significant threat to the stability of South Vietnam.

The first documented indication of American awareness of that danger appeared in a report to Washington, from the 'country team' of the Saigon embassy, dated 7 March 1960. By then, as we have seen, the Communist strategy of combining 'mass uprisings' with sporadic guerrilla attacks – together with a growing number of political assassinations – was already under way. The poor performance of ARVN units in the two engagements of 26 September 1959 and 25 January 1960 was cause for concern at MAAG headquarters and a new American strategy seemed called for. On 26 April the Pacific Command in Honolulu (CINCPAC) forwarded to the Pentagon a MAAG recommendation for co-ordinated national counterinsurgency plans in both Laos and South Vietnam.[12] That, in effect, was the start of a long period of debate and planning, whose first fruit was the Vietnam counterinsurgency plan signed by President Kennedy during his first week in office. The situation inside South Vietnam, however, was deemed too critical to await the outcome of a long debate. On 5 May 1960 it was announced that the size of MAAG would immediately be doubled, to a level of 685 men, apparently with the agreement of the International Commission and despite objections from its Polish member.[13] On that basis the Americans accepted the condition that TERM must complete its work by the end of the year, at which time its remaining 89 members would be allowed to transfer to MAAG within the new ceiling. Another element in this expansion of MAAG was the deployment of 30 US special forces instructors to South Vietnam to train ARVN's own special forces. These moves, rather than Kennedy's decisions a year later, represent the real starting point for the 'escalation' of American involvement.

They were made against an international background in which the 'spirit of Camp David' had conspicuously failed to achieve a reduction of tension in other spheres of East-West relations. Indeed by May 1960 it seemed to have evaporated altogether. The Vietnam decisions formed one element of a new global strategy which, in the eyes of Washington, had become a necessary response to the Communist threat in several areas of the world. Relations with Cuba, for example, entered a new and more bitter phase following the visit of Mikoyan to Havana from 4 to 13 February 1960. While Castro was demanding more favourable economic treatment by the United States, and at the same time nationalising more American property, the Central Committee of the People's Socialist Party passed a resolution (published 16 March) urging him to seek arms from Eastern Europe. Castro's rejection of an apparently conciliatory approach by the United States on 17 March led Eisenhower to approve a secret CIA plan to train Cuban exiles for anti-Castro guerrilla operations. Cuba meanwhile began to develop economic relations with the USSR and Soviet oil began to arrive on 19 April; diplomatic relations with Moscow were established on 7 May.[14] This sequence of events must have caused alarm and despondency in Washington. Nor were the Americans comforted by the 'hardline' speech on Berlin which Khrushchev made at Baku on 25 April, and which (even before the U-2 disaster of 1 May) seemed to leave little room for compromise at the forthcoming Paris summit meeting.

At this juncture Vietnam's importance for the United States had three separate aspects, each of which involved an American commitment. First, as an American ally South Vietnam had received nearly US$1.4 billion in various forms of aid since 1955 and had become a test case for the concept of 'defence support', making it essential to prove that aid on such a scale was not in vain. This was not mere symbolism, for South Vietnam was by now the weak link in a chain of American alliances with anti-Communist states across Asia. Both sides knew that, given the strategy the Americans had chosen to adopt, the 'loss' of Vietnam would have serious practical consequences. Second, the fact that South Vietnam and Laos bordered directly onto the socialist camp gave them a special status in the American theory of 'containment'. Whatever the legal ambiguities of military partition, the United States was by now committed to respond to any unilateral attempt to reverse the status quo at the edge of the 'free world' – whether in Indochina, West Berlin or South Korea. Whilst the intrinsic worth of South Vietnam might be much less than that of the other two areas, the parallel had a decisive effect on the way its security was viewed by the Pentagon and the State Department. Third, Vietnam belonged to the Afro-Asian world and was a logical target for revolutionary armed struggle of a kind not easily countered by conventional military means. The success of Castro in Cuba, coinciding with an apparent change in the Communist line on 'national liberation' wars, meant that the Americans must find new ways of meeting their self-imposed obligation to 'contain' Communist expansion. In one sense

Castro's triumph in Cuba was more alarming than anything that had so far happened in Indochina, since it brought a Soviet presence into the Western Hemisphere and seemed to threaten other parts of Latin America. But the fact that Laos and South Vietnam lay on the sacred line of 'containment' gave them an importance which no president could afford to ignore.

### III

The different contexts in which the Vietnam problem arose, and in which United States policy had to be formulated, may explain some of the ambiguities which were to characterise Washington's decision-making about Indochina throughout the 1960s. This was not just a matter of logical contradictions between different levels of analysis, but also of bureaucratic conflict between separate agencies within the American government and armed forces, whose representatives saw the problem in quite different terms.

The need for close co-operation between departments and agencies was a central theme in the Draper Reports, which among other things demonstrated the extent to which the Defence Department's responsibility for military aid had already brought it into the sphere of 'international security affairs'. Whilst economic aid and cultural activities, as well as diplomacy, came under the aegis of the State Department and its subsidiary agencies, the various MAAGs throughout the world were directly answerable to the Pentagon. Decision-making in the field of 'defence support' was thus already an inter-agency affair, quite apart from the role of the CIA in assessing the political circumstances of a given country and if necessary recommending specific actions. In consequence all these departments and agencies had to be brought into the policy process – either through the NSC, whose structure had grown increasingly elaborate under Eisenhower, or through *ad hoc* task-forces directly responsible to the White House, which became the rule under Kennedy. In Saigon, inter-agency co-operation was the responsibility of the 'country team', headed officially by the ambassador but liable to be strongly influenced in its reporting by both MAAG and the CIA station-chief. According to one source, this interdependence permitted the CIA virtually to dominate Vietnam policy in the early 1960s.[15]

There was always a potential conflict between the State Department and the Pentagon. Diplomacy being a game which never ends, the main concern at the State Department was how to find policies for Vietnam which would not interfere with American objectives in other parts of the world. It was necessary to avoid losing Vietnam, but not at the price of losing opportunities in other spheres. In certain circumstances, of course it might be necessary to take a 'hard' line in South-East Asia for reasons which had more to do with a general heightening of world tension than with events in Vietnam itself. The generals, however, more used to solving specific problems by bringing to bear whatever form of military strength seemed most appropriate, were likely to concentrate on Vietnam as a distinct problem. They felt that by regarding it as primarily a 'political' or 'diplomatic' question, the State Department was seeking to impose constraints which interfered too much with the military task in hand. But when asked to comment on Indochina generally, the JCS were also liable sometimes to question whether it was really sufficiently important to justify the level of military commitment that had been required in Korea, or might be needed in the event of another war in Europe. The notorious 'domino theory' may have been invoked to convince faint-hearted generals rather than as a realistic assessment of the anticipated consequences of the 'loss' of Vietnam.

The doctrine of counterinsurgency again involved fundamental differences of approach between the agencies required to co-operate in order to make it work. Everyone was aware that on the Communist side success depended on the ability to integrate political mobilisation with armed struggle, in accordance with the teachings of Mao Zedong. But in Washington and Saigon each agency was bent on pursuing its own perception of the problem and its own contribution to the response. Civilian aid specialists – and perhaps some Pentagon theorists – laid special stress on 'nation-building' and the need for a sound political structure. They might sometimes argue among themselves about the relative importance of particular institutions and personalities, but they were inclined to see the problem as primarily 'political'. In the circumstances of 1959–60 in South Vietnam this approach led to a growing demand for political and administrative reforms. At the other extreme the practitioners of 'special war' preferred to concentrate on the security aspect of the situation, seeing the problem as primarily a 'military' one, albeit of an unconventional kind. They were anxious to avoid experimental reforms which might weaken the security effort in the short term. Historians given to explanations based on 'bureaucratic determinism' might be tempted to argue that, from the beginning, the United States failure in Vietnam arose from inability to develop a sufficiently coherent inter-agency response to the Communist challenge. For their part the Communists were often able to turn these 'contradictions' on the American side to their own advantage.

Tension between different American schools of thought on Vietnam was becoming serious by autumn 1960. It was reflected in the conflicting assessments of Ngo Dinh Diem's performance contained in reports and recommendations from the then ambassador in Saigon (Durbrow) and from Diem's original sponsor General Lansdale, now working in a special section of the Pentagon.[16] Ambassador Durbrow argued that many of Diem's problems in the countryside stemmed from his own political failings; that he was losing the support even of the urban élite in Saigon; and that increased military and technical assistance would produce results only when placed in the hands of a South Vietnamese government enjoying popular approval. He did not call explicitly for withdrawal of support from Diem, but he wanted Washington to put pressure on him to introduce a programme of reform. It is hardly likely that the State Department idealists were so naïve as to imagine that South Vietnam could be run on precisely the same constitutional lines as the democracies of North America and Western Europe. Nevertheless the concept of 'nation-building' required a political leader capable of commanding respect.

In the Spring of 1960, moreover, a non-Communist opposition had begun to make its presence felt. On 26 April a number of leading politicians outside the presidential clique (known as the 'Caravelle Group' because they met in the Saigon hotel of that name) signed the 'Manifesto of the Eighteen': a plea to Diem to adopt economic and administrative changes which would restore the sense of national purpose that had supposedly existed during the early years of his rule.[17] One American commentator has suggested an analogy between these demands and those of the student movement against Syngman Rhee in South Korea, which brought about the overthrow of the latter at precisely the same time. But there were no student demonstrations in Saigon, and at this stage no open indication that Washington was losing faith in its South Vietnamese protégé. The only possible vehicle of effective opposition lay in the armed forces, where a dissident movement did begin to develop in the autumn, leading – as we shall see – to the abortive coup of 11 November 1960. Carried out by relatively junior officers it was easily crushed, and in the aftermath several members of the Caravelle Group were arrested and imprisoned until 1963.

At that point the Americans made up their minds to commit themselves firmly to the Diem regime, although Durbrow continued to urge reform so long as he remained ambassador. The CINCPAC recommendations of 26 April had by now made their way to the JCS, where they were approved on 6 June. A counterinsurgency plan, which was submitted to the State Department in mid-September, had begun to take shape.[18] Meanwhile General Williams was replaced by General Lionel McGarr as commander of MAAG with responsibility for implementing the new strategy. The military advocates of counterinsurgency were keen supporters of political continuity in Saigon, believing that Diem could still govern effectively so long as he solved the security problem. What he needed was more military and police aid.

Durbrow's disagreement with Lansdale revealed a paradox in the whole American approach to military aid to 'free Asia'. Much more was involved than a sense of frustration at being unable to exert sufficient leverage to force Diem to accept proposals for reform. The ambassador's cable of 16 September raised the possibility that an Asian regime, installed with strong American backing in 1955, might at some stage cease to be an adequate instrument for United States policy and might no longer qualify for support. The purpose of counterinsurgency was not merely to 'help a friend' (as John McNaughton put it in 1964) but to defend the 'free world' as a whole. What happened if the 'friend' proved inadequate to the larger task? At what point did the military and political commitment justify intervention in the internal affairs of an individual member-country of the 'free world', to ensure that its government remained not only well-disposed towards the West but also capable of the measures which Washington deemed necessary for that country's survival? On the one hand it could be argued that 'freedom' always implied the possibility of political ineffectiveness; or for that matter, the freedom of every country to change its government and its foreign policy at will. On the other hand South Vietnam was by now part of a global system, for whose defence Washington had an ultimate responsibility extending beyond the boundaries of any one country. The American failure to resolve this paradox became more and more apparent as the military commitment steadily increased in scale. In the end the Americans became locked in to a strategy of keeping Diem in power for reasons which had little to do with either his own virtues as a national leader or the general principles of democracy in an individual state.

# Part IV
## 1960–1

Part IV

1960

# 12 Towards a New Cold War?

The struggle of the Vietnamese people for the peaceful reunification of the fatherland is surging ahead. This struggle has now become an important part of the stormy struggle of the people of the whole world against US imperialism.

Zhou Enlai, 2 September 1960

Our time . . . is a time of struggle between the two opposing social systems, a time of socialist revolutions and national liberation revolutions, a time of the break-down of imperialism, of the abolition of the colonial system, a time of transition of more peoples to the socialist path, of the triumph of socialism and communism on a world-wide scale.

The Communist Parties . . . have always been against the export of revolution. At the same time they fight resolutely against the imperialist export of counter-revolution. They consider it their internationalist duty to call on the peoples of all countries to unite, to rally all their internal forces, to act vigorously and, relying on the might of the world socialist system, to prevent or firmly resist imperialist interference in the affairs of any people who have risen in revolution.

At a time when imperialist reaction is joining forces to fight Communism it is particularly necessary to consolidate the world Communist movement . . . Communists throughout the world are united by the great doctrine of Marxism–Leninism and by the joint struggle for its realisation.

Moscow Statement of
Communist and Workers' Parties,
6 December 1960

# I

One important factor in Soviet politics in 1960, if not itself a central issue, was the ongoing debate about military strategy. On 14 January Khrushchev had announced to the Supreme Soviet a massive reduction in the size of the armed forces from 3.7 million to 2.5 million men. This would have increased the size of the civilian skilled-labour force by over a million people; militarily, it implied greater reliance on strategic nuclear weapons. In that respect Khrushchev may have been trying to follow the American example by adopting a parallel strategy of 'massive retaliation' – at the same time reassuring Washington that the Soviet Union had no plans for the kind of limited war in Europe which Kissinger and other analysts were now writing about. But he was also threatening the conventional assumptions of many Soviet generals and it would not be surprising if some of them tried to resist the proposed change.[1] In the same speech, perhaps in order to appease his critics, Khrushchev returned to the theme of a separate peace treaty with East Germany. Although at that stage he was probably winning the battle for military contraction, the acquiescence of his colleagues may have been conditional on the achievement of a German treaty – despite Western opposition to a change in the status of Berlin. The German question was in any case an issue of some importance.

So too was the question of relations with China. The Sino-Soviet debate entered a new phase on 4 February at a meeting of the Warsaw Pact countries in Moscow attended by Chinese and North Vietnamese observers. The Chinese delegate Kang Sheng made a sharp attack on United States imperialism in Asia, focusing especially upon Taiwan, Korea and Laos – as well as on Japan, whose new security treaty had been signed in Washington two weeks before.[2] (Interestingly, he still made no comparable references to South Vietnam.) China's aim may have been to persuade the Russians to take a similarly tough line in Europe. On that score Kang Sheng's views may have been quietly shared by some Soviet leaders, and Khrushchev was certainly open to criticism from 'hardliners' who argued that Soviet enthusiasm for détente ought not to be carried to the point of precipitating an open split with Peking. Khrushchev was nevertheless pressing ahead with plans to meet Eisenhower and other Western leaders at a summit conference in Paris in the middle of May. He was also continuing to develop the Soviet strategy of alliance with genuinely independent regimes in Asia, some of which no longer had cordial relations with Peking. From 11 February to 5 March he undertook a second tour of India, Burma, Afghanistan, and this time also Indonesia, which the Hanoi media followed with enthusiasm but which the Chinese virtually ignored until it was over.[3] Following his return from Asia, however, the Soviet leader faced increasing pressure from his colleagues on the issue of détente.

March and April were critical months for the socialist camp. On one level they saw the start of an overt ideological dispute (as opposed to semi-traditional rivalry) between Moscow and Peking. Equally important was the conflict which seems to have been going on between Khrushchev and his critics within the Soviet leadership. The first secretary was absent from public view twice during that period: from 19 to 22 March, after postponing a visit to Paris on the grounds of 'influenza'; and again from 12 to 20 April, when he was 'on holiday' at Gagra on the Black Sea.[4] Both were probably moments of acute crisis in the Soviet Politburo, although Western historians can only guess what may have happened and what issues were involved.

We cannot dismiss without further evidence the possibility that Khrushchev's difficulties were due in part to the harder line being taken by the United States at that point. There is no reason to suppose that the Russians immediately became aware of Eisenhower's authorisation for the CIA to train anti-Castro exiles (17 March); but the American decision to prepare a further series of underground nuclear tests was announced publicly on 16 March. It was also known by then that the West German armed forces were negotiating supply-base agreements with neighbouring countries, which no doubt worried the Russians. These Western moves may themselves have been occasioned by intelligence implying the adoption already of a harder Soviet line, but so far that has not been demonstrated. At such critical moments it is impossible, without detailed inside information, to apportion blame for a deteriorating situation. What is clear from the point of view of Soviet politics is that during the next month or so the Kremlin certainly did harden its positions, in relation to both arms control and the German issue. Khrushchev's visit to France, which finally took place between 23 March and 2 April, produced nothing to alter the trend; and on 2 April the Western powers saw fit to repeat publicly that they would accept no change in the status of Berlin. After another apparent crisis in Moscow, Khrushchev responded with a speech at Baku on 25 April which left hardly any room for compromise.

The divergence between Khrushchev's views and those of the Chinese leadership became even more apparent on the occasion of the 90th anniversary of Lenin's birth, celebrated in all Communist capitals around 22 April 1960. It was then that the Chinese journal *Hong-qi* produced its first major theoretical attack on 'revisionism' in terms which could be applied to the Soviet Union as easily as to Yugoslavia. Under the title 'Long live Leninism!' it concentrated on two fundamental themes: the unchanging nature of imperialism, which made further wars inevitable regardless of the invention of nuclear weapons; and the necessity of revolutionary violence against a world bourgeoisie that would not give up power without a fight.[5] Both ideas were justified in terms of Lenin's own thinking; but the article also dwelt on the experience of the Paris Commune, which was to become a favourite theme of Chinese radicals in later years. The contrast could not have been greater between all this and the speech given in Moscow for the same anniversary by the veteran Comintern leader Otto Kuusinen. Although Khrushchev himself was not present, the themes were those which he approved: the need to apply Lenin's thought 'in a creative way'; the possibility of avoiding war through negotiation; and the value of collaboration with non-Communist Asian leaders who have 'cast off the yoke of colonialism'. The speech was balanced, it is true, by an article in *Kommunist* calling for 'vigilance' in foreign relations; but the same journal refused to publish an article containing Molotov's ideological views.[6]

It would appear therefore that Khrushchev was able to resist the ideological challenge from Peking; his 'revisionist' position was sustained within the CPSU. But he seems to have been obliged to harden his stand on negotiations with the West. On 4 May, barely a week after the Baku speech, there was a significant reshuffle of the Soviet leadership which left Kozlov in a strong position in the Secretariat (virtually Khrushchev's deputy) and promoted Kosygin and Podgorny within the Politburo. A few days later it became known that Brezhnev, who had been a rising star in the Secretariat in January, would succeed Voroshilov as head of the Supreme Soviet – a less powerful position. No doubt these changes had a bearing on internal Soviet policy; their international effect was probably to tie Khrushchev's hands in dealing with Eisenhower. By then too, on 1 May, the Russians had brought down an American U-2 spy-plane over Sverdlovsk and had captured the pilot: a fact which allowed Khrushchev to make capital out of Eisenhower's unconvincing and embarrassing denials. In the fullness of time it is likely that access to American archives will permit us to know more about that incident, but its main consequences are already clear. Khrushchev, unable to appease his colleagues, used it as an excuse to wreck the Paris summit conference on 17 May. Although he was able to keep the door open for eventual talks with Eisenhower's successor, to be elected the following November, there were to be no serious negotiations in the meantime. During that fateful interval, between Spring 1960 and early 1961, the conflict in Indochina got out of hand.

## II

The continuing partition of Vietnam had not figured significantly in Kang Sheng's speech of 4 February 1960, even though he paid some attention to Laos. The Chinese seem at that stage to have been less interested in expanding the revolutionary struggle in South Vietnam than in promoting a harder Soviet line in Europe, if not an actual confrontation over Berlin. What is more difficult to assess is the Soviet attitude to the Vietnamese situation at that time: the Warsaw Pact meeting was also attended by Truong Chinh and Vo Nguyen Giap, who presumably had talks with Soviet leaders about their own problems. Possibly the Russians had become convinced that some form of armed struggle in South Vietnam was now unavoidable. But they may have disapproved of the current tactics of mass struggle and guerrilla warfare, preferring a low-key strategy less likely to interfere with Soviet – American relations in other spheres – but more likely to succeed in the end. At some point the Russians seem to have made *some* move which again increased Le Duan's influence within the Hanoi leadership. For whilst Truong Chinh played an important role in the VNWP anniversary celebrations at the beginning of January 1960, and went to Moscow a month later, it was Le Duan who made the keynote speech for the Lenin anniversary (on 20 April) and who subsequently emerged as the Party's first secretary at the Third Congress in September.

Sometime between early February and mid-April therefore, Truong Chinh lost ground to Le Duan. The likeliest moment, if one dare pinpoint an exact date, was 21 March when Le Duan produced a major report on agricultural collectivisation which reversed the line advocated by Truong Chinh during 1958–9.[7] There was no question of North Vietnam going back on the measure of co-operativisation already achieved or planned; but Le Duan argued that the next stage must wait until industrial development had progressed far enough to allow the mechanisation of agriculture. In the meantime what mattered was the 'struggle for production', and he saw no danger in permitting an element of private peasant production if that would contribute to higher output. As on many other occasions during the next twenty years, Le Duan was more concerned with combining ideology and technology to establish the long-term goals of the revolution than with ideological purity as the sole means of protecting socialism. What is significant in the present context is that his ideas were published at that critical moment; for the change in agricultural strategy almost certainly had wider implications. It occurred, moreover, at precisely the moment when the crisis in Moscow first came to a head – when Khrushchev himself disappeared for three days (19–21 March).

A month later Le Duan's speech of 20 April had a more direct bearing on the question of the South. He succeeded in avoiding the contentious themes of both Kuusinen's speech and 'Long live Leninism!'. Instead he drew upon a number of less controversial ideas in the Leninist canon to justify an anti-imperialist line which had profound relevance for Vietnam's own situation. One section of the speech applied Lenin's thinking to the problem of economic transformation in the North, coming out in favour of priority for the development of heavy industry. Other passages dealt with various aspects of the nature of revolution, emphasising the need for proletarian leadership in any united front – and the essentially subordinate role of the 'national bourgeoisie'. He also made a pointed reference to Lenin's remarks of 1919 on 'the role played by the Eastern peoples in deciding the fate of imperialism'. At another point he dwelt on Lenin's theory that the international nature of imperialism makes it not only possible but necessary for revolution to break out at the weakest point in the imperialist chain (as happened in Russia itself in 1917). Had he wished to be more controversial, Le Duan might have applied that idea more explicitly to the circumstances of Vietnam itself in the world of 1960: was it not now the weakest link of imperialism? But he was careful to avoid anything which might conflict with known Soviet positions.

Perhaps the most important section of the speech was that which analysed the current state of the Vietnamese revolution. Despite the ultimate unity of the revolution in North and South, its two halves were now in different stages: the North having begun to 'build socialism', whilst the South had not yet completed the 'national democratic' revolution. They must therefore be treated separately for the time being. As in his earlier analysis of November 1956, Le Duan was anxious to reconcile his desire to continue and expand the revolution in the South with the need to maintain 'peaceful co-existence' in the international sphere. Now he introduced a new argument which was to be of fundamental importance to Vietnamese Communist strategy throughout the following decade:

> In the present conjuncture, when the possibility exists to maintain lasting peace in the world and create favourable conditions for the world movement of socialist revolution and national independence to go forward, we can and must guide and restrict within the South the solving of the contradiction between imperialism and the colonies in our country.[8]

Therein lay the essence of the revolutionary line subsequently adopted by the Third Party Congress, leading directly to the creation of a separate National Liberation Front for the South at the end of the year.

A significant change in the Vietnamese Communist line was indicated more precisely in a letter circulated to southern Party branches by the Nam-Bo Regional Committee on 28 March 1960.[9] After praising the achievements of the mass struggle movement inaugurated the previous November, it went on to criticise three serious shortcomings in the way the situation had been allowed to develop. They can be construed as criticisms of Truong Chinh and possibly of Nguyen Chi Thanh, and thus reflect the same caution instilled more than three years earlier by Tran Van Giau's article of November 1957. First, said the letter of 28 March, it was wrong to behave as though the Diem regime had already reached the point of collapse. The long-term struggle would involve a very gradual change in the balance of forces; too precipitate actions against 'the enemy' were therefore inappropriate. Second, the Party must not at this stage seek to *replace* political struggle by armed struggle; the role of the latter was to protect and support an essentially political movement. Third, more attention must be given to the task of winning over members of the Diem regime's own armed forces and civil service, rather than merely spreading propaganda indiscriminately. To correct these shortcomings the Party must strengthen both its own network and also various specialist groups capable of organising opposition to the regime on specific issues. The document set forth a virtual blueprint for political struggle, designed to exploit all identifiable grievances – or 'contradictions' – within South Vietnamese society and so to undermine Saigon's control of its own countryside. The object was not to expand the area under direct Communist control; nor to bring about a full-scale war between 'liberated' and 'occupied' zones, such as had existed during the Viet-Minh struggle before 1954. The gradual creation of armed units must proceed alongside the political mobilisation of opposition to Diem in as many different spheres as possible, often embracing groups whose opinions were not in any sense 'Communist'. Revolutionary skill lay in ensuring that this many-sided struggle remained under the leadership and control of the Party, so that only its aims were actually fulfilled.

This attempt to put a brake on the mass struggle movement may have been prompted partly by fears that the Party itself was not yet sufficiently well developed, or perhaps had suffered too many losses during 1958–9, to be capable of maintaining disciplined control over the expanding movement. However, now that more is known about the complexity of relations between Hanoi and Peking (as well as between Peking and Moscow) another possibility must also be mentioned. As early as 26 May 1959 an American intelligence estimate had observed 'recent indications of Chinese Communist participation' in the Communist apparatus of South Vietnam.[10] Since the 'indications' were not specified, it is impossible to assess their true significance. But given the presence of a large overseas Chinese community in South Vietnam, it would have been logical for the CCP to establish its own clandestine network among them; indeed it had probably begun to do so as early as the 1940s. From Hanoi's point of view, such a network would be a valuable asset so long as no tension existed between the Chinese and Vietnamese Parties. But by early 1960, when Sino-Soviet differences had begun to surface, the Vietnamese may have become anxious to avoid letting their own struggle in the South become totally dependent on Chinese participation. Whether or not that hypothesis can eventually be sustained, there is little doubt that the developments of the spring of 1960 amounted to a determined effort to strengthen the foundations of the 'national liberation' movement in the South and to prepare for a long-term political and armed struggle. This reflected a change in the Soviet attitude. Faced with the danger that the Chinese might seize the initiative throughout Asia, the Russians were at last willing to support a more active revolutionary line in Indochina whilst still pursuing détente in Europe.

The Chinese seem also to have changed their position on the question of Vietnam sometime during 1960. Hoang Van Hoan, writing in 1979, reported that for several years Chinese leaders had disagreed with the Vietnamese about whether the time was ripe for 'revealing the strength' of the Communist position in South Vietnam; not until 1960 did they come round to Hanoi's view and offer to support a resumption of armed struggle.[11] Hoan did not say precisely when the change took place, but possibly it came as a direct response to greater Soviet interest in South Vietnam. The Vietnamese 'White Book', to which Hoan was replying, insisted that as late as May 1960 the Chinese were still advising Hanoi to provide only political and not military support to the southern struggle, and were advocating guerrilla warfare based on 'self-reliance' rather than larger-scale operations. We know from another source that Ho Chi Minh paid a visit to Guangxi province on 17–19 May 1960, to celebrate his official birthday there in the company of Wei Guoqing; possibly that was the occasion when such advice was given.[12] (The visit occurred, it will be noted, immediately after the breakdown of the Paris summit.) As Soviet support for the Le Duan line increased, however, the Chinese probably revised their opinion.

Thus by mid-1960 the North Vietnamese were actually benefiting from Sino-Soviet rivalry, since neither of the major Communist powers could afford to be excluded from the next phase of the Vietnamese revolution. It was these developments, rather than any fundamental change inside South Vietnam, that allowed Hanoi to throw off some of the constraints imposed on it since 1954. The one condition, it would seem, was that the southern struggle must be carried on ostensibly as a separate 'national liberation' movement, with no public acknowledgement of Hanoi's responsibility.

Ironically, having insisted in 1954 that Vietnam was politically one country, the North Vietnamese were now obliged by their own allies to adopt the fiction that an entirely separate South Vietnamese polity and society was capable of generating its own 'national' revolution.

## III

During the three months following the collapse of the Paris summit the world situation deteriorated sharply. The optimism of the previous summer, such as it was, had evaporated completely and the Americans were quick to blame Moscow for the intensification of anti-American action in several different areas of the world. Cuba, having established diplomatic relations with the USSR on 7 May 1960, now felt strong enough to challenge the most powerful of all American enterprises. The oil companies Esso and Texaco were informed that they would soon be obliged to process Soviet oil; when they refused, Castro took over their refineries at the end of June. A week later Eisenhower signed a measure cutting Cuba's quota of American sugar imports, which amounted to the imposition of economic sanctions. Thereupon Khrushchev announced Soviet willingness to import extra Cuban sugar, and on 9 July promised military support in the event of an American invasion of the island; to which Washington responded with a reaffirmation of the Monroe Doctrine.

Almost simultaneously, trouble broke out in the former Belgian Congo (Zaire), which at the end of June became independent under a government headed by the radical Patrice Lumumba. Like Castro he may or may not already have had secret Communist affiliations; certainly he was willing to make friends with Moscow. The result was panic among the European community during the week from 7 to 14 July. The crisis was only partially resolved by the arrival of United Nations forces on the 15th, since it was still possible that Lumumba and the left would eventually establish themselves in power. Whilst the degree of actual Soviet involvement is not easy to ascertain, the Americans held Moscow to be responsible. Fifteen years later it was revealed that in autumn 1960 the CIA began plotting to assassinate both Castro and Lumumba.[13]

Another area of potential crisis was Indonesia, where a confrontation seemed to be looming between the Communists and the armed forces. Incidents in early July, involving the apparent persecution of Chinese residents in West Java, not only produced Chinese protests but also coincided with a hardening of the PKI anti-imperialist line. On 14 July 1960 D. N. Aidit and other Communist leaders were placed under virtual house arrest and for a time their newspaper was closed down. In the upshot Sukarno succeeded in re-establishing national unity on the basis of a more conciliatory line towards the Chinese, combined with a vigorous attack on the continuing Dutch presence in New Guinea (West Irian). On 17 August the Indonesian president broke off relations with the Netherlands and launched an all-out campaign to recover West Irian; he also ordered an end to attacks on Chinese residents.[14] The United States was not yet the main target of anti-imperialism in this case and there was no danger to American oil interests in Sumatra; but Washington was blamed indirectly for supporting the Dutch.

Finally mention must be made of events in Japan, where the revised security treaty was due to be ratified by the Diet in mid-June 1960. The compaign of protest against it now reached a climax, forcing President Eisenhower to cancel a planned visit to Tokyo on 19 June. The treaty was in fact ratified, but Kishi was forced to resign and was succeeded by Ikeda on 18 July. Although the latter remained pro-American in his policies, he could not ignore a public so obviously opposed to any further moves in the direction of Japanese rearmament or of any closer alliance with the United States. Meanwhile Eisenhower's visit to Taiwan (17–18 June) served to remind Peking that the American commitment to Chiang Kaishek was as strong as ever.

During the same period, in the midst of what seemed like a 'high tide' of anti-imperialism, Sino-Soviet relations continued to deteriorate. At a meeting in Peking of the World Federation of Trade Unions (6–9 June 1960) a Chinese delegate insisted that even if world war could now be avoided, there would still be wars of national liberation: a view which the Soviet leadership still rejected. Further exchanges took place in Bucharest during and after the Romanian Party Congress (20–26 June), when Khrushchev made a strong attack on the Chinese 'Long live Leninism!' and persuaded most delegates of other parties – except the Albanians – to condemn the Chinese line on imperialism and war. Peng Zhen, representing the CCP, did not attempt a detailed defence of the *Hong-qi* article on that occasion, but concentrated rather on the importance of international Communist unity. He accused the CPSU of having diverged from the line agreed at the time of the Moscow Declaration of 1957. Quite possibly the Chinese had still to make up their minds on some issues and were genuinely taken by surprise; afterwards they circulated a memorandum charging the Russians with having behaved improperly at Bucharest.[15] Following the Soviet leader's return home, a plenum of the CPSU Central Committee in mid-July decided to withdraw 1390 Soviet experts from China – perhaps as a means of putting pressure on Mao and his colleagues rather than with the intention of permanently severing economic relations. In the event, Mao used this as an argument for economic 'self-reliance' and the experts never returned. There must have been a lively debate in Peking about China's next move in response to Soviet pressure, with the majority in the leadership probably opposing an open and final breach with Khrushchev. There was still some hope that the Russians would agree to change their line, at least in relation to the third world, in which case some kind of *rapprochement* might still be possible.

In this context North Vietnam appears to have made a fresh attempt to secure public Chinese endorsement both of its demand for reunification and of the revolutionary struggle in the South. On 24 June 1960 (while the Bucharest meeting was in session) Pham Van Dong wrote to Chen Yi enclosing copies of Hanoi's latest protests to the Geneva Conference Co-chairmen; to which the Chinese foreign minister replied on 11 July promising full support for the North Vietnamese position. Not long afterwards, on 19 July, Peking marked the sixth anniversary of the Geneva Agreements with a rally of 10,000 people and a strongly worded editorial in *Renmin Ribao*. The growing importance of South Vietnam in Chinese policy seemed to be confirmed by Zhou Enlai's speech at the Vietnamese national day reception on 2 September, which linked the 'struggle for peaceful reunification' to the 'stormy struggle of the people of the whole world against American

imperialism'.[16] Perhaps the Chinese had already reached the point
indicated by Hoang Van Hoan: that of recognising that the time
was 'ripe' for armed struggle in South Vietnam.

By August there were already signs of an intensification of the
struggle on the ground in South Vietnam. One later account
indentified a clash between ARVN and Communist Troops on 20
August 1960, at Hiep-Duc in Central Vietnam, as the first serious
engagement of the war.[17] In Long-An province, a propaganda
leaflet dated 19 August – the 15th anniversary of the August
Revolution – emphasised the success of the armed struggle that had
been going on since January. Almost simultaneously, on 23 August,
an American intelligence estimate drew attention to the deteriorating security situation since January and to the danger of growing
non-Communist opposition to Diem in the towns.

Even more important was the sudden change in the situation in
Laos on 8–9 August, when a group of young officers in the Royal
armed forces led by Captain Kong Lae seized control of Vientiane.
His motives have never been adequately explained, and it is
impossible even now to know whether the coup itself had inter-
national dimensions.[18] The consequences are not in doubt.
Although the rightist leaders escaped capture, being in Luang
Prabang at the time, the government was forced to resign on 14
August and to permit the return to power of Souvanna Phouma.
The new government, which included the leftist (but non-
Communist) Quinim Pholsena, immediately declared in favour of a
neutral policy: a first step towards restoring the national coalition
which had collapsed in mid-1958.

It should be mentioned in passing that on 23 May 1960 Prince
Souphanouvong and his colleagues, after being detained in
Vientiane for almost a year, had succeeded in escaping once again
to the maquis. Their whereabouts in early August were not certain,
but on 24 August a new Pathet Lao radio station broadcast a
message from the prince welcoming the change of policy and regime
in Vientiane. Phoumi Nosavan, for his part, declared outright
opposition to Kong Lae and joined forces with Prince Boun Oum (of
the southern ruling family of Champassak) at Savannakhet.
Nevertheless an effort was made to reconcile Souvanna Phouma
and the Phoumist faction, and for a brief moment at the end of
August it seemed as though the rightists might accept a reduced role
in a new coalition. Precisely how that attempt failed, on 31 August

or 1 September, is still not wholly clear; but in the event Phoumi again took refuge in Savannakhet and the Pathet Lao resumed its operations in Sam Neua province.

During the first week of September, Souvanna Phouma and Quinim Pholsena made contact with the Pathet Lao and on the 7th announced a new ceasefire. The next step, an agreement on military collaboration between the Pathet Lao and Kong Lae against the Phoumist forces, was worked out during the next ten days. Meanwhile on 10 September Phoumi Nosavan and Boun Oum formed a new Revolutionary Committee with the aim of overthrowing Souvanna Phouma and recovering control of Vientiane. The Savannakhet group had strong support from Bangkok, which imposed a blockade on the neutralist areas of Laos; and by mid-September it was receiving military aid from the CIA. This critical turning-point, it will be noted, occurred immediately after the failure of the 100th Sino-American meeting of 6 September and while the VNWP Third Congress was still in session.

## IV

If there was a real danger of Sino-Soviet rivalry developing into enmity between the two Communist powers, the Soviet Union needed to reassert its own influence in Indochina; unless, that is, they were willing to let the whole of South-East Asia become an exclusively Chinese sphere of influence. The absence of Ho Chi Minh from public view between 3 and 24 August appears to have coincided with yet another visit to Moscow, where he was casually reported attending an exhibition on the 15 August. At about the same time the Soviet news agency TASS (but not NCNA) reported Hanoi's first reactions to the Bucharest debate: a *Nhan-Dan* article, appealing for international Communist unity without committing itself to the Khrushchev line.[19] Possibly this reflected some development in Moscow itself, where the 'hardliners' may have secured a decision in favour of greater support for North Vietnam. The outcome of the Soviet debate on Vietnam became clearer at the Third Congress of the VNWP, held in Hanoi from 5 to 12 September 1960. Not only did Le Duan emerge as the dominant figure in the Party, reading the main political report in his new capacity as first secretary, but the Congress also adopted the principles outlined in his 'Lenin anniversary' speech in April. The new five-year plan (1961–5) would give priority to heavy industry, presumably on the basis of a substantial increase in Soviet economic aid, and the South Vietnamese people would be encouraged to expand their own revolutionary struggle against Diem. This implied Soviet as well as Chinese endorsement of that struggle, so long as it was pursued as an 'internal' affair of the South.

The emergence of Le Duan as Ho's 'number two' in the Party was now complete. His success, however, was but one element in a wider reorganisation of responsibilities which established a balance between the various leaders that would last for the next decade. Changes affecting state appointments had been announced on 15 July at the end of the first session of the new National Assembly, elected in May in North Vietnam's first full-scale election since 1954.[20] Pham Van Dong remained prime minister, with five deputy premiers (including Nguyen Duy Trinh and Le Thanh Nghi, as well as Giap and Pham Hung); but Truong Chinh ceased to be a deputy premier and became instead chairman of the National Assembly standing committee. His old associates were likewise excluded from government appointments: Hoang Quoc Viet becoming chief procurator, and so (under the new constitution) directly responsible to the Assembly, whilst Le Van Luong returned to the Party Secretariat in September; neither of them was allowed to rejoin the Politburo.

This apparent defeat of Truong Chinh, at a time when Le Duan was gaining power, fuelled the impression of some Western observers that a 'pro-Chinese faction' had lost ground to a 'pro-Soviet faction'. This was not necessarily the case. We now know that, if anyone, Hoang Van Hoan was the leading 'pro-Chinese' figure. Not only did he retain a key role in the National Assembly, as first deputy chairman, but his close associate Nguyen Khang was given an important position in the premier's office; and Hoan retained his Politburo position, albeit with reduced status. Nguyen Chi Thanh, also thought to have had friends in Peking, remained a member of both the Politburo and the Secretariat. The new pattern of responsibilities thus enabled North Vietnam to maintain a balanced relationship with its two major allies despite the new prominence of Le Duan. Both Moscow and Peking sent high-powered delegations to the VNWP Third Congress, led respectively by the Soviet Party secretary Mukhitdinov and the Chinese planning chief Li Fuqun. Their speeches, somewhat selectively

reported by TASS and by NCNA, followed essentially the lines of
the ideological conflict already evident at Bucharest. But in Hanoi
questions about the inevitability of war and the unchanging nature
of imperialism had a rather more immediate relevance.

The Americans watched the proceedings with interest, drawing
the conclusion that they amounted to international endorsement of
the expansion of the conflict in South Vietnam. Equally important,
however, was the 100th Sino-American ambassadorial meeting
which took place in Warsaw on 6 September 1960, while the
Vietnamese Party Congress was still in session.[21] The two sides
discussed new proposals for exchanging newsmen; but the
Americans again rejected a Chinese draft communiqué which
would have linked agreement on that issue to a recognition of
Peking's claim to Taiwan. The trouble taken by the two sides to
justify their opposing stands, in separate statements on 8 and 13
September, suggests that both appreciated the long-term significance of their failure to reach a compromise at this point. It is just
possible that some dramatic American concession on this occasion
might have enabled Zhou Enlai to recover lost ground in Peking,
and might even have prevented an absolute Chinese commitment
to the new struggle in Vietnam. The presence of another Japanese
Socialist Party delegation in China at precisely that moment may
also have been more than a coincidence. But no conciliatory move
was made, and by the time of the 101st meeting on 18 October it was
too late.

## V

The period between mid-September and late October 1960 was
again one of crucial importance in the evolution of the global
conflict. Whilst Nixon and Kennedy were sparring in the final run-
up to the American presidential election, a battle seems to have
been fought out in the State Department and the Pentagon which
resulted in the adoption of a tougher anti-Communist line than at
any time since 1954. There was no doubt that the Communist
'threat' to American interests around the world had been growing
more serious throughout the preceding six months. Whether the
policies advocated by the 'hawks' represented the most effective
possible response is more debatable.

TABLE 12.1 *The sharpening of global conflict, September–October 1960*

| East–West relations | International Communist relations | Indochina conflicts | Other areas of tension |
|---|---|---|---|
| | | | 2 Sept.: Castro's 'Declaration of Havana' speech, accepting Soviet support, recognising Peking. |
| | 5–12 Sept.: Third Congress of VNWP, Hanoi. | | |
| 6 Sept.: 100th Sino-American ambassadorial meeting, Warsaw. | | 7 Sept.: Ceasefire between Pathet-Lao and Souvanna Phouma's government. | |
| | | | 8–14 Sept.: Climax of Lumumba's bid for power in Congo, and overthrow by Mobutu. |
| | 10 Sept.: CCP letter to CPSU, continuing the ideological attack. | 10 Sept.: Savannakhet Revolutionary Committee, set up by Phoumi Nosavan and Boun Oum. | |
| | | 16 Sept.: Durbrow cable from Saigon, urging reforms by Diem regime. | |
| | 17–22 Sept.: Deng Xiaoping in Moscow for Sino-Soviet talks. | | |
| 19 Sept.: Khrushchev arrived in New York. | | | 18–28 Sept.: Castro in New York; Khrushchev promised more Soviet aid. |
| | | 20 Sept.: Phoumist forces failed to break through towards Vientiane, retreated from Paksane. | |
| 23 Sept.: Khrushchev speech at United Nations urging reorganisation of its secretariat, opposing US line in Congo. | | | |

TABLE 12.1 (*Contd.*)

| East–West relations | International Communist relations | Indochina conflicts | Other areas of tension |
|---|---|---|---|
| 29 Sept.: Khrushchev–Macmillan meeting at United Nations. | | 27 Sept.: Anglo-French–American statement supporting Souvanna Phouma government. | 28 Sept.: USSR recognised provisional Algerian government. |
| | | 28 Sept.: Pathet Lao retook Sam Neua. | 29 Sept.–5 Oct.: Ferhat Abbas received in Peking. |
| | 1 Oct.: Mao Zedong's selected works, fourth volume, published; Lin Biao praised it in *Hong-qi* article. | 30 Sept.: Congress of Kampuchean Communist Party: split between Pol Pot and other leaders. | 1 Oct.: Sino-Burmese Boundary Treaty signed in Peking. |
| | 1–20 Oct.: Further Sino-Soviet talks in Moscow; progress towards a compromise. | 5 Oct.: Souvanna Phouma announced diplomatic relations with USSR. | |
| | | 7 Oct.: US aid to Laos suspended. | |
| | | 11 Oct.: Souvanna Phouma had talks with Phoumi Vongvichit (Pathet Lao). | 11 Oct.: Cuba: start of new phase of nationalisation. |

| | | |
|---|---|---|
| 13 Oct.: Khrushchev left New York after final outburst at UN session on 12th. | 13 Oct.: Soviet ambassador arrived in Vientiane.<br>12–14 Oct.: Parsons in Laos, then flew to Bangkok.<br>17 Oct.: US resumed aid to Laos, but sending some directly to Savannakhet. | 13 Oct.: US imposed trade embargo on Cuba. |
| 18 Oct.: 101st Sino-American ambassadorial meeting, Warsaw. | 19 Oct.: Minh Tranh's article on the revolution in South Vietnam and the question of reunification. | 28–9 Oct.: US accused Russians of sending arms to Cuba: withdrew its Ambassador from Havana. |
| 2 Nov.: Ho Chi Minh, Le Duan in Peking, on way to Moscow Conference. | | |

Further evidence will be needed before historians can determine whether a genuine opportunity to revive the 'Camp David spirit' was lost during Khrushchev's second visit to the United States between 19 September and 13 October 1960. At a time when it was still not known who would be the next American president – although it certainly would not be Eisenhower – the Soviet leader did not visit Washington at all. His main purpose was to address the United Nations and to meet other world leaders then present in New York. But the talks he had in private with Western leaders, notably Macmillan, failed to achieve whatever objectives may have been collectively decided on in Moscow; and in public he was aggressive and bad-tempered. In the end Khrushchev left for home empty-handed and with bad grace, and afterwards he seems to have been obliged to capitulate even further to his 'hardline' colleagues.

American intransigence, however, must also be related to what was happening at that point in various parts of the third world. In the Congo, Washington's fears had been eased slightly following a crisis in early September. Lumumba, encouraged by a Soviet promise of support on 20 August, had tried to seize dictatorial powers only to be overthrown on 14 September in a right-wing coup led by Colonel Mobutu. But in Cuba the situation was going from bad to worse from the American point of view. Castro's 'Declaration of Havana' on 2 September proclaimed his willingness to accept Soviet military aid and to recognise Peking. He received further promises of assistance from Khrushchev in New York, and in mid-October the Cuban authorities moved to nationalise both indigenous and American private enterprises. The Americans retaliated with a complete trade embargo. At the end of October, after making a formal protest to Moscow alleging large-scale deliveries of Soviet arms, Washington withdrew its ambassador from Havana. By then the CIA had already begun to supply arms to the Cuban exiles training in Guatemala. In early November, following the collapse of a nascent guerrilla movement on the island, Washington decided to support an actual invasion by anti-Castro forces: the first moves towards what would become the 'Bay of Pigs' fiasco. Here too the precise sequence of events may one day be unravelled when scholars have full access to the relevant United States archives.[22]

The conflict in Laos also became more critical during these weeks, producing a serious clash of opinion on the American side between the new ambassador in Vientiane (Winthrop Brown) and his superior J. Graham Parsons, who had himself been in Vientiane

before becoming Assistant Secretary of State for the Far East.[23] On
28 September the Pathet Lao moved to recover control of Sam
Neua town, making that province virtually a 'liberated area'.
Immediately afterwards the government of Souvanna Phouma
agreed to establish diplomatic relations with the USSR and
announced its intention publicly on 5 October. The connection
between the two events is not certain; but together they alarmed the
State Department, which once again suspended aid to Vientiane.
On 11 October Souvanna Phouma received a high-level delegation
from the Pathet Lao led by Phoumi Vongvichit; and on 13 October
the first Soviet ambassador arrived in Laos. Meanwhile the
Russians were airlifting supplies into the country via Hanoi, in
order to defeat the Thai blockade along the Mekong. In spite of all
this, Ambassador Brown was still advocating Western support for
Souvanna Phouma in keeping with a joint Anglo-French-American
statement on 27 September. He was overruled when Parsons himself
flew to Laos on 12 October (the last day of Khrushchev's stay in
New York) and then, having failed to obtain satisfaction there, flew
on to Bangkok to organise more support for the rightists. The
outcome was that aid deliveries were resumed on 17 October, but
on condition that substantial supplies of military equipment were
sent directly to Phoumi Nosavan at Savannakhet – which in time
would make him strong enough to overthrow Kong Lae. There was
a direct parallel between this decision and the plan for an invasion
of Cuba: indeed American policies towards Cuba and Laos
continued to run in parallel from then till the following spring, when
Kennedy backed away from a direct confrontation in both areas.

We have already seen that in Saigon at this time Ambassador
Durbrow was trying to persuade his superiors to adopt a more
critical attitude towards Ngo Dinh Diem.[24] He too found himself at
loggerheads with the 'hawks' in Washington and was eventually
overruled. On 19 October, the ambassador received a cable from
the State Department, instructing the 'country team' to formulate
detailed procedures to implement the counter-insurgency plan.
Whilst the situation in Laos required more urgent attention, it was
becoming increasingly likely that before long Diem's position would
also be seriously challenged. With the benefit of hindsight it can be
argued that the 'hawks' were right to give Phoumi Nosavan
sufficient aid to hold southern Laos, if only to secure the western
borders of Vietnam south of the 17th Parallel; that objective could
probably have been achieved. If there was a serious American error,

it was to imagine that the Phoumist forces could ever become strong
enough to recover and pacify northern Laos; or that the Communist
powers would allow it to happen. In accepting the need to restore
the political unity of Laos – which was still required by the Geneva
settlement – the Americans abandoned the possibility of a *de facto*
partition. They thus embarked on a gamble that national unity
could ultimately be maintained under a pro-American regime. But
in so doing they challenged a vital interest of Peking. They also
ignored the danger that the Chinese and Russians, despite other
differences, might at last form an anti-American coalition to support
both the Pathet Lao and North Vietnam.

A new consensus seems to have been emerging in Peking by this
time. Zhou Enlai was still able to press ahead with his 'Bandung'
strategy in relation to 'genuinely independent' Asian regimes. In
Indonesia it had already been possible to work out a *rapprochement*
with Sukarno in August, allowing Chinese residents and the PKI to
continue to play a role in national life. At the end of September, the
Burmese leader Ne Win visited Peking to sign the final text of the
boundary agreement worked out earlier in the year, and by
November it was even possible for Sino-Indian border talks to open
in Rangoon, although they made little progress.[25] Side by side with
these developments, however, Lin Biao continued to pursue the
theme of 'people's war'. The fourth volume of Mao's selected
writings appeared on 1 October 1960, and for the occasion Lin
contributed to *Hong-qi* a eulogy on the Chairman's military
thought. The importance of national liberation wars was further
emphasised by the special honour paid to the Algerian leader
Ferhat Abbas when he attended the Chinese national day celebrations on that day.[26] (On his way through Moscow, Abbas had
at last secured the *de facto* Soviet recognition of his provisional
government which had been withheld two years earlier.) The new
line no longer precluded violent struggle against the imperialists.
What Zhou was trying to do now was to build up a new kind of
international united front, embracing the various nationalist
governments in Asia and supporting 'national liberation' wars in
areas of acute conflict with the West: for example, Indochina.
    The Soviet Union itself now seemed more willing to move in that
direction. During Khrushchev's absence from Moscow his col-

leagues held new talks with a Chinese delegation led by Deng Xiaoping, which visited the Soviet capital twice, from 17 to 22 September and again from 1 to 20 October. The deadline for their attempt to find some formula for ideological *rapprochement* was the meeting of world Communist leaders due to take place in Moscow in November.[27] When Khrushchev returned, unable to report any sign of compromise on the part of the Americans, the Chinese position and that of the Soviet 'hardliners' could begin to converge. No action could be taken on Germany or on disarmament until the United States had a new president. But in the third world it might be possible for some kind of *rapprochement* to emerge, permitting at least a truce in the ideological dispute and an end to open polemics. By 20 October that had probably been achieved. The 101st Sino-American meeting two days earlier proved conclusively that there was no likelihood of any change in the American and Chinese positions on Taiwan.

In due course Liu Shaoqi led a Chinese delegation (also including Deng Xiaoping, Peng Zhen and Kang Sheng) to the full-scale Moscow meeting which opened on 11 November. Also present were Ho Chi Minh, Le Duan and Nguyen Chi Thanh. The Vietnamese must surely have found comfort in the new polarisation of the world situation and in the fact that the Moscow meeting was able to work out a new international Communist line which recognised 'national liberation' wars as a legitimate form of struggle. The constraints of 'peaceful co-existence' no longer applied to South Vietnam.

# 13 The National Liberation Front

To ensure the complete success of the revolutionary struggle in South Vietnam, our people there – under the leadership of the Marxist–Leninist Party of the working class – must strive to establish a united bloc of workers, peasants and soldiers, and to bring into being a broad National United Front directed against the US and Diem and based upon the worker–peasant alliance . . . . This Front must carry out its work in a very flexible manner in order to rally all forces that can be rallied, win over all forces that can be won over, neutralise all forces that should be neutralised, and draw the broad masses into the struggle against the US and Diem.

Le Duan's Report to the VNWP
Third National Congress,
5 September 1960

The urgent tasks of national rebirth facing the countries that have shaken off the colonial yoke cannot be effectively accomplished unless a determined struggle is waged against imperialism and the remnants of feudalism by all the patriotic forces of the nation, united in a single national democratic front.

The aims of the Communists accord with the supreme interests of the nation. The reactionaries' effort to break up the national front under the slogan of 'anti-communism' and to isolate the Communists, the foremost contingent of the national liberation movement, weakens the national movement. It is contrary to the national interests of the people and threatens the loss of national gains.

Moscow Statement of
Communist and Workers' Parties,
6 December 1960

I

The Conference of 81 Communist and Workers' Parties held in Moscow from 11 to 25 November 1960 was described by one Marxist commentator as an attempt to revive the spirit of the Comintern debates of the 1920s, on an even grander scale.[1] The debate was lively, even bitter, and it took until 6 December to work out the final version of what became known as the Moscow Statement. One of the principal issues was that of 'fractionalism': whether the Chinese should be allowed to express publicly ideas which diverged significantly from the Soviet line. Khrushchev, along with some of his supporters among the European Parties, would probably have liked to force the Chinese to conform or leave. But that view was firmly overruled by the majority opinion, and absolute conformity was no longer demanded. Nevertheless the Sino-Soviet talks in September and October appear to have succeeded in narrowing the differences between the two principal Parties, with the result that the Statement itself amounted to a serious attempt at compromise in the interests of international unity. In the final text, Western observers had little difficulty in identifying what they believed were the respective Soviet and Chinese contributions. They also detected a marked contrast between the interpretations of the Statement given by Khrushchev to a meeting of Soviet Marxist–Leninist intellectuals on 6 January 1961, and by Deng Xiaoping in a report to the CCP's 9th Plenum a week later. But it is important not to underestimate the degree of genuine unity that emerged, which was none the less real for being shortlived.

The line represented by the Moscow Statement was by no means incoherent, even though it differed in fundamental respects from that which had prevailed in 1955–6. The Chinese now accepted that negotiations with the imperialists on such issues as trade and disarmament might not be entirely futile. In theoretical terms that meant a retreat from their previous insistence on the unchanging nature of imperialism. In practice it allowed Khrushchev room to negotiate with the new American president, who it was now known would be Kennedy and not Nixon. The Chinese themselves seem to have had no plans for serious talks with Washington at this stage: détente would be an area for Soviet initiative. Nor was there any question now of the Russians making commitments on behalf of the

Chinese. On the issue of national liberation struggle, however, it was the Soviet leaders who gave way. The Moscow Statement recognised this as a distinct (and inevitable) form of warfare; and Khrushchev seemed to accept that view in his speech of 6 January. Sino-Soviet agreement on this meant that the revolutionary movement in South Vietnam could now be legitimised as a 'national liberation struggle' in a sense acceptable to both Moscow and Peking. What the Statement did, therefore, was to separate completely the two conflicting aspects of Marxist–Leninist strategy towards the West. The pursuit of détente on the diplomatic level no longer precluded Communist encouragement of anti-imperialist revolutions in the third world. Even after the Sino-Soviet 'dispute' developed into a virtual 'split' in 1961, this dichotomy would persist in Soviet global thinking.

Ngo Dinh Diem, as head of a 'feudal' regime created by 'imperialism', was a suitable Communist target from all points of view. His defeat, as well as destroying another link in the 'imperialist' defence system, would severely damage American prestige in Asia without any harmful implications for the Communist line towards 'bourgeois nationalist' regimes elsewhere. The Vietnamese struggle might even become a logical focus for international solidarity within the 'socialist camp', despite continuing Sino-Soviet differences on other issues. Given all this, it was difficult for the Americans to regard the National Front for the Liberation of South Vietnam, when it was finally unveiled, as anything more or less than a specific application of the international Communist line contained in the Moscow Statement.

Practical Chinese and Soviet support for North Vietnam found expression in further promises of economic aid, as well as political and probably military consultations. Ho Chi Minh visited China in early November and again in early December, on his way to and from the Moscow Conference, and was accompanied for part of the time by Le Duan and Nguyen Chi Thanh. On 4 December, while Ho was still in Peking, planning chief Nguyen Duy Trinh arrived at the head of an economic delegation which later went on to the Soviet Union. A new agreement on Soviet economic and technical aid to North Vietnam was signed in Moscow on 23 December; and when Trinh returned to Peking in late January he secured an agreement for a Chinese seven-year loan equivalent to 140 million roubles.[2] It is not known whether any parallel arrangements were made for military assistance at this time; but economic aid was probably enough to give Hanoi the confidence it required for a more adventurous strategy in the South.

## II

The formal establishment of the National Liberation Front took place at a meeting of representatives from various provinces and organisations said to have been held somewhere in the 'liberated area' of South Vietnam on 19–20 December 1960: the fourteenth anniversary of the 'general uprising' against the French in Tongking at the end of 1946. The Front's public debut was nevertheless delayed until the end of January and its manifesto and programme were not published by the VNA until 3 February 1961 – the newly designated official anniversary of the foundation of the Indochinese Communist Party in 1930. In the interval between 20 December and 20 January, meetings and demonstrations were held in various parts of the South to welcome the new organisation and to install Liberation Front Committees at provincial and lower levels. In southern Central Vietnam, especially the former Viet-Minh strongholds of Quang-Ngai and Binh-Dinh, it was claimed that as many as three million people participated in anti-Diem demonstrations between 25 December and 8 January. In Nam-Bo, where the peak of activity seems to have come around 15–20 January (exactly one year after the 'mass struggle' movement of 1960), meetings involving several tens of thousands of people were reported from at least six provinces. An important area of Communist support was the province of Ben-Tre, where Diem's governor Pham Ngoc Thao is now thought to have been himself a secret supporter of the Party.[3]

The stated aims of the new Front were straightforward. The principal objective in its ten-point programme was the overthrow of Ngo Dinh Diem and the formation of a 'National Democratic Coalition Administration', which after an unspecified period would negotiate with the North to bring about 'peaceful reunification'. Most of the other points were designed to appeal to various sections of the southern population by playing upon such specific issues as democratic rights, living conditions, rent-reduction and the elimination of 'gangster-style' American culture. The basic strategy of the programme had already been spelled out in an article broadcast by Hanoi Radio, for internal consumption, on 19 October 1960. Whilst the North remained ready in principle to hold talks with the South on the question of reunification, that required the existence in Saigon of a regime willing to negotiate on Hanoi's terms. The only way to achieve reunification by that means, therefore, was to overthrow Diem: that is, to defeat the Americans by revolutionary struggle. Consequently, 'the problem of the struggle for reunification and that of the revolution in South Vietnam are inseparable'.[4]

Thus Hanoi abandoned its earlier strategy of pursuing a diplomatic and political struggle to secure 'implementation' of the Geneva Final Declaration. There was no longer any question of demanding nation-wide elections under international supervision as the means of re-establishing national unity. The future of Vietnam would now be settled by a two-stage process: revolutionary struggle in the South, already defined as armed struggle; to be followed by 'peaceful' negotiations once that struggle had been won by the Front. It was now expedient for Hanoi to accept the partition whose validity it had previously denied, and to treat South Vietnam as a separate 'nation'. The aims of the Front could then be presented as a purely 'internal' revolt against Diem and his American allies. But the creation of the Front, as an organisation with its own military arm, was an open breach of the most fundamental element in the Geneva Agreement: the ceasefire. The Vietnamese Communists in effect abandoned the 1954 settlement, whilst still claiming to uphold it; and did so with the full backing of both Peking and Moscow. The question of the precise meaning of the Geneva Agreement and Declaration thus became academic, although it continued to be debated among Western intellectuals long after it had ceased to be of any political consequence. It remained important as a propaganda issue, in that the Communist side still needed to justify its own decision to abandon the Geneva framework by arguing that the Americans had refused to implement its political terms.

The NLFSVN presented itself to the world as a 'national' movement, divorced from both the VNWP and the government of the DRVN in Hanoi. It evoked comparison with the Algerian FLN which we have seen was a genuinely nationalist movement at war with France, and not in any sense a tool of the Algerian Communist Party. But the Vietnamese reality was very different from that of Algeria. The fact that the most prominent members of the NLFSVN were all natives of South Vietnam, and that none of them could immediately be identified as Communist, helped to sustain the myth that it was a spontaneous and wholly southern-based organisation inspired only by the repressive rule of the Saigon regime. However, after its victory in 1975 Hanoi openly admitted that the key role in the leadership of the revolution in the South had been played by senior members of the Party who had secretly guided its strategy throughout the fifteen years of the Front's existence. Nor was there ever really more than one Marxist – Leninist Party in Vietnam, with its Central Committee and Politburo in Hanoi. The NLFSVN was thus a 'front' in the sense understood by the authors of the Moscow Statement. Its relationship to the Party was not unlike that of the VNFF in the North; indeed in all important respects it was heir to the southern branch of the VNFF formed in 1955, and in 1976 it was reabsorbed into the parent organisation.

Like the Fatherland Front, the NLFSVN embraced a number of existing political and religious organisations. Among the southern sects there were still substantial elements which, despite their alienation from the Diem regime, refused to join a Viet-Minh organisation. But other groups did join the Front, notably the Tien-Thien ('Former Heaven') branch of the Cao-Dai, whose principal centre was in Ben-Tre province. A grassroots study of a Vietnamese village in the Mekong Delta found that particular sect enjoying a period of unusual prosperity and expansion around 1957. It may in fact have served as a cover for the early growth of the 'liberation' movement in some places.[5] Survivors of the Binh-Xuyen also joined the Front, led by Vo Van Mon who remained an important figure in the PLAFSVN until at least 1972. Catholic and Hoa-Hao representatives were also drawn in at a later stage; but only a minority of converts to those religions can have been whole-hearted supporters. The one political party ostensibly present at the Front's creation was the Democratic Party whose leaders included Huynh Tan Phat, later the prime minister of the Provisional Revolutionary Government formed in 1969. Down to 1958 his party had claimed to be anti-Communist, but it then went underground after Diem had begun to suspect its true affiliation. Another existing group to be absorbed into the NLFSVN was the Saigon Peace Committee formed in 1954 by Nguyen Huu Tho, who in early 1961 was sprung from a prison in Phu-Yen province to become Chairman of the Front's Central Committee. But the Radical Socialist Party (which joined the Front later) and the People's Revolutionary Party (a supposedly separate Communist movement in the South) did not emerge until 1962 and played no part in the foundation meeting of December 1960.[6]

Behind the scenes the Nam-Bo Regional Committee of the VNWP continued to function, becoming the 'Central Office for South Vietnam' in late 1961, and it was there that real power lay. Following Le Duan's departure for Hanoi in 1957, the key figure in the committee was Nguyen Van Linh: a man whose name was virtually unknown in the West until he surfaced in 1975. Originally a native of Bac-Bo (Tongking) he had been imprisoned on Con-Son island along with Le Duan and Le Duc Tho between 1930 and 1936, and again from 1941 to 1945. Since then he had worked entirely in the South, and at the Third Congress of the Party in September 1960 (if not earlier) had become a secret member of the Secretariat. But even now the details of his career over the next fifteen years have not been revealed.[7] Among other Party figures mentioned in connection with the Front from time to time was Vo Chi Cong, a native of Quang-Nam province and probably also an associate of Le Duan or of Nguyen Duy Trinh.

What is not certain is which Politburo member in Hanoi had special responsibility for the South in the early 1960s. Le Duan himself may conceivably have gone there from time to time. But several other leaders formerly active in the South seem by 1960 to have been concerned primarily with the task of building socialism in the North. Pham Hung spoke on agriculture at the Third Congress; he does not appear to have had much to do with southern affairs again until 1967. Le Duc Tho reported to the Congress on the new VNWP constitution, implying that now his main work was to assist Le Duan in Party reorganisation. The one man whose role at that period is unclear was Nguyen Chi Thanh, who had accompanied Ho and Le Duan to Moscow in November but who was mentioned only very occasionally by the Hanoi media between then and 1963. By the latter year, and even more certainly from 1964 until his death in 1967, his main preoccupation is believed to have been with South Vietnam; but precisely when he was assigned military responsibilities in that area is still not known. In a series of military appointments approved on 3 March 1961, Thanh's position as head of the PAVN political department was given to another general (Song Hao) without any mention of his own new post.[8] Whilst he seems to have done some work in the field of agricultural co-operatives in the early 1960s, it is not impossible that he already had the additional task of supervising the military side of the struggle in the South. Any such role would certainly have been kept a close secret.

In public the Front was essentially a political organisation, but its programme also stressed the need for 'an army for the defence of the fatherland and people' without specifying whether that meant a separate southern army or merely referred to the existing People's Army of Vietnam. Ten years later, on 14 February 1971, the Chinese defence minister Lin Biao sent greetings to the PLAFSVN to mark the tenth anniversary of its 'unification'.[9] It would appear that in mid-February 1961 a new command was created in order to bring together the various armed units which had been drawn into the Front organisation: for example those formerly belonging to the sects and the Binh-Xuyen, as well as Viet-Minh veterans. It must also have had the delicate task of integrating into southern units the troops being gradually reinfiltrated from the North. The main function of the PLAFSVN at this stage was to reinforce the political struggle, by challenging the Saigon security forces in areas where they were at greatest disadvantage and so destroying peasant confidence in the regime.

Vietnamese Communist thinking was now somewhat different from both Chinese and Viet-Minh strategy in the 1940s and early 1950s, when the 'three-stage' concept of people's war had prevailed. In 1951, when it had been decided to advance to the 'higher' stages in northern Indochina, the South (along with Cambodia and the rest of South-East Asia) had been kept at the 'first' stage. But in the thinking of those days, the essential purpose of 'first-stage' guerrilla warfare and political activity had been to prepare the ground for the two 'higher' stages. It was not expected that such operations would in themselves be sufficient to overthrow the colonial regime, or even to force it into negotiations. In South Vietnam in 1960, however, there was every prospect that a combination of guerrilla warfare and political mobilisation might destabilise a government which depended on American aid but was in other respects independent. The Communist aim was not so much a spontaneous revolt of the masses as the spontaneous collapse of the Saigon regime.

## III

The complex relationship between the international role of the NLFSVN and its overtly 'national' character presents the historian with one of his most difficult problems. There is now sufficient evidence to demonstrate that the Front's claim to be essentially non-Communist and entirely independent of Hanoi was as bogus as the American intelligence community claimed; and that much of its impact on world opinion, especially in the liberal West, was achieved through skilful misrepresentation of the truth. Nor can its emergence during 1959–60 be attributed to subsequent American decision-making: for example the policies of the Kennedy administration, so often identified as the 'cause' of the war. On the other hand the Front could not have presented a serious challenge to the American presence in South Vietnam unless it had been able to mobilise substantial grass-roots support by exploiting economic and political grievances not entirely of its own making. It is unlikely that either the Russians or the Chinese would have given encouragement to North Vietnamese ambitions unless they had been satisfied that the new movement had deep roots. That in turn raises the question whether the southern struggle would have been able to expand into a full-scale guerrilla war if Ngo Dinh Diem and his American allies had succeeded in finding an effective means of coping with it during 1960. The fundamental basis of the Marxist–Leninist approach to revolution is the analysis and exploitation of 'contradictions' in a given society. On the ideological plane these must be defined in terms of class, with the Party as the vanguard of the 'worker–peasant alliance' in opposition to whatever class has to be defeated in the current stage of the revolution: in this case, the 'feudalists' and 'comprador bourgeoisie' which were the elements in South Vietnamese society most willing to collaborate with the Americans. The task of Party cadres in practice was to identify conflicts and grievances of all kinds and work out plans for organised action.

In debates about the effectiveness of the NLFSVN much has been made of the importance of the land question, and those who have tried to pretend that it was insignificant have on the whole failed to prove their case. But it is not necessary to accept at face value the Front's own interpretation of the agrarian issue. It has generally been assumed that Diem's programme of land redistribution was miserably ineffective. It might be more accurate to say that it moved too slowly: it had barely begun to gain momentum by the time the rural situation became critical in 1960. Of the 452,000 hectares of riceland eventually confiscated from large Vietnamese landowners under Ordinance 57 of 1956, over 300,000 hectares were in fact taken over during the years 1959–60; and of that total nearly 130,000 hectares were actually redistributed during the same two years.[10] Another important step (in October 1958) was an agreement between the South Vietnamese government and France under which all French-owned ricelands were to be bought up and transferred to Vietnamese owners. But precise terms were not finally worked out until the end of 1959, and much of the land was in any case cultivated in the form of plantations. Its main value would have been for large resettlement areas, if security conditions had allowed. Only in 1960, therefore, was it possible to embark upon a serious land programme which in other circumstances might have served to increase the government's popularity.

It was precisely then that the Communist side, as well as mounting the 'mass struggle' movement, began to implement its own plans for agrarian reform. The programme of the NLFSVN was very cautious, proposing land-rent reduction as a general rule and promising actual redistribution only of land 'usurped by the US imperialists and their agents'. The Front had no more desire than Diem to alienate small owners, who between them held a substantial part of the Mekong Delta ricelands. Evidence from Long-An province suggests none the less that some redistribution did occur, and that from about April 1960 onwards the Communist side began to place greater emphasis on the agrarian issue in order to sabotage the government programme.[11] The Saigon authorities had to be prevented from resolving the 'contradiction' in their own terms; and since the government programme had not achieved real changes during the years when it might have made significant progress, peasant grievances remained strong. Whether those grievances were sufficiently great to have produced serious unrest on their own, however, is by now an impossible question to answer.

Another key element in the political struggle was opposition to the Diem regime's repression of the population at large. Considering the circumstances of his accession to power it is not surprising that Diem and his advisers were obsessed with the problem of security, and this undoubtedly produced a number of measures which fell harshly on many people who were neither

Communists nor any real threat to the regime. The notorious Law 10/59 was itself a response to Communist activity; but earlier anti-Communist 'denunciation campaigns' had already led to many arrests and to the establishment of 're-education' centres like that at Phu-Loi. As time went on, government action against individual Communists and suspects was followed by more general security measures designed to make it more difficult for anyone to subvert the rural population. An important step along that road was the decision (announced in July 1959) to create eighty large 'agrovilles' in the next four years, together with 400 smaller settlements which would regroup scattered communities into locations where they could more easily be defended.[12] Such a policy tended to exacerbate the social 'contradictions' which the NLFSVN sought to exploit; but the fact that new settlements became targets for disruption and propaganda suggests also that they may sometimes have been effective in preventing revolutionary mobilisation.

It is too facile to argue that all Diem's moves were misguided and inevitably doomed to fail; nor is it necessary to accept all the claims and allegations of the Front at face value. The situation of 1960 must be studied in its own terms rather than as a prelude (and an explanation) for what came later. Grievances and 'contradictions' were undoubtedly present in South Vietnamese society, and were especially acute under a regime more preoccupied with security than with social welfare. But the fact that it was necessary for the Communist side to resume the armed struggle at all in 1959–60 suggests that the purely political struggle had not been sufficient to translate the 'contradictions' into successful revolution. From that point on, the critical factor was the developing armed struggle itself and the American failure to deal with it in time. The resulting insecurity in rural areas made it easier for the Communist side to exploit a wide variety of grievances in order to build up its own destructive potential; a process for which it had been preparing the ground ever since the end of 1956.

The effect of this strategy was already being felt in Saigon by the autumn of 1960. The mere possibility that the government might in the end prove incapable of defeating the guerrillas was enough to create uncertainty about the future amongst non-Communist Vietnamese; and their fears were compounded by uncertainty among the Americans themselves about whether the existing government deserved absolute support. It was this situation which produced the abortive military coup of 11–12 November 1960, when a group of dissident colonels – who may or may not have been encouraged by American contacts – almost succeeded in capturing the presidential palace. They were prevented from doing so by troops loyal to Diem, which advanced on the capital whilst the colonels were still hesitating. Evidence that a CIA officer was responsible for delaying their final attack on the palace until it was too late suggests that the Americans did not really intend the coup to succeed.[13] Its failure forced them to make up their minds to 'sink or swim with Ngo Dinh Diem'. The colonels were allowed to escape to Phnom Penh, but the incident was made an excuse to arrest the Caravelle group and other dissident politicians, whom Diem suspected of planning to participate in a new government after his own removal. Henceforth the non-Communist political élite became more divided than ever.

The failure of the coup also convinced Hanoi that more pressure was needed to bring about the ultimate crisis in Saigon. Had Diem been overthrown, the Communists might have been able to take advantage of the ensuing chaos to disrupt security programmes and so further destabilise the situation. As it was they were obliged to proceed to the next stage of revolutionary mobilisation: the creation of the Front. Meanwhile Diem and the Americans began to implement the first steps of what would become the initial counterinsurgency plan. The National Assembly had already voted to expand the South Vietnamese armed forces on 5 November; on 22 November it decided to call up reserve officers and NCOs. On 1 December the Pentagon approved a request for helicopters to improve ARVN's mobility in counter-guerrilla operations.[14] Saigon's military response was thus already taking shape even before Kennedy signed the formal counter-insurgency plan at the end of January 1961.

Comparisons have sometimes been made between the conflict in South Vietnam at the end of 1960 and that in Malaya ten years before. In certain respects they were similar. The NLFSVN was believed by now to have increased its armed forces from around 3000 (in 1955–6) to nearly 10,000, including perhaps 4500 southerners re-infiltrated from the North. In Malaya (as it then was) the 'liberation' forces had grown from perhaps 4000 fighting men in 1948 to an estimated 8000 three years later, before again declining under the impact of the British security campaign.[15] But South Vietnam in 1960 differed from Malaya in three respects: the political context was different, since there was no longer a colonial government; the Communist forces, although numerically similar, were strategically stronger in that they had already 'liberated' certain areas and possessed bases of a kind the Malayan guerrillas never succeeded in creating; and most important of all, South Vietnam did not yet have an effective counter-guerrilla campaign. If the Malayan war can be said to have been won by the British at the critical turning-point of 1951–2, it might almost be true to say that the Vietnam War was lost at the point where Diem and the Americans failed to defeat the guerrillas in late 1960 and early 1961. From that point onwards American action was always too much, too late.

## IV

The Communist decision to treat South Vietnam as a separate entity with its own 'liberation' movement had implications for the rest of Indochina. Chinese support for an intensification of armed struggle in the southern half of Vietnam did not in itself require any modification of Zhou Enlai's earlier strategy of seeking separate relations with Laos and Cambodia; indeed Hanoi's creation of a separate NLFSVN implied an acceptance, at least for the time being, of the Chinese concept of the Indochinese revolution. Moreover the new international line established by the Moscow Statement continued to respect genuinely neutralist regimes like those of Souvanna Phouma and Sihanouk.

In Cambodia there were nevertheless indications of a serious split within the People's Revolutionary Party on the issue of armed struggle. Many years later, the Pol Pot regime would commemorate the seventeenth anniversary of the Kampuchean Communist Party on 30 September 1977 on the grounds that it had been 'founded' on 30 September 1960. Later still, in 1981, the revived Kampuchean People's Revolutionary Party insisted that what had really happened on that day was a clash of opinion at its own Second Congress. (The first had been held in June 1951, when the Party was founded.) According to this latter version Pol Pot challenged the leadership of the 'old comrades' and attempted to change the name of the Party, but was overruled by the majority who continued to support Tou Samut as secretary-general. Only after the murder of Tou Samut in July 1962 did Pol Pot and Ieng Sary actually seize control.[16] There

TABLE 13.1  *Developments in Indochina, November 1960–January 1961*

| Laos | Cambodia | South Vietnam |
|---|---|---|
| | | 11–12 Nov.: Abortive coup against Diem regime.<br>November: Decision to expand ARVN military system. |
| 18–20 Nov.: Souvanna Phouma and Souphanouvong met at Sam Neua, agreed on restoration of coalition, recognition of Peking. | | |
| 28 Nov.: Phoumi Nosavan began offensive to retake Vientiane. | 28 Nov.: Sihanouk arrived in Moscow. | |
| 6 Dec.: Phoumist forces took Paksane. | | 1 Dec.: Pentagon decision to supply helicopters to ARVN |
| 9 Dec.: Souvanna Phouma withdrew to Phnom Penh | | |
| 10 Dec.: Quinim Pholsena went to Hanoi to negotiate Soviet arms airlift. | 10–14 Dec.: Sihanouk in Mongolia. | |
| 13–16 Dec.: Battle of Vientiane; Kong Lae forced to withdraw. | 14–19 Dec.: Sihanouk in Peking; leading to: | |
| | 19 Dec.: Sino-Cambodian Treaty of Friendship. | 19–20 Dec.: Meeting to found the NLFSVN. |
| 22 Dec.: Soviet Note to Britain proposing a new conference on Laos. | | 25 Dec.–8 Jan.: NLF Meetings in southern Central Vietnam. |
| End Dec.: Kong Lae forces moved to Plaine des Jarres to join Pathet Lao; both forces re-equipped and reorganised, with Soviet arms. | | |

1 Jan.: Sihanouk called for new Geneva conference on Laos.

Early Jan.: US sent AT-6 aircraft and more advisers to Laos.

January: Diplomatic moves continuing, in atmosphere of growing crisis.

2–14 Jan.: Col. Lansdale visited South Vietnam to assess situation.

January: NLF meetings and demonstrations in Nam-Bo.

28 Jan.: Kennedy signed Counter-insurgency Plan.

29 Jan.: Hanoi Radio reported formation of NLFSVN: programme published in early February.

is not yet sufficient evidence to reconstruct what actually took place; but a split of some kind undoubtedly occurred, and it marks the origin of the conflict between 'pro-Vietnamese' and 'pro-Chinese' elements for control of the Kampuchean Party. As in the case of the VNWP itself however, it is unlikely to have been a simple 'two-line struggle'; more probably several Cambodian factions were involved, and possibly also inter-regional conflicts.

The Second Congress does appear to have rejected any idea of embarking on an immediate armed struggle against Sihanouk, but there is one small piece of evidence to suggest that the prince was seriously worried by that possibility. A declassified American document records a conversation he had with President Eisenhower in New York on 27 September 1960 in which he seemed at last to be coming round to the need for more American military assistance in order to counter a potential guerrilla threat.[17] In the event, however, Sihanouk did not seek more aid. On his way home from the United Nations he stopped in both Moscow and Peking and appears to have secured assurances that his own position would not be threatened.

On 19 December the Cambodian prime minister Pho Preung, who accompanied Sihanouk to Peking, joined with Zhou Enlai to sign a Treaty of Friendship and Non-aggression which established the basis of relations between the two countries until the end of the 1960s. This enabled Sihanouk to continue to maintain friendly relations with North Vietnam as well. The only price he might have to pay, as time went on, was the use of border sanctuaries by Vietnamese guerrilla units; but on the scale of military activity contemplated in late 1960 that was not difficult for him to accept so long as no Cambodians were harmed.

In Laos on the other hand a civil war was already under way, involving a rapid increase in Soviet as well as North Vietnamese assistance to the Pathet Lao. Towards the end of November, using recently delivered American artillery and tanks, Phoumi Nosavan began his march on Vientiane. Kong Lae's neutralist forces were in no position to resist; nor was there a great deal the Pathet Lao could do to help unless North Vietnamese regular troops went to their aid. By 8 December, partly as a result of moves by Phoumi's allies in Vientiane, it was clear that the capital would fall. At that point Souvanna Phouma withdrew to Cambodia, leaving the government in the hands of Quinim Pholsena; and two days later Quinim went to Hanoi to negotiate Soviet military support. To overcome the

Thai blockade of normal supply routes through Bangkok, the Russians were already airlifting petroleum and other essential supplies to Vientiane; Soviet military equipment began to be sent in soon afterwards. But it arrived too late to save the neutralists' position in Vientiane, which was captured by Phoumi Nosavan on 17 December. The king, still in Luang Prabang, thereupon agreed to install a new government with Boun Oum as premier; and Kong Lae was forced to retreat northwards to a point midway between the administrative and royal capitals.

Nevertheless Soviet aid prevented Kong Lae's complete annihilation, and whilst he regrouped his forces there was now scope for diplomatic activity. On 22 December, following statements by the Indian and Chinese governments, a Soviet Note to Britain proposed that the Geneva Co-chairmen reconvene the Conference on Indochina in order to restore 'normality' in Laos. In the meantime they should also appeal for an end to 'foreign intervention' – namely that of the United States. On 1 January, in an urgent letter to several heads of government including Britain and the USSR, Sihanouk called for a new and enlarged version of the Geneva Conference.[18] Although the British were unable to accept either proposal immediately (or in its initial form), these moves reopened the possibility of a diplomatic solution to the crisis.

Soviet aid was not sufficient to enable the neutralists, with or without Pathet Lao help, to recover control of Vientiane or any other part of the lowlands close to the Mekong. The Phoumist forces were too well armed for that. As well as having the support of several hundred American special forces, they also – according to Chinese accounts – had military backing from Thailand; and in early January the Americans added further to their strength by sending in a number of AT-6 fighter-bombers. The main Soviet objective was to make it impossible for Phoumi Nosavan, even with all this extra support, to advance beyond the lowlands and take over the rest of Laos. In a five-day campaign at the beginning of January 1961 the Pathet Lao 'liberated' a series of towns in the north, including Phong Saly and Xieng Khouang, whilst Kong Lae's units broke through into the Plaine des Jarres to join up with the Pathet Lao. The latter were at this stage reorganised and re-equipped with heavy Soviet weapons; and it would appear that North Vietnamese officers virtually took over command as well as training duties. The neutralists likewise received Soviet weapons and were now ready to fight alongside the Pathet Lao.[19] Thus when the Phoumists resumed their advance in early February and tried to penetrate eastwards into the Plaine des Jarres they were unable to make much headway. By 7 March the Pathet Lao and Kong Lae were ready to counterattack.

The new Kennedy administration faced the difficult question whether to increase its own military involvement – possibly by sending in regular combat divisions – or to seek a diplomatic solution. In the end, as we shall see, it chose the latter course. The eventual outcome of this first phase of the Laotian civil war was thus a virtual partition of the country, which was probably what the North Vietnamese and Russians had been trying to achieve – but not along the 17th parallel. They now had control of a long corridor of territory embracing the whole of the Vietnam – Laos border area, which could be developed on a substantial scale as an infiltration route from North to South Vietnam.

Between mid-November 1960 and the end of January 1961 therefore, the new pattern of conflict in Indochina finally assumed the shape it was to retain during the next four or five years. Cambodia would stay genuinely neutral, maintaining relations with China and the Soviet Union as well as with the West. But it was a neutrality which might be ended at any time by a Communist decision to promote a revolution against Sihanouk; and the prince, aware of that danger, had no choice but to allow border sanctuaries inside his country to be used by the Vietnamese Communists. In international law, however, his neutrality was substantial enough to prevent South Vietnamese government forces or their American advisers from operating beyond the frontier even on the grounds of 'hot pursuit'. Laotian neutrality, by contrast, had broken down: in its original form the Geneva Agreement was no longer respected by either side. Whilst some kind of neutralisation might yet be restored through international negotiations, there was no longer any real possibility of establishing the precise frontier between Communist North Vietnam and non-Communist Laos which the Americans had been trying to create since 1954. Diplomacy might succeed in averting an escalation of the conflict in Laos, and so ensuring its separateness in principle from the growing crisis in Vietnam. But Laos was likely to remain an area of confrontation for as long as the issue in Vietnam was unresolved, and the Communist side would be able to go on using not merely border sanctuaries but an actual corridor for infiltration between the two zones of Vietnam – unless the Americans took some drastic preventive action.

The main focus of attention now, however, was South Vietnam, where the conflict had begun to take the form of an internal 'liberation' struggle: on one side a Communist-led Front, pursuing armed revolution with the full support of Hanoi and at least the acquiescence of Moscow and Peking; on the other an established government in Saigon, receiving economic and military assistance from the United States. Hanoi had abandoned for the time being its insistence on a single Indochinese revolution; or at least it had acknowledged that separate strategies were appropriate for the three areas of Indochina not yet under Communist rule. To that extent the Geneva Settlement continued to impose certain constraints on Hanoi's policy, even though the ceasefire no longer held; the question was whether the Americans would accept the same constraints and try to defeat the Front on its own terms.

# 14 Kennedy's Dilemma

How could we work anything out (said Khrushchev) when the United States regarded revolution anywhere as the result of Communist machinations? It was really the United States which caused revolution by backing reactionary governments: look at Iran, look at Cuba . . . Kennedy's assumption that revolution was the consequence of intervention was dangerous.

This, Kennedy protested, was not the issue. The issue was the disruption of the existing equilibrium of power. The Castro regime was objectionable not because it expelled American monopolies but because it offered Communism a base in the Western Hemisphere. . . . What would Khrushchev do if a pro-American government were established in Warsaw?

Kennedy brought up Khrushchev's pledge to support wars of national liberation in his speech of January 6. Was this non-interference? Obviously both nations were helping groups in other countries. The problem, while we backed our respective movements, was not to clash ourselves. Khrushchev vigorously defended his speech. . . . Wars of national liberation, he said, were 'sacred' wars and the Soviet Union was certainly going to support them.

> Arthur M. Schlesinger, Jr.,
> on the exchanges at Vienna,
> June 1961 (*A Thousand Days*)

It is clearer than ever that we face a relentless struggle in every corner of the globe, that goes far beyond the clash of armies or even nuclear armaments . . . Too long we have fixed our eyes on traditional military needs, on armies prepared to cross borders, on missiles poised for flight. Now it should be clear that this is no longer enough: that our security may be lost piece by piece, country by country, without the firing of a single missile or the crossing of a single border. . . . We intend to re-examine and reorient our forces of all kinds.

> John F. Kennedy, to the
> American Society of Newspaper Editors,
> 20 April 1961

I

During the first few months of his presidency Kennedy was determined to reverse the tough anti-Communist line that had emerged in Washington in the second half of 1960. Anxious not to jeopardise the possibility of new negotiations with Khrushchev by overreacting to the Communist 'threat' in any specific area of the globe, he was determined above all to avoid committing American combat troops in circumstances where that might lead to a local war. The president probably still believed in the 'missile gap' which as a senator he had been among the first to identify, and which was not finally shown to be a fallacy until September 1961. He was also painfully aware that the United States strategic reserve of conventional forces was not large enough to permit the deployment of a substantial number of troops to any one part of the world without endangering the security of other areas.[1] One of the principal tasks he assigned to Secretary of Defence McNamara was that of reorganising and expanding the American capability for 'limited war'. Nevertheless his main hope was that bilateral negotiations with the Soviet Union would lead not only to mutual restraint in the field of nuclear weapons but also to an easing of tension throughout the world. In the meantime, having been converted to Maxwell Taylor's ideas about 'flexible response', he was inclined to favour wherever possible covert operations rather than overt military intervention as a method of countering any actual threat to American interests. Kennedy was well aware of the risks to American global power – as well as to his own reputation – of failing to make any response at all whenever that power seemed to be challenged.

By early March the new administration faced difficult decisions in two key areas of inherited crisis: Cuba and Laos. Both situations had to be handled in ways that would not impede the three-power talks on banning nuclear tests due to be resumed in Geneva on 21 March. In the case of Cuba, Kennedy had to decide whether to proceed with existing plans to use exile forces to provoke an uprising against Castro; and if so, how far to allow United States combat forces to become directly involved. A series of top-level meetings between 11 and 15 March 1961 worked out a compromise plan which permitted the operation to go ahead, on condition that it was strictly covert and deniable. With that in mind it was decided that the exiles would land in the relatively secluded 'Bay of Pigs' rather than at the point originally designated on the south-eastern coast of the island.[2] Without more substantial evidence it would be going too far to suggest that Kennedy deliberately allowed the operation to fail; certainly he was determined to prevent it becoming the excuse for direct American military involvement. It is not clear whether he knew for certain that Castro could not be dislodged without such intervention; but he had some idea of the scale of Soviet arms deliveries since October. The president may have decided that if the CIA could bring about a change of regime by means which required *only* the training and supply of indigenous forces, the result would be welcome. He was not prepared to accept the diplomatic repercussions of direct military action, however, and he intended to draw a clear distinction between the two. At a news conference early in April he explicitly ruled out action by American combat forces against Cuba, and he refused to be swayed from that position when the 'covert' operation went ahead on 15–19 April and proved a fiasco.

The situation in Laos was more complicated. In Cuba, where a Soviet ally was already in power, there was no question of convening an international conference to guarantee the island's neutrality. Laos on the other hand had already been the subject of international guarantees, whose reaffirmation in some form was the only way to avert deeper external involvement in an ongoing civil war. It could be argued that not only the United States but also the Soviet Union and North Vietnam had by now violated the Geneva settlement beyond redemption. But so far they had done so only in ways which amounted to indirect interference in Laotian politics and the provision of aid to Laotian armies; they had not sent in their own combat forces. The problem for the Americans was that their intervention had not worked: rightist forces were still not strong enough to restore the situation of early 1960. Here too, Kennedy had to decide whether to deploy American troops in order to secure the southern half of Laos once and for all.

The advice he received from the JCS was probably ambivalent. There was no doubt that a Communist Laos, under the full control of the Pathet Lao and closely allied with North Vietnam, would pose a potential threat to the security of both Thailand and South Vietnam. Militarily therefore if it ever became necessary to deploy combat units at all in the Indochinese Peninsula, Laos was the logical place for them to go. But the generals were far from enthusiastic about risking another major land war in Asia,

TABLE 14.1 *Laos, Vietnam and Cuba, March–May 1961*

| Diplomacy | Laos | Vietnam | Cuba |
|---|---|---|---|
| *A Mar.: 1961* | | | |
| 7 Mar.: US and Chinese ambassadors held 103rd meeting, Warsaw, US warning that ceasefire must precede conference on Laos. | 9 Mar.: Start of offensive by Pathet Lao and Neutralist forces. | 9 Mar.: NSAM-28, on planning for guerrilla operations in 'Viet-Minh territory'. | 11 Mar.: White House meeting reviewed plans for covert operation (worked out since Nov. 1960). |
| | 10 Mar.: Souvanna Phouma and Phoumi Nosavan, in Phnom Penh, called for international conference on Laos. China and North Vietnam denounced this statement. | | 14–15 Mar.: Revision of plans: Kennedy approved landing at 'Bay of Pigs', but rejected any idea of US military action to support it. |
| | 14 Mar.: Start of evacuation (by US planes) of KMT forces from Laos to Taiwan. | 15 Mar.: Decision to replace Durbrow by Nolting, as US ambassador in Saigon. | |
| 21 Mar.–18 Apr.: Resumption of three-power conference (Geneva) on ending of nuclear tests. | 20–1 Mar.: US NSC decided on military moves affecting Okinawa and north-east Thailand; but no direct intervention in Laos. | | |

22 Mar.: Formation of 'Revolutionary Council' in Miami, followed by final stage of preparations.

15 Apr.: Preliminary air strikes by Cuban-flown planes from Nicaragua.

16 Apr.: Kennedy vetoed second air strike.

17–19 Apr.: 'Bay of Pigs' landings, easily defeated by Castro.

23 Mar.: Kennedy news conference warning of possible US intervention, but in principle agreeing to ceasefire and Laotian neutrality.

27 Mar.: SEATO Meeting, Bangkok: discussion of Laos.

23 Mar.: British Note to USSR calling for ceasefire in Laos, to be followed by an international conference.

24 Mar.: Harriman visited Delhi, seeking Indian action to persuade Moscow to accept ceasefire in Laos.

24 Mar.: US dropped spying charges against Soviet official at United Nations.

24 Mar.: Gromyko requested meeting with Kennedy.

27 Mar.: Kennedy met Gromyko in Washington; some easing of tension.

27 Mar.: *Pravda* accepted principle of ceasefire in Laos.

B  *April–May 1961*

16 Apr.: China supported call for conference on Laos, in communique after Zhou Enlai–U Nu talks.

18 Apr.: Exchange of messages between Kennedy and Khrushchev, relating to Cuba.

TABLE 14.1   (Contd.)

| Diplomacy | Laos | Vietnam | Cuba |
|---|---|---|---|
| | 19 Apr.: Kennedy ordered US special forces in Laos to put on uniforms; Programs Evaluation Office replaced by MAAG for Laos. | 20 Apr.: DRVN protested to Geneva Co-chairmen about possible combat role of US advisers in Laos.<br>20 Apr.: Deputy Defence Secretary Gilpatric convened task-force to recommend US action in Vietnam. | 20 Apr.: Kennedy speech on the significance of Cuba, and the new threat to American power in the world. |
| | | | 23 Apr.: 'Bay of Pigs' Board of Enquiry appointed: context for debate on CIA role in covert paramilitary operations. |
| | 22 Apr.: Neutralist forces again on the offensive.<br>22–25 Apr.: Laotian leaders in China. | | |
| 24 Apr.: Joint appeal by Geneva Co-chairmen (UK and USSR) for ceasefire in Laos, followed by conference. | 26–29 Apr.: Further consideration of US military intervention in Laos. | 26–27 Apr.: Gilpatric task force produced its first memorandum, including leading role for Lansdale.<br>29 Apr.: National Security Council approved limited | |

actions in Vietnam; question of sending troops still under discussion.

2 May: G. Ball moved to amend report of Gilpatric task force.

3 May: Durbrow handed over Saigon embassy to Nolting.

6 May: Final version of task-force report, more acceptable to State Department; role of Lansdale eliminated.

10 May: JCS recommended deployment of US troops to South Vietnam and Thailand; State Department opposed this.

11 May: NSAM-52 approved 'Program of Action' for Vietnam, but deferred question of troop commitment.

12 May: Vice-President Johnson met Diem in Saigon to explain decisions.

1 May: US decision not to deploy forces to Laos at present.

3 May: Ceasefire due to come into effect throughout Laos.

8 May: International Control Commission reconstituted in Laos: verified ceasefire by 11 May.

12 May: Geneva Conference on Laos due to meet; it actually opened on 16 May.

12 May: Khrushchev letter to Kennedy, reviving idea of a meeting and proposing Vienna as site for talks. (They met there, 3–4 June.)

especially in a country whose existing communications and logistic facilities were as primitive as those of Laos. They insisted that any operation there would require a force of at least 60,000 men; and by April they were talking about 140,000.[3] That order of commitment, they well knew, was impossible without calling up reserves and embarking on an immediate military build-up. Kennedy realised that such action would not only destroy the Geneva framework irreversibly but would also damage the prospect for East–West negotiations on any other issue. Indochina was not worth such extreme consequences.

Therein lay the essence of his dilemma. Military action was impracticable from almost all points of view – unless he wished to plunge the world into crisis at a time when the United States could no longer take for granted the superiority of its own nuclear forces. Negotiations of some kind were therefore imperative; but would negotiations produce a long-term solution? It was by no means certain that *both* Communist powers would be willing to negotiate an agreement acceptable to the United States. Even if they were, would the resulting neutralisation of Laos provide adequate protection for South Vietnam and Thailand? For better or for worse Kennedy decided, as in the case of Cuba, to adopt a policy of restraint – but without any guarantee of success.

On 7 March 1961, at the 103rd ambassadorial meeting in Warsaw, the United States warned China that it would be compelled to intervene in strength in Laos unless all sides accepted the principle of an enforceable ceasefire.[4] That same day the combined forces of the Pathet Lao and Kong Lae began a counteroffensive against Phoumi Nosavan's army, not only preventing him from taking over the rest of Laos but driving him back from the approaches to the Plaine des Jarres and Sam Neua province. After two weeks of fighting the situation became critical, forcing Washington to make up its mind on further action. An NSC meeting on 21 March decided to alert special forces in Okinawa; to send the seventh fleet to the Gulf of Thailand and establish a helicopter base in north-east Thailand; but for the time being not to move troops into Laos itself. Two days later the President went on television to explain his desire for a 'truly neutral' Laos and his willingness to negotiate on that basis. At the same time he warned that if there were no ceasefire the Americans would have to 'consider their response'. That it would have to be a unilateral response, rather than one in conjunction with SEATO allies, became clear at a meeting in Bangkok on 27 March when both France and Britain showed extreme reluctance to implement the organisation's contingency plans in existing circumstances. Moreover, an article in *Pravda* that day seemed to accept the principle of a ceasefire in Laos, which further weakened the argument for American military intervention. Possibly under European pressure, the Americans were now willing to abandon their exclusive support for Boun Oum and Phoumi Nosavan so long as they could re-establish friendly ties with Souvanna Phouma, thus reversing the policy of J. Graham Parsons which had prevailed six months earlier. To that end Averell Harriman made contact with the neutralist prince in late March. There were also signs of a more general improvement in Soviet–American relations about that time, including a visit to the White House by foreign minister Gromyko (at his own request) on 27 March.

Kennedy thus had some reason to hope that restraint on the part of the United States would now lead to corresponding restraint on the Communist side. But much would depend on the Chinese. On 1 April they signalled their rejection of Kennedy's insistence that a ceasefire must take effect before negotiations began. But there does not appear to have been any significant new breach between Moscow and Peking at this stage; the signing of a trade and credit agreement between them on 8 April suggests that their relations were still relatively calm. Mao's final acceptance of a preliminary ceasefire in Laos probably came during a visit to Hangzhou by Souvanna Phouma and Souphanouvong (on their way home from Moscow) between 22 and 25 April. On 24 April 1961 the Geneva Co-chairmen at last felt confident enough to appeal formally for a ceasefire – to be verified by the reconvened International Commission – and invited fourteen nations to send representatives to Geneva on 12 May. At that point the Americans debated one last time whether to send troops into Laos. They had decided on 19 April to put into uniform the 400 special forces already operating there, and to transform the Program Evaluation Office into a full MAAG comparable with that in Saigon.[5] But that was as far as they would go. The ceasefire came into effect on 3 May and was confirmed by the International Commission on the 11th. On 16 May Sihanouk himself inaugurated the second Geneva Conference on Indochina.

The American decision not to put combat units into Laos had immediate consequences for Vietnam. Pathet Lao and North

Vietnamese control of Eastern Laos, extending to areas bordering
directly on South Vietnam, had made it difficult if not impossible to
devise any form of 'neutralisation' which in practice, as opposed to
international law, would prevent the expansion of covert infiltration routes from North to South Vietnam. On the other hand, a
new international agreement would effectively preclude the
Americans themselves from taking retaliatory action beyond the
Vietnamese border. Unless they intended to abandon South
Vietnam altogether, they must therefore find ways of strengthening
both the political confidence and the material capabilities of the
Diem regime. Saigon must be provided with the means to cope with
both existing guerrilla activity and a possible expansion of the
armed struggle. Kennedy may have hoped that his own restraint in
Laos would be met by some attempt on the part of the Soviet Union
and China to avert an escalation of the conflict in South Vietnam. If
so he was proved wrong.


## II


In the aftermath of the 'Bay of Pigs', the Americans had to accept
that national liberation struggles of the kind which had brought
Castro to power could not easily be reversed once they had
succeeded. A revolutionary regime already in control could
legitimately declare itself an ally of the Soviet Union and China,
and obtain sufficient economic and military support to resist any
'covert action' against it. Kennedy was alarmed at the prospect of
similar struggles in other countries of the third world leading to a
gradual expansion of the 'socialist camp'. In a speech to the
American Society of Newspaper Editors on 20 April 1961, he
defined what he saw as the changing nature of the 'Communist
threat' to the existing global balance of power. On the same day he
instructed his deputy secretary of defence, Roswell Gilpatric, to
convene an interagency task-force which would recommend a new
programme of action for Vietnam.[6] Throughout the next few
months, decision-making on Vietnam was paralleled by a more
general discussion of American capabilities in the field of
counterinsurgency.

Kennedy was already a convert to Maxwell Taylor's ideas about
the need for 'flexible response' rather than total reliance on the

nuclear deterrent. He had appointed Taylor his special adviser on military affairs and had assigned to McNamara the task of reviving and developing an American capability to wage 'limited war'. But the president was also convinced that conventional military action by regular combat divisions was inappropriate to situations of the kind that had arisen in Cuba, Laos or Vietnam. He sought to build on ideas about counterinsurgency that had begun to emerge from Pentagon and CIA planning during 1960. At the same time he was determined to avoid any repetition of the Cuban fiasco, where the CIA had been allowed to devise and execute its own paramilitary attack, far beyond the scale of operations originally envisaged for that agency. The board of enquiry set up on 23 April to examine the lessons of the Cuban adventure devoted much of its time to working out a more effective doctrine of counterinsurgency, and to discussing a new pattern of responsibility. What emerged was a policy requiring the participation of all the main agencies of government concerned with foreign affairs. The JCS were given greater powers in the paramilitary field and under their direction a new office was created in the Pentagon: the Special Assistant for Counterinsurgency and Special Activities, whose chief was to become a leading figure in waging the type of 'special warfare' soon to develop in South Vietnam. The reorganisation was probably completed by late June, when a series of NSAMs defined the responsibilities of the JCS in this field and made it – theoretically at least – impossible for the CIA to have independent control of large-scale operations.[7] Unfortunately, having solved one set of problems, Kennedy found it impossible to prevent the new programme from acquiring a momentum of its own and becoming even more difficult to handle than the old type of covert operation.

Meanwhile the Gilpatric task-force spent the last ten days of April developing a set of recommendations on Vietnam predicated on the assumption that American troops would not be sent into Laos. Its preliminary memorandum of 26 April argued for a programme to be carried out by the task-force itself, which would include an important (if not predominant) role for Lansdale. As the Laos ceasefire took shape, however, the State Department began to assert a claim to more influence in Vietnam decision-making; and in early May Under-secretary of State Ball intervened to oblige the task-force to revise its memorandum. There was to be no weakening of the essential commitment to South Vietnam; but the task-force itself, and particularly Lansdale, would no longer have responsibility for action on the ground. This gave Kennedy greater freedom to relate Vietnam decisions to the wider themes of his global strategy. But the principle of interagency control, with stronger participation by the State, meant in the long run that strategy for Vietnam would develop in a less personalised, more bureaucratic fashion. The question whether things might ultimately have gone better for the United States in Vietnam if Lansdale had been allowed to take charge at this point must remain one of those 'ifs of history' which no amount of speculation can resolve. Certainly the delay between then and the final approval of a more systematic American policy in October gave the Communist side time to consolidate its position and so keep the initiative.

Kennedy's first substantive decisions on Vietnam (apart from his endorsement of the Eisenhower counterinsurgency plan in January) were formalised in NSAM no. 52 of 11 May 1961. He overruled a proposal from the JCS to deploy United States forces to South Vietnam immediately, to be there in the event of a subsequent crisis. Instead he approved measures to strengthen the Saigon army and civil guard, backed by an expanded programme of operations by American special forces, which would now include more careful surveillance of the Laos border and the infiltration of intelligence teams north of the 17th parallel.[8]

In order to reassure South Vietnam and other friendly governments in the region that the decision on Laos did not imply a general weakening of American commitments, Vice-President Johnson was sent on a tour of South-East Asia which took him to Saigon on 12 May. Among the questions he discussed with Diem was that of a bilateral treaty between the Republic of Vietnam and the United States, which would have guaranteed military support in case the SEATO allies again refused to act collectively in a crisis. Any formal treaty, however, would have been a flagrant violation of Article 19 of the Geneva Agreement and the Americans eventually decided against it. They preferred to justify the further expansion of military assistance to Saigon by arguing that the Communist side had violated the ceasefire, rather than by themselves renouncing any specific clause of the Agreement.[9] Future relations between the United States and South Vietnam would be based on a simple exchange of letters between the two presidents defining their respective needs and commitments. Later on, American opponents of the war would emphasise the fact that there had never been a formal treaty obligation – nor even a specific request for

Washington to send troops. But in 1961 Kennedy had no intention of becoming so deeply involved; the legality of commitment was less important than the diplomacy of restraint.


## III


On the day originally fixed for the Laos conference to open (12 May), Khrushchev wrote a personal letter to Kennedy proposing a meeting in Vienna the following month. Kennedy's first reaction was one of optimism, but when the encounter actually took place on 3–4 June it proved considerably less productive than he had hoped.[10] Cuba was no longer a problem; and on the question of Laos the Soviet attitude still permitted a measure of conciliation. During the first sessions at Geneva (16 May–26 June) progress was made on a number of issues. But those were areas where the Americans had backed away from active military involvement. Kennedy was no doubt hoping for something in return – if only a tacit understanding that in other areas the Soviet Union would refrain from actions calculated to disturb the global balance of power. Had such reassurances been forthcoming the United States might have been willing to co-operate more fully in spheres where the Russians sought bilateral agreements: trade and credit relations, normalisation of consular arrangements, and control of nuclear weapons. However, Khrushchev denied the possibility of a status quo if it meant an end to revolutionary activity throughout the world. He compared Kennedy's proposal with the nineteenth century concept of a 'holy alliance' against political change of any kind. Given the current international line agreed between Moscow and Peking the previous autumn, the Soviet leader could hardly have done otherwise. He also reiterated the demand for a German peace treaty, including a revision of the status of West Berlin; there too he may have been under pressure from 'hardline' colleagues in Moscow. The effect of the summit in Vienna was to convince Kennedy that direct negotiations with the Soviet Union could not immediately resolve outstanding problems in areas of East–West tension. He must therefore brace himself for a war of nerves, if not for more serious conflict.

The danger of a crisis over Berlin had already been foreseen in an NSAM of 25 April 1961, authorising contingency planning which was by now under way.[11] In mid-June the Russians began to force the pace, setting in train the confrontation which led to the building of the Berlin Wall in mid-August and which did not finally die away until late October. Yet despite its apparent seriousness, the Berlin crisis was a controlled international game in which each side could make up its mind how far to go – and could equally rapidly retreat if the conflict threatened to get out of hand. At Vienna, Kennedy expressed fears of 'miscalculation' in such situations, but on this occasion there was probably no real danger of war. The same controlled conditions had characterised the Taiwan Straits crisis of 1958. But in South-East Asia there was a far greater danger of the conflict developing in ways the superpowers could not control.

By July it was also obvious that the Geneva Conference would not produce rapid results in Laos. Compared with the conference of 1954, that of 1962 lacked any sense of urgency; there was consequently little hope of agreement within a specified time limit. Nor was formal partition a possible solution by this stage. The declared object of the negotiations was to bring the three 'parties' in Laos together in order to reunify the country, and then to neutralise it on terms acceptable to both China and the Soviet Union as well as to the Western powers. On 22 June Sihanouk managed to arrange a meeting in Zurich between the 'three princes' (Souvanna Phouma, Souphanouvong and Boun Oum), which led to an agreement in principle to work together. But much still remained to be settled when the Geneva Conference itself adjourned four days later. Part of the blame for this may have rested with the Americans, but the Chinese attitude was equally important. Peking's refusal to agree to strong international machinery – on the grounds that it would deprive the Vientiane government of its sovereignty – seems to have arisen from the fear that a virtual Soviet–American condominium in Laos might exclude China's own influence there.[12] Since the Americans insisted on proper international guarantees, the result was stalemate.

The impossibility of achieving rapid agreement on Laos was part of the reason why it also proved impossible to stabilise the situation in Vietnam. On 9 June Ngo Dinh Diem drafted a letter asking Kennedy for increased military support, which his minister of defence delivered in Washington a week later. Kennedy thereupon agreed to set up a joint economic commission composed of American and Vietnamese officials to work out the economic implications of a further expansion of South Vietnam's military capabilities. Presided over by the economist Eugene Staley – but also including several military advisers – it set to work in Saigon during the second half of June and reported at the end of July.[13]


In late July and early August 1961 the various strands of the global conflict came together. On 25 July, just as the American disarmament negotiator John J. McCloy was arriving in Sochi for talks with Khrushchev, Kennedy went on television to announce a call-up of military reserves and an increase in United States military expenditure. Although the president also expressed interest in further negotiations on the German question, Khrushchev was bound to react sharply. In conversation with McCloy, he accused Kennedy of declaring 'preliminary war' on the Soviet Union. Two weeks later, on 7 August, the Soviet leader made his own television broadcast which all but reversed the decision of January 1960 to reduce the size of the Soviet armed forces. This amounted to another set-back for his ideas about both 'peaceful co-existence' and Soviet economic development. It must also have convinced Washington that Khrushchev alone was not the arbiter of Soviet policy and that the Moscow 'hardliners' were still influential.

It is beyond the scope of the present study to determine whether this impasse might have been avoided by some more 'moderate' American approach; but the consequences for Soviet and American decision-making on Vietnam are clear. Also in late July 1961, Khrushchev received at Sochi the Vietnamese premier Pham Van Dong, who had arrived in Moscow in late June and had since been touring Eastern Europe. By the time he left for home on 12 August, Dong had secured not only public Soviet endorsement of the revolutionary struggle in South Vietnam but also another major agreement on economic aid.[14] Kennedy meanwhile reached the conclusion that he had no choice but to 'make a stand' in Vietnam. Even so, when he came to consider the Staley Report at the beginning of August he was still inclined to accept its 'minimum' rather than its 'maximum' recommendations. On 11 August another NSAM (no. 65) authorised the support required to increase South Vietnam's regular forces to a level of 200,000, and to accelerate various economic and social programmes. If the North Vietnamese had been obliged at that point to submit to renewed Soviet and Chinese constraint, the 'Staley programme' might just possibly have been adequate to enable Diem to cope with his difficulties. But by now such constraint seemed less likely than ever. The situation on the ground in South Vietnam continued to deteriorate during August and September, and by October Kennedy found himself endorsing a programme for even greater United States involvement.


## IV

Could Kennedy have done anything to avoid this greater level of commitment? It is easy enough to criticise his actions by invoking generalities: that he overestimated the importance of Indochina in American global strategy; that he was too concerned with theoretical 'anti-Communism' and failed to recognise the specific realities of Vietnam; or even, following Khrushchev's line of thinking, that he ought not to have tried to stem the 'tide of revolution' in Asia at all. But international decision-making does not allow world leaders the luxury of reassessing basic principles – or redefining the realities of power politics – at every turn of events. If the historian wishes to suggest that Kennedy made some specific error of judgement, it must be identified in terms of the day-to-day sequence of his actual decisions within the limits of choice open to him.

China was probably the key to the situation. The one thing the United States was free to do in mid-1961, and which *might* have made a significant difference to the subsequent course of events throughout Asia, was to permit the Chinese People's Republic to take its seat at the United Nations. In terms of American domestic politics that decision was all but impossible for Kennedy to take: it would have been opposed not only by the extreme right but even by Eisenhower, and his own position as president was still too insecure. When Kennedy and his advisers met on 5 August at Hyannis Port to discuss tactics for the autumn session of the General Assembly, it was taken for granted that they would continue to recognise Chiang Kaishek: a decision which probably determined the shape of China's policy for the next four or five years.[15] Khrushchev himself had appealed to Kennedy at Vienna to recognise Peking; he probably knew better than his adversary the risks that would be run if it did not happen. The Sino-Soviet *rapprochement* of 1960 had been possible only because Deng Xiaoping and Liu Shaoqi had been able to persuade their colleagues to compromise with Khrushchev's line. During the spring and early summer of 1961, Zhou Enlai and Chen Yi had likewise persuaded the leadership to accept the ceasefire in Laos and to participate in the conference at Geneva. But the situation was one in which moderation could be justified only by success, and Lin Biao was almost certainly ready to seize any opportunity to reassert the anti-imperialist, anti-revisionist line. Once it became clear that entry into the United Nations was still barred, the 'moderates' again lost ground.

On the Soviet side it was beginning to be apparent around the middle of August 1961 that Khrushchev might after all persuade the Soviet Central Committee – and ultimately the CPSU 22nd Congress – to continue its support for détente; the building of the Berlin Wall (17 August) marked the essential turning-point of the crisis there. Two days later the withdrawal of the Soviet ambassador from Tirana represented one more step towards making condemnation of Albania a vehicle for indirectly criticising the Chinese line on imperialism and war. At the Congress itself, between 17 and 31 October, Khrushchev launched a major ideological attack on Albania.[16] The Chinese were thus forced to decide whether to follow suit or to reaffirm their independent anti-imperialist line. Zhou Enlai, who led the Chinese delegation to the 22nd Congress, failed to secure any modification of the Soviet line – and on 23 October he made a dramatic exit and left for home.

Ho Chi Minh and Le Duan also went to Moscow again in October for the CPSU Congress. They were careful not to criticise Albania, but paid a tactful visit to the Baltic states when Zhou Enlai went home. There was no question of a Soviet–Vietnamese 'split', and North Vietnam succeeded in remaining on good terms with both the Soviet Union and China throughout the 1960s. Ironically, whereas in 1960 a Sino-Soviet *rapprochement* had helped North Vietnam to secure international Communist support for a return to armed struggle, the Sino-Soviet breach of 1961 helped them even more. The Chinese were now more inclined than ever to give Hanoi moral support, if not actual military aid; in such circumstances Khrushchev could not afford to sacrifice Vietnam in the cause of détente. Meanwhile a political work conference of the PLA meeting in Peking from 18 October to 4 November probably endorsed a strongly anti-imperialist line, as well as the 'Maoist' line on people's war.[17] Zhou himself is said to have addressed the PLA conference on his return. The Sino-Soviet conflict thus came out into the open; but in a form which entirely precluded any détente between China and the United States or Japan.

From Hanoi's point of view international conditions were now favourable for an expanding struggle against Diem. The Americans had therefore to work out an appropriate response or allow South Vietnam to collapse. Between 18 October and 1 November 1961, coinciding precisely with the Soviet Party Congress and the military conference in Peking, Maxwell Taylor undertook a mission to Indochina to find ways of further strengthening South Vietnam. There was no longer any reason to hope that negotiations with Moscow would lead to any significant Soviet restraint of Hanoi, and the immediate security situation was deteriorating rapidly.

In Laos, Kennedy was satisfied that a combination of diplomacy and covert operations would be sufficient to prevent the fall of Vientiane; and short of an American invasion, there was little to be done about the 'Ho Chi Minh trail' along which Communist infiltration was continuing at a growing rate. In Vietnam, however, something more was required. The president was still determined not to commit regular combat troops, and in early November he rejected Taylor's advice to send even a token force of 8000 men whose presence might have been justified by a need for flood relief operations. Instead he approved a new form of counterinsurgency which for the first time would involve a direct role for United States special forces and logistic support units. This was to lead to the deployment of 10,000 Americans during the next twelve months, but all operating within (or in conjunction with) the South Vietnamese command structure.[18] It remained to be seen whether such a programme of 'limited partnership' with the Vietnamese would prove an effective counter to revolutionary warfare. But by refusing to send combat units to any part of Indochina and by entering into negotiations on Laos, Kennedy had (if nothing else) averted the possibility of a wider war. The struggle would now be confined to South Vietnam. Win or lose, there was still some hope that he and Khrushchev could between them prevent Vietnam from becoming a serious obstacle to negotiation on major bilateral issues when the opportunity returned.

Kennedy was anxious above all to avoid a sequence of moves and counter-moves which might unravel the whole framework of international relations that had evolved since the Second World War. Throughout the years since 1945 the United States had adhered to the principle of upholding the various agreements which had established the geopolitical pattern across the globe after the Second World War, and the ceasefire agreements on Korea and Indochina in 1953–4 had been treated as an extension of the same pattern. The Americans thus found themselves applying the same criteria of importance to Indochina as to other key areas in their global system; the commitment to South Vietnam was in many respects precisely the same as that to the non-Communist halves of Germany and Korea. But militarily, the actual threat to South Vietnam was more comparable with revolutionary struggles elsewhere in the third world. The problem for Kennedy was whether the United States could fulfil its commitment by successfully responding to that threat in its own terms. Hence the vital importance of his strategy of counterinsurgency.

In all this it is not necessary to suppose that Kennedy saw his own decisions as the first rung on a ladder of 'escalation'. The subsequent influence of Hermann Kahn's doctrines, and the application of that term to Johnson's strategy after 1964, should not deceive us into thinking otherwise. Kennedy himself made no assumption that if counterinsurgency failed it would then be logical to proceed to more conventional operations, including the deployment of ground troops. His objective, in Vietnam as elsewhere, was to find a new method of defeating a new type of 'threat' to an American ally: a substitute for, not a prelude to, the conventional action which he knew to be inappropriate. Nor is there any reason to suggest that either Kennedy or his generals deliberately *chose* to make Vietnam their 'test case' for the doctrine of counterinsurgency, in preference to some other country that would have been more suitable. Those who have suggested that Vietnam was 'the wrong war at the wrong time in the wrong place' have ignored the fact that Kennedy was responding to a situation where most of the initiative lay with the Communist side. Vietnam became important in 1960–1 for reasons which had more to do with the global strategies of the Soviet Union and China, and with American vulnerability, than with the exercise of options on the part of the United States. Trouble in Vietnam – or alternatively in Vietnam and Laos together, if there had been no Geneva Conference in 1961 – was avoidable only in the same sense that the Korean War might have been avoided: by surrender, in circumstances where negotiation was impossible. There was a war in Vietnam because that was where the challenge arose, at a moment when Kennedy could not ignore the challenge.

# Appendix: The Vietnam Workers' Party and its Leaders

There is still no adequate history of the Indochinese Communist Party and its successors, based on all available source material. The following notes may be useful as background for references to the Party in the present work. They are based partly on the author's own research in the Paris Archives.

*Foundation*

During the summer of 1929, two Communist Parties were founded and for a time were in competition with one another: the 'Indochinese Communist Party', with its leadership in Bac-Bo (Tongking) but with a following in other areas too; and the 'Annam Communist Party', with its leadership in Hong Kong but also with a following inside the country, especially the Centre and South. (A third group also emerged in Central Vietnam, but little is known about it in detail.) Ho Chi Minh was most closely associated with the 'Annam' group, whilst Truong Chinh is probably a survivor of the 'Indochina' group. After a period of rivalry, involving several appeals to the Comintern Executive Committee in Moscow, the three groups were obliged to merge at a 'reunification meeting' which took place in Hong Kong early in 1930. Ho Chi Minh (then Nguyen Ai Quoc) played a key role in that process; he was not, however, secretary-general of the new Party.

Confusion has arisen about the date of this meeting. Down to early 1960, the Party (except for a few years in the 1950s) commemorated the foundation anniversary on 6 January. It is possible that some kind of internal reorganisation of the Tongking-based ICP occurred on 6 January 1930. But at the Third Party

Congress (in September 1960), it was decreed that the 'correct' date of the Party's foundation was 3 February 1930, which appears to be the true date of the Hong Kong unification meeting. The only conclusion to be drawn is that the 'reunification' was not very successful, but that it became recognised as the occasion of the Party's foundation when Ho Chi Minh (Nguyen Ai Quoc) effectively became leader of the Party after 1945. There was also disagreement about the Party's name. The Hong Kong meeting established the 'Vietnam Communist Party'. But in October 1930, following the arrival in Vietnam of the Comintern-designated secretary-general of the new Party (Tran Phu) the name was again changed to 'Indochinese Communist Party'.

*1932–45*

The new Party suffered severe repression in 1930–1, with the result that many of its leaders (including Tran Phu) died or were sent for long terms of imprisonment – often on the island of Con-Son (Poulo Condore). In 1932–3 a new leadership of Moscow-trained intellectuals emerged in the South, including Tran Van Giau; whilst a new exile leadership based itself in Macau under a new secretary-general, Le Hong Phong (d. 1941). The latter organised a meeting in Macau in 1935, now recognised as the First Congress of the Party. Following an amnesty of many leading Communists in 1936 there was a period of legal and semi-legal activity, but the Party still retained its clandestine structure. A new period of suppression in 1939–41 again decimated the leadership, and the Party suffered especially severely in the South as a result of the abortive uprising of November 1940.

In 1941 Ho Chi Minh (alias Nguyen Ai Quoc) returned to the Vietnam–China border area and made contact with the new secretary-general of the Party inside Vietnam (Truong Chinh) with the result that the 8th Plenum of the first Central Committee was held at Pac-Bo in May 1941. It decided to set up a united front, and out of that decision emerged the Viet-Nam Doc-Lap Dong-Minh (Vietnamese Independence League), known as the 'Viet-Minh'. During the years 1941–5, four groups can be identified:

(a)  The group close to Ho Chi Minh (including Hoang Van Hoan, Pham Van Dong and Vo Nguyen Giap), who established a base area in the far north in Cao-Bang province. (Ho himself went to China and was imprisoned there, 1942–4.)

(b)  The group close to Truong Chinh, operating an underground network in the area north of Hanoi; it included Hoang Quoc Viet and several other natives of Bac-Bo.

(c)  The Moscow-trained group, inactive in this period if not actually in prison, which included Tran Van Giau and several others who had been trained in Moscow in the years 1929–33 and who were generally 'leftist'; they re-emerged in 1945 – mainly in the South, but following the August Revolution were excluded from the top leadership.

(d)  Several leaders in prison on Con-Son (including Le Duan, Pham Hung and Nguyen Duy Trinh), who were to play an important part in the Nam-Bo (Cochinchina) after their release in 1945; they were not especially close to Ho Chi Minh, but had known Pham Van Dong during the latter's (earlier) imprisonment on Con-Son.

In the August Revolution of 1945, the first and second groups took over leadership in the North; the fourth group eventually (certainly by 1950) emerged as the leading element in the South. But the ICP itself was formally dissolved in November 1945 and went underground, leaving the Viet-Minh as the principal overt organisation until 1951.

*From 1951*

The Party re-emerged in February–March 1951, as the Vietnam Workers' Party, again with Truong Chinh as secretary-general (until 1956). Its new name implied acceptance of the Stalinist theory that in the current stage of its revolution Vietnam did not need a full Communist Party, but only a Party of labour. (The same rule was applied in Korea and in Eastern Europe after 1945.) The new name also indicated an intention to found separate Parties in Laos and Cambodia. These eventually emerged (certainly by 1955), but remained secret organisations; and they took the name 'People's Party' which implied an even less advanced type of revolutionary vanguard than the 'Workers' Party'. In principle the Cambodian and Laotian Parties were expected to work closely with the Vietnamese; but by 1960 there was room for friction between them, which in the case of Cambodia, became serious later on.

The Vietnam Workers' Party retained that name until 1976, holding its Third Congress in September 1960 and its Fourth in

December 1976. (At the latter it became the Vietnamese Communist Party.) Meanwhile a new united front was founded in 1946, the Lien-Viet, which for five years existed alongside the Viet-Minh. Following the re-emergence of the Party (i.e. the VNWP) in 1951 the two were merged as the Lien-Viet Front, renamed the Fatherland Front in 1955. Separate Fronts developed in Laos and Cambodia.

Both the VNWP and the VNFF were originally intended to serve the whole of Vietnam, and no separate organisations were created for the South until 1960. At that point, following the adoption of a new strategy, the 'National Front to Liberate the Southern Region of Vietnam' was founded (Mat-Tran Dan-Toc Giai-Phong Mien-Nam Viet-Nam), but the Party remained unified – with a southern regional office which followed directives from the Centre in Hanoi. In 1962 a supposedly separate People's Revolutionary Party was created for the South, but its status has never been clearly defined. Ostensibly it was on a par with the People's Party in Laos and Cambodia; in practice it was almost certainly the southern branch of the VNWP in disguise. It ceased to have any separate identity at all long before 1975.

TABLE A.1    *The Communist Parties of Indochina and their Front Organisations, 1951–60*

| Vietnam | | Cambodia, Laos | |
| --- | --- | --- | --- |
| **1951** | Feb.: VNWP (Lao-dong Dang) inaugurated at the 'Second' Congress (as continuation of ICP). | | |
| | Mar.: Merger of 'Viet-Minh' and 'Lien Viet' Fronts, to form new Lien-Viet National United Front. | **1951** | 3 Mar.: Creation of Joint Committee to embrace national united fronts of Vietnam (Lien-Viet), cambodia (Khmer Issara) and Laos (Lao Issara). |
| | | | June: First Congress of Khmer People's Revolutionary Party (indicated in Hanoi press, 1981). |
| **1955** | Sept.: Lien-Viet became the VNFF: First Congress held in Hanoi. | **1955** | Mar.: Secret inauguration of Lao People's Party (Phak Pasason Lao). |
| | | **1956** | Jan.: Lao Issara reorganised as Lao Patriotic Front (Neo Lao Haksat). |
| **1956** | Sept.–Oct.: VNWP Central Committee: 10th Plenum. (Truong Chinh removed as Party secretary-general; other changes). | | |
| **1959** | Jan.: VNWP Central Committee: 15th Plenum. (Decision to step up struggle in South; not published until May that year.) | | |
| **1960** | Sept.: VNWP held its Third National Congress. New Central Committee and Politburo. | **1960** | Sept.: Khmer People's Party held its Second Congress: split between 'pro-Viet-Minh' and 'anti-Vietnamese' (Pol Pot) groups. (Later counted as date of foundation of Pol Pot's Kampuchean Communist Party.) |

TABLE A.2    *Leading figures of the Vietnam Workers' Party, 1956–60*

| Order of precedence, 1956–7 | Origins | Prison experience | Party work |
|---|---|---|---|
| 1. Ho Chi Minh ( = Nguyen Ai Quoc) | b. 1894 (?) Nghe-An | Hong Kong, 1931–2 Guangxi, 1942–4 | French CP, 1920 Comintern, 1925–43 ICP etc., 1930 |
| 2. Truong Chinh ( = Dang Xuan Khu) | b. 1909 Nam-Dinh | Son-La, 1931–6 | ICP, probably 1929 Politburo by 1940 Secretary-general, 1941–56 |
| 3. Le Duan | b. 1908 Quang-Tri | Con-Son, 1931–6 and 1941–5 | ICP by 1931 Central Committee by 1939 Acting Secretary, 1957–60 Secretary-general, 1960 |
| 4. Pham Van Dong | b. 1908 Quang-Nam | Con-Son, 1931–6 | ICP, 1930 Politburo by 1951 |
| 5. Vo Nguyen Giap | b. 1912 Quang-Binh | Central VN, around 1930–2 | ICP by 1933 Politburo by 1951 |
| 6. Nguyen Duy Trinh | b. 1910 Nghe-An | Kontum, then Con-Son, 1932–45 | ICP by 1932 Central Committee by 1951 Politburo by 1957 |
| 7. Hoang Van Hoan | b. 1905 Nghe-An | ? | Liaison work in China and Siam, 1930s, and early 1940s Central Committee, 1951 Politburo by 1957 |
| 8. Pham Hung | b. 1912 Vinh-Long | Con-Son, 1931–45 | ICP, 1930 Central Committee by 1951 Politburo, 1957 Secretariat, 1960–82 |

| Government posts | National Assembly (Standing Committee) | Army positions |
|---|---|---|
| President, 1945–69<br>Prime Minister, 1945–55 | — | — |
| Deputy Premier, 1958–60 | Chairman, 1960–81 | — |
| — | — | Police Commissar in South, around 1950 |
| Finance Minister, 1945–6<br>Deputy Premier, 1949–55<br>Prime Minister, 1955→<br>Foreign Minister, 1954–61 | — | — |
| Interior Minister, 1945–6<br>Defence Minister, 1946–80<br>Deputy premier, 1955 → | — | Commander-in-chief of PAVN, 1947–80 |
| Premier's office, 1954–8<br>Chairman, State Planning Commission, 1958–65<br>Deputy premier, 1960→ | — | — |
| Ambassador to China 1950–7 | Deputy chairman, 1958–76 | — |
| Premier's office, 1955–60<br>Deputy Premier, 1958→<br>Chairman, Agricultural Board, 1960–3 | — | — |

TABLE A.2   (*Contd.*)

| Order of precedence, 1956–7 | Origins | Prison experience | Party work |
|---|---|---|---|
| 9. Le Duc Tho | *b.* 1910 Nam-Ha | Con-Son, 1930s | ICP, 1929? Central Committee, 1944 Politburo by 1955 Secretariat by 1960 |
| 10. Le Thanh Nghi | *b.* 1911 (North?) | ? | ICP by 1930 Politburo by 1958 Specialist in labour activities |
| 11. Nguyen Chi Thanh | *b.* 1915 ? Thua-Thien | ? | ICP by 1945; early career uncertain Politburo by 1960 Leader of Youth movement, 1950s |
| 12. Hoang Quoc Viet (demoted, 1956) | *b.* 1905 Bac-Ninh | Con-Son, 1930–6 | ICP, 1929 Central Committee by 1941 Politburo, 1951–6 (Secretary-general of Viet-Minh 1951; leader of trade union federation, 1951–76) |
| 13. Le Van Luong (demoted 1956) | *b. ca* 1912 (North ?) | Saigon, 1930–4 Con-Son, 1934–45 | ICP, 1929 (labour organiser, 1929–30) Politburo and Secretariat by 1956 Secretariat, 1960–82 |

| Government posts | National Assembly (Standing Committee) | Army positions |
|---|---|---|
| — | — | — |
| Industry Minister, 1955–60<br>Deputy Premier, 1960–82 | — | — |
| — | — | Head of Political Department of PAVN, 1950–61; commander or commissar in South, 1964–7 |
| — | Chief Procurator (under Standing Committee) 1960–76 | — |
| Deputy Minister of Interior, ?–1956<br>Premier's office, 1955–6 | — | — |

# Notes

NOTES TO CHAPTER I: INTRODUCTION

1. This applies especially to the Gravel Edition of the *Pentagon Papers* (1971) and to the analysis by Gelb and Betts (1979). It is also true of the selection of documents by Porter (1979), where, out of a total of 765 documents for the period 1941–75, only ten belong to the two-and-a-half years between mid-1956 and the end of 1959. Nor has much effort been made to secure declassification of American official documents from the later Eisenhower years.

2. One important exception, for the period down to 1959, is Thayer (1977). Nothing comparable appeared while the war was still going on. The official 'White Paper' published by the State Department in 1965 to demonstrate 'aggression from the North' was remarkably superficial, considering the extreme American measures it was intended to justify. Nor did Pike's study of the 'Viet-Cong' (1966) reveal very much of what American intelligence analysts must by then have known about the activities of the Party (as opposed to the Front) in South Vietnam. A more serious attempt to provide documentary evidence of Hanoi's involvement in the South, going back, to the late 1950s, was produced in a State Department 'Working Paper' of 1968; but although the main text was later reprinted by R. A. Falk (1969) in *The Vietnam War and International Law*, vol. II, pp. 1183–1205, the documentary appendix is still extremely rare. The *Pentagon Papers* analysis of the origins of the insurgency is also somewhat thin, depending to a considerable extent on published secondary works.

3. I have used the BBC version in the present work: *Summary of World Broadcasts*, Part V, *Far East* (*SWB/FE*). It can be consulted in the British Library, London. Much of the material included there, however, derives from monitoring by the FBIS.

4. The most important example so far is probably D. Yergin, *Shattered Peace: The Origins of the Cold War and the National State* (New York, 1977; repr. in paperback, Harmondsworth, Middx. 1980). Like the majority of accounts of American policy in Vietnam, it concentrates on a detailed analysis of United States debates and decisions and pays virtually no attention to Communist strategy in the years 1945–8.

5. The conflict between Stalin and Zhdanov is hinted at by Conquest (1961), but not fully explored in ideological terms. For the thesis that Stalin's purges were related to his determination to prevent a deepening commitment to Spain, see Slusser (1973); and for an account of the Communist side in the Greek war, extremely critical of the official Party line dictated by Stalin, see D. Eudes, *The Kapitanios: Partisans and Civil War in Greece, 1943–49* (New York, 1972).

NOTES TO CHAPTER 2: THE GENEVA PARTITION

1. The details of the regroupment are covered by the interim reports of the International Commission in Vietnam, notably the *Fourth Interim Report* (London: HMSO, December 1955) Cmd 9654, covering the period 11 April–10 August 1955. For an estimate of 10,000 Viet-Minh personnel left behind, see US National Intelligence Estimate 63. 1–3–55 of 11 October 1955 (declassified 4 November 1975), partly reprinted in Porter (1979) vol. II, pp. 13–14.
2. Young (1968) pp. 44 ff.
3. *People's China*, September 1954, Supplement.
4. VNA, 4 October 1979: *SWB/FE/6238/A3/1* and 8–10.
5. See Chapter 5.
6. The text of the 4 June 1954 Treaty appears in Cameron (1971) pp. 268–9; it was accompanied by a second treaty of association with the French Union, which could be separately abrogated by the State of Vietnam (and was) without affecting the grant of independence.
7. The analogy is explicitly made in a telegram from Dulles to Saigon, 6 April 1955, and in a National Security Council Study of 17 May 1955, both printed in Porter (1979) vol. I, pp. 603–4, 697–702.
8. *Documents Relating to British Involvement in the Indochina Conflict 1945–1965* (London: HMSO, December 1965) Cmnd 2834, pp. 101–5.
9. This interpretation is developed by Ra'anan (1969) ch. iv, with special reference to the decision to supply arms to Egypt in 1955; the same author demonstrates the growing importance of Indonesia in Soviet thinking after about April 1956.
10. See Young (1968) chs iii–iv. The talks were secret; his account merely pieces together published information and suggests an interpretation.
11. The contrast between the joint communiqués at the end of the two visits (Peking, 7 July 1955; Moscow, 18 July 1955) was noticed by Porter (1979) vol. I, pp. 705–9, where the relevant passages are reprinted.
12. *Documents Relating to British Involvement in the Indochina Conflict*, Cmnd 2834, pp. 124–5.
13. Messages from the Co-chairmen dated 8 May 1956, ibid., pp. 96–9.

NOTES TO CHAPTER 3: THE UNITED STATES AND NGO DINH DIEM

1. A telegram of 9 April 1955 from Dulles to Lawton Collins, US special envoy in Saigon, leaves no doubt that Dulles was determined to end the situation where the Americans were paying the bill and the French calling the tune: *USVNR*, Bk 10, pp. 907–9, reprinted in Porter (1979) vol. I, pp. 696–7. For the 'tripartite meeting' of 8–11 May 1955, see *PP* (Gravel), vol. I, pp. 235–9.
2. *PP* (Gravel), vol. I, pp. 224–5.
3. McCoy (1972) pp. 93–4, 115ff. Also the principal source for information on the Binh-Xuyen, below; based on memoranda by Savani and interviews with former members of the Binh-Xuyen group.
4. For accounts of the religious background and political role of the Cao-Dai sects, see R. B. Smith, 'An Introduction to Caodaism', *Bulletin of School of Oriental and African Studies*, vol. XXXIII (1970); and also Werner (1976).

5. A detailed history of the Hoa-Hao sect and its antecedents has been made by Hue-Tam Ho Tai, 'The Evolution of Vietnamese Millenarianism 1849–1947', unpublished PhD thesis, Harvard University, 1977 (to be published by Harvard University Press). For a brief introduction to the various sects, see B. B. Fall, 'The Political–Religious Sects of Vietnam', *Pacific Affairs*, September 1955.

6. For the background to these events, see R. B. Smith, 'The Japanese Period in Indochina and the Coup of 9 March 1945', *Journal of Southeast Asian Studies*, vol. IX (1978).

7. For the background to the Can-Lao Party, officially founded in September 1954, see Donnell (1964); also his contribution to Fishel (1961).

8. Lansdale's report, *PP* (Gravel), vol. I, pp. 577–8. For the American role in the rise of Nasser, which the CIA obviously did *not* regard as a model for Vietnam, see M. Copeland, *The Game of Nations* (London, 1969).

9. They were Tran Van Soai, Nguyen Van Hinh and Nguyen Van Vy; see Lancaster (1961) p. 396. The date of Diem's formal appointment is given correctly by Lancaster (1961) p. 328, and by Fall (1967) p. 244. The date of 7 July, given in *PP* (Gravel), vol. I, p. 204 (and later celebrated as the 'double seventh' anniversary of his accession to power), was that on which he announced his first cabinet. Lancaster is used as the principal source for the paragraphs which follow.

10. The *coup* plan is indicated by Jean Leroy in his memoir *Fils de la Rizière* (Paris, 1977) pp. 267ff; and by Lansdale (1972).

11. For an account of the efforts of Spellman and the International Rescue Committee (including Joseph Buttinger) to mobilise support for Diem in America during 1954–5, see R. Scheer, *How the United States Got Involved in Vietnam* (Santa Barbara, 1965), of which the relevant section is reprinted by Gettleman (1966) pp. 246ff.

12. Lansdale's version of these events, which makes no mention of Savani, is given in his memoir (Lansdale, 1972). The interpretation of a 'proxy war' is developed by McCoy (1972) on the basis of information gleaned from Savani's papers.

13. The story of Michigan State University involvement is summarised in Montgomery (1962) pp. 64ff.; the same work covers numerous other aspects of the aid question.

NOTES TO CHAPTER 4: HANOI AND REUNIFICATION

1. This point is made by Hue-Tam Ho Tai in 'The Evolution of Vietnamese Millenarianism 1849–1947', unpublished PhD thesis, Harvard University, 1977. There is still no adequate study of the Nam-Ky rising of 1940, but see *Thirty Years of Struggle of the Party* (Hanoi, 1960) pp. 68–9; the same source (p. 67) notes that Le Duan and several others were arrested by the French shortly before the rising occurred.

2. Taipei Radio, 5–6 January 1952: *SWB/FE/*143, p. 36.

3. VNA, 18–20 December 1951: *SWB/FE/*140–1; also 'Voice of the Nam-Bo' (radio station), 4 January 1952: *SWB/FE/*143, p. 81. For the subsequent death of Nguyen Binh, see VNA, 12 and 13 January 1952: *SWB/FE/*144, p. 85.

4. Cf. A. Short, *The Communist Insurrection in Malaya* (London, 1975) pp. 318–21.

5. For biographical notes, see Appendix Table A. 2.
6. VNA, 4 October 1979: *SWB/FE/6238/A3/*1 and 8–10; cf. Chapter 1 above.
7. *Beijing Review*, 7 December 1979, pp. 11ff.
8. Ho Chi Minh, *Selected Works*, reprinted in Porter (1979) vol. 1, pp. 632–7.
9. The importance of this period was first demonstrated by Thayer (1977) Ch. iv, to which the following paragraphs are very much indebted.
10. Thayer (1977) pp. 181–2, based on an interrogation of two Communist prisoners, 1956, and a South Vietnamese intelligence report of November 1955 referred to also in Falk (1969) p. 1188: 'Working Paper', items 17 and 205; the second source indicated the reinfiltration of 50 or more cadres from the north in October 1955. Thayer (1977) also notes the proclamation by Ba Cut of his own 'national liberation front' on 10 October 1955.
11. Falk (1969) p. 1188; and Thayer (1977) pp. 189–90, citing 'Working Paper', items 16, 21 and 22.
12. Thayer (1977) pp. 200ff., relying on 'Working Paper', items 30, 31 and 204.
13. *SWB/FE/*550, pp. 53–8. For the VNWP Central Committee 9th Plenum, see *SWB/FE/*557, pp. 57–9. Note also the Soviet–DRVN protocol on commodity deliveries, signed in Moscow on 5 May 1956: *SWB/FE/*Economic Suppl./216, p. 41.
14. Thayer (1977) pp. 202–3, relying on 'Working Paper', item 31.
15. For an account of Diem's land policies, see Fishel (1961), which includes a chapter by Ladejinsky; also Scigliano (1964) pp. 120ff. On the regulation of village councils, see Scigliano (1964) p. 32.
16. The document was captured in Long-An province in 1957, and was later located there by J. Race; its text appears as no. 1002 in the Race Collection, deposited with the Center for Research Libraries in Chicago; Race (1972) pp. 75–81, provides a summary; extracts are translated in Porter (1979) vol. 11, pp. 24–30.

NOTES TO CHAPTER 5: LAOS AND CAMBODIA: THE SEARCH FOR NEUTRALITY

1. *Bangkok Post*, 1 July and 3 August 1975.
2. Fifield (1958) pp. 385–7; Norodom Sihanouk and Burchett (1973) pp. 76–82.
3. Details of the various meetings in 1955–6 are given in *Second* and *Third Interim Report of the International Commission for Supervision and Control in Laos*, respectively Cmd 9630 and Cmnd 314 (London: HMSO, 1955, 1957). For details of Laotian political changes, see Toye (1968) ch. v.
4. Lee (1970) pp. 30ff. On the return of Phetsarath to Vientiane, see 'Phetsarath' (1978) pp. 93ff.
5. In hearings before the US House of Representatives Committee on Governments in 1959, as cited in Toye (1968) p. 112.
6. NSC Policy Statement, 5612/1, 5 September 1956; printed in *USVNR*, Bk 10, V.B. 3, p. 1091.
7. For his own account of American attempts to influence him after 1955, see Norodom Sihanouk and Burchett (1973) chs v–vii.
8. For the changes in the Party's name, see *Thirty Years of Struggle of the Party* (Hanoi, 1960).

9. *SWB/FE/*151, pp. 68–9; the foundation of the Lao Issara Front (as a Communist organisation) was noted in a broadcast of 1953, which also said that delegates from the three fronts in March 1951 had set up the liaison committee: *SWB/FE/*251, p. 46. For references to the Cambodian united front in July 1951 and March 1952, see *SWB/FE/*128, p. 70 and *SWB/FE/*153, p. 80.
10. See the account in *Nhan-Dan*, 26 May 1981.
11. Zasloff (1973) pp. 13–15; cf. also Langer and Zasloff (1970). The documents referred to are: the notebook of a Vietnamese cadre serving in Laos in 1968, and a training document of the Lao People's Party dated July 1960. For Pol Pot's version of the history of the Kampuchean Communist Party, put out by Radio Phnom Penh in September 1977, see *SWB/FE/*5629/C2/1–9.
12. RIIA, *Documents on International Affairs 1955* (London, 1958) p. 426; the relevant passage is quoted at the head of this chapter.

NOTES TO CHAPTER 6: VIETNAM AND THE COMMUNIST WORLD CRISIS

1. Micunovic (1980) pp. 26–32.
2. See Ho Chi Minh, *Selected Works*, vol. IV (Hanoi, 1962) pp. 153–6; the 9th Plenum communiqué was published by VNA on 27 April 1956: *SWB/FE/*557, p. 57. Truong Chinh made an important report at the same meeting, dealing with the progress of land reform: cf. Thayer (1977) pp. 220–6. For Poland at this period see Fejtö (1974) p. 81; and for China, Rice (1974) p. 143.
3. *SWB/FE/*585, p. 34, and 587, p. 36; and Econ. Suppl. no. 228, p. 38.
4. The most useful summary of the '*Nhan-Van* Affair' is in Thayer (1977) pp. 322–9; see also Nhu Phong (1962) pp. 58–60.
5. Ho Chi Minh's birthday has been celebrated on 19 May every year since 1946, when his year of birth was given as 1890. But a document in the French archives, based on information available to the Sûreté in 1922, gives the date of birth of Nguyen Ai Quoc as January 1894. For other biographical data, together with notes on the history of the Party, see Appendix.
6. None of the accounts of this controversial aspect of the Vietnamese revolution is completely satisfactory; the subject has been distorted by the question of how many people were killed, following allegations by South Vietnamese psychological warfare specialists designed to blacken the Communist regime rather than to elucidate the actual sequence of events. The issue is too complex to be resolved in the present study, but the paragraphs which follow are based on reading contemporary monitored radio reports, rather than on any of the secondary works. Among the latter the most useful is that of Moise (1976); see also Gittinger (1959) and Porter (1972).
7. NCNA and Peking Radio, 25 November; VNA, 24–5 November 1955: *SWB/FE/*514, p. 39; for the departure of the French representatives at Haiphong, VNA, 2 December 1955: *SWB/FE/*516, p. 41.
8. Summarised by Turley (1972) pp. 100ff. Porter (1972) has challenged interpretations of Giap's speech which claim that he admitted the execution of large numbers of people; but that issue is irrelevant to the main burden of the speech.

9. That, moreover, was the day Mikoyan arrived in Hanoi. See Turley (1972) p. 132; Tran Do's article appeared in *Nhan Dan*, 26 October 1955, *ibid.*, pp. 134ff. Turley does not emphasise sufficiently the threat to the army in 1956, but he covers in some detail the modernisation of 1957.

10. Scalapino and Lee (1972) vol. I, pp. 510–15.

11. *SWB/FE*/supplements on CCP Congress, nos 1–3; cf. Rice (1974) p. 141. In the Cultural Revolution period Liu, Deng and Peng Dehuai were severely criticised for the line they advocated on this occasion and for seeking to push Mao to one side.

12. The October meetings were reported by Hanoi Radio, 3i October and 9 November 1956: *SWB/FE*/610, p. 43 and *SWB/FE*/614, p. 32. For the 10th Plenum communiqué, *SWB/FE*/610, pp. 39ff.

13. For the official report of his death by Hanoi Radio (22 October 1956) see *SWB/FE*/608, p. 42; for reports put out by Saigon Radio (14 November) see *SWB/FE*/614, pp. 33–4. The story about Nguyen Son's dying of cancer is given by Hoang Van Chi, *From Colonialism to Communism* (London, 1964) p. 126, who says that he returned to Hanoi in August and died 'two days after his arrival'. It is curious that Chi, so eager to make capital out of the subsequent Quynh-Luu uprising and the *Nhan-Van* affair, should not only fail to pick up the possibility of a major political conflict involving Nguyen Son but even reports the date of his death inaccurately.

14. The most useful summary of the details is once again that in Thayer (1977) pp. 315–8, based mainly on *Nhan-Dan*, 18 November, and Hanoi Radio broadcasts of 20–1 November 1956; see *SWB/FE*/616, pp. 23–7.

15. *SWB/FE*/615, 617; Thayer (1977) pp. 338–51.

16. These developments are covered by Thayer (1977) pp. 351–61; the communiqué of the 11th Plenum, published on 12 January 1957, refers to 'winning over the South' rather than to revolution as such.

17. See Thayer (1977) pp. 460–5, 488–5, 488–9, etc.

NOTES TO CHAPTER 7: ASIA AT THE CROSSROADS

1. NSC 5612/I, 5 September 1956, of which the text is given in *USVNR*, Bk 10, V.B. 3, pp. 1082–5. An even sharper definition of the 'threat' will be found in US Department of State, *The Sino-Soviet Economic Offensive in the Less Developed Countries* (Washington, D.C., 1958; reprinted New York: Greenwood Press, 1969).

2. See especially Yanaga Chitoshi, *Big Business in Japanese Politics* (Yale, 1968) ch. viii.

3. These events cannot be covered in detail; for brief reference to them, see Fleming (1961) pp. 888–93; and R. Stephens, *Nasser* (London, 1971) pp. 271–4.

4. See Ra'anan (1969) for an account of the Indonesia arms purchase.

5. Freedman (1977) p. 69.

6. RIIA, *Documents, 1957*, pp. 112–13; cf. also Yahuda (1978) p. 66.

7. See Young (1968) pp. 123ff.

8. Borisov and Koloskov (1975) pp. 121–7.

9. For the start of the attack on Ding Ling, see *SWB/FE*/8 August 1957, pp. 15–16; for the decree on socialist education, MacFarquhar (1974).

10. See Ambekar (1964) p. 274.
11. See the *Fourth Interim Report of the International Commission . . . in Laos*, Cmnd 541 (London, HMSO, 1958); also Fall (1969) pp. 76–7.
12. *Fourth Interim Report* (Laos), pp. 11–13 and 57ff.
13. See M. Nishihara, *The Japanese and Sukarno's Indonesia* (Tokyo, 1976); also Ra'anan (1969).
14. The fullest account of the diplomacy of the crisis is in H. P. Jones, *Indonesia: The Possible Dream* (Stanford, 1971). A brief glimpse of the CIA operation is given by L. F. Prouty (1973) pp. 323–7, presumably based on inside information. It is also mentioned by V. Marchetti and J. D. Marks, *The CIA and the Cult of Intelligence* (New York, 1975) pp. 51–2; but references to it were among the passages challenged in court by a CIA lawyer before the book was allowed to appear.
15. For the text of the agreement, together with background on the Sino-Japanese trade relations in the 1950s, see R. K. Jain (1977) pp. 207–14. Its economic implications, had it been implemented, are discussed in *Far Eastern Economic Review* (*FEER*), 13 March 1958, p. 336. See also *FEER*, 18 September 1958, pp. 360–1; and *Peking Review*, 22 April and 13 May 1958.
16. *Fourth Interim Report* (Laos), pp. 15ff.
17. The text of the Chinese-Cambodian statement of 24 August 1958 appears in Ambekar (1964) pp. 32–5. Cf. also R. M. Smith (1965) pp. 142–3; Norodom Sihanouk and Burchett (1973) p. 103.
18. Thayer (1977) pp. 450 and 564ff.
19. *SWB/FE/*752, p. 31. An earlier agreement had been signed in May 1956.

NOTES TO CHAPTER 8: THE EMERGENCE OF LE DUAN

1. See, for example, Honey (1963); but his failure to press the evidence as far as it would go led Thayer (1977) to dismiss the idea that any crisis occurred at all. Neither author attempts to relate events in North Vietnam to the wider Communist picture.
2. Micunovic (1980) pp. 197–9.
3. The most useful account of these events is still that of Conquest (1961) pp. 292ff. Additional insight is provided by the account of the Yugoslav ambassador in Moscow at that period: Micunovic (1980) pp. 160–312; see also Khrushchev (1974).
4. For a detailed account of this movement, see MacFarquhar (1974); Mao's principal speeches of 1957 eventually appeared in his *Selected Works*, vol. v (1977).
5. The administrative debate is analysed by Schurmann (1968); see especially pp. 195ff. It is necessary to read MacFarquhar and Schurmann together to gain a full picture of what was happening at this time.
6. This was revealed in the polemics of summer 1963; see *Peking Review*, September 1963; also Halperin (1967). For Khruschev's tour of Asia, see *SWB/ FE/*697ff.
7. The text of the Moscow Declaration is reprinted in Hudson *et al.* (1961) pp. 46–56.
8. Covered by Thayer (1977) pp. 567–71.
9. Covered in some detail by both Turley (1972) and Thayer (1977).

10. *SWB/FE/*703, pp. 36–7. There is no basis for supposing his death was other than natural, but his disappearance from the scene may have had important consequences; for his appointment in May, see Turley (1972) p. 141. For the *Nhan-Dan* article of 5 November 1957, mentioned later, see *SWB/FE/*715, p. 45.

11. For Aristov's visit, see *SWB/FE/*710–12; for that of Yugov, *SWB/FE/* 706–07.

12. Peking Radio, 18–19 February 1981: *SWB/FE/*6656/A3/1.

13. Le Duan, *On the Socialist Revolution in Vietnam*, vol. 1 (Hanoi, 1965) p. 84. Much of the speech was a theoretical analysis of proletarian leadership, which included the passage quoted at the head of this chapter. For Giap's speeches, see Thayer (1977) pp. 549–55 and *SWB/FE/*703, pp. 36–7.

14. Race (1972) pp. 86–7, citing a reference in Race Document no. 1009, dated 30 November 1957; cf. also Werner (1976) p. 486, citing an American military document referring to it in July 1957.

15. Thayer (1977) pp. 494–5; for the 'extermination of traitors', *ibid.*, pp. 507ff.

16. *SWB/FE/*721, pp. 46–7; extracts are translated in Porter (1979) vol. II, pp. 33–4.

17. *SWB/FE/*716, p. 41.

18. *SWB/FE/*722, p. 35.

19. *SWB/FE/*733, p. 40; *SWB/FE/*737, pp. 34–5. It was also noticeable that Hoang Van Hoan had by that time lost status within the Politburo, whilst Pham Hung had risen in rank.

20. *SWB/FE/*766, p. 29; 767, p. 29; and 773, pp. 39–40.

21. *SWB/FE/*759; 760; 761; 764.

22. *SWB/FE/*749, pp. 41–3; *SWB/FE/*752, pp. 33–5; cf. Thayer (1977) pp. 658–62. Other important developments at that time were a meeting of the Fatherland Front Committee, and a conference of North Vietnamese Buddhists.

NOTES TO CHAPTER 9: THE CHANGING PATTERN OF WORLD TENSION

1. *Peking Review*, 5 August 1958; cf. Deutscher (1970) pp. 157–62.

2. The proposal is noted by Khrushchev (1974) pp. 306ff. (Penguin edn).

3. Young (1968) covers the crisis from the diplomatic point of view (see Chs vi–viii); see also the analysis in Kalicki (1975).

4. C. Mullin, 'Tibetan Conspiracy', *FEER*, 5 September 1975. For Sino-Indian relations, see N. Maxwell, *India's China War* (Harmondsworth, Middx., 1972) pp. 84, 91ff.

5. *Peking Review*, 25 November 1958. For Fujiyama's talks in Washington, see *American Foreign Policy Current Documents: 1958*, pp. 1214–6.

6. *Peking Review*, 16 December 1958: *SWB/FE/*838–9.

7. Thomas (1971) provides the best general account of events in Cuba at this period; whilst the author himself is at pains to minimise the role of the Communists, he offers evidence which could easily be interpreted in the opposite direction, especially on pp. 1002–3, 1006–7 and 1010–11. The Party's deliberate adoption of a low profile proves nothing.

8. See Horne (1977) pp. 371, 404ff.; and on South Yemen, see F. Halliday, *Arabia without Sultans* (Harmondsworth, Middx., 1974) p. 183.

9. *Peking Review*, 27 January 1959.

10. Conquest (1961) pp. 364–70.

11. This conclusion was based on an analysis of different Soviet views of the Arab world in the late 1960s: see I. Kass, *Soviet Involvement in the Middle East 1966–73* (Boulder, Col., 1978).

12. Schram (1974) Text 6; for discussion of Chen Yun's views at this period, see Moody (1973) p. 136. The 6th Plenum was reported in *Peking Review*, 23 December 1958, but in terms which avoided any open criticism of the 'great leap' or of Mao.

13. See articles given full prominence in *Peking Review*, 17 and 31 March 1959.

14. These visits, together with Ho's trip to Indonesia, were reported in regular VNA transmissions: *SWB/FE/852–60*. For Soviet–Vietnamese co-operation and aid agreements, see *SWB/FE/852*, p. 37. Equally important economic and technical aid agreements were signed with China on 18 February: *Peking Review*, 24 February 1959, p. 26.

15. Young (1968) pp. 221–3; for Zhou's report to the NPC, see *Peking Review*, 21 April 1959.

NOTES TO CHAPTER 10: THE RETURN TO ARMED STRUGGLE

1. NCNA, 6 March 1959: *SWB/FE/851/China*, p. 8.

2. Norodom Sihanouk and Burchett (1973) ch. vii. On events in Laos in early 1959, see Toye (1968) pp. 124–5.

3. *USVNR*, Bk 10, V.B. 3, pp. 1156–82. For events in Quang-Ngai and other upland areas, see Ta Xuan Linh (1975), Vu Can (1968) and Thayer (1977) p. 538.

4. Thayer (1977) p. 506.

5. VNA, 18 January 1959: *SWB/FE/838*, pp. 35–6. The formation of a 'People's Organization to Investigate the Phu-Loi Mass Murder' was announced in Hanoi on 25 February 1959: *SWB/FE/849*, p. 41.

6. Thayer (1977) pp. 664–7. For the article of Giap and Thanh, see Turley (1972) pp. 150–5.

7. *SWB/FE/27/A3/1–3*. Several American sources, including the *Pentagon Papers*, erroneously place the 15th Plenum itself in May 1959, despite the fact that the 16th Plenum was held in April that year. For the correct dates of both, see Truong Chinh, *March Ahead under the Party's Banner* (Hanoi, 1963) pp. 30, 110.

8. US State Department, *The Situation in Laos* (Washington, September 1959) p. 16; and Dommen (1971) pp. 338–9, 348–51.

9. *Peking Review*, 17 March 1959; cf. Chapter 9 above.

10. The most detailed accounts of this crisis are those contained in statements by the Laotian and Chinese governments on 17–18 May 1959: *SWB/FE/29/A3/6–7*, and *Peking Review*, 26 May 1959, p. 13.

11. Zasloff (1973) p. 15; see also, for biographies of Kaysone and other Pathet Lao leaders, ibid., pp. 109–14. The Neo Lao Hak Sat congress, held in September 1959, was reported by VNA on 28 October: *SWB/FE/168/A3/6–7*.

12. US State Department, *Working Paper on the North Vietnamese Role in the War in South Vietnam* (May 1968), reprinted in *Vietnam Documents*, nos 37–8. For the report of actual infiltration from July 1959, see Warner (1964) pp. 154–5.

13. C. Yanaga, *Big Business in Japanese Politics* (Yale, 1968) p. 227.

14. Dommen (1971) pp. 119–24. For a US intelligence report on the situation in Laos, 18 September 1959, see *USVNR*, Bk 10, V.B. 3, pp. 1242–7; also printed in Porter (1979) vol. II, pp. 46–51.

15. Ho's tour is indicated by reports in *SWB/FE/69*, W16, 104, 109, 111, 115.

16. For Mao's speech on that date, see Schram (1974) Text 6; other documents relating to the fall of Peng are included in Union Research Institute, *The Case of Peng Teh-huai* (Hong Kong, 1968). For the Soviet refusal to supply an atomic bomb, see the Chinese statement of 15 August 1963, *Peking Review*, 16 August 1963.

17. See commentary in Deutscher (1970) pp. 186ff., originally published on 15 December 1959; also Zagoria (1962) p. 259.

18. For details of the American response, see below, Chapter 11.

19. Borisov and Koloskov (1975) pp. 156ff. Writing in 1971, they defend the Soviet refusal to support China against India.

20. *SWB/FE/121/C/1*; besides Nguyen Chi Thanh the promotions also involved Van Tien Dung and Chu Van Tan.

21. Jain (1977) pp. 40 and 225–9; the Japanese visitors were obliged to endorse statements opposing the existing policy of Tokyo towards Peking. For the Senate studies in 1959, see S. D. Backrack, *The Committee of One Million* (New York, 1976) pp. 154–6.

22. *Peking Review*, 6 October 1959; the same issue contained a national day article by Lin Biao on Mao's military thinking – possibly a direct challenge to the Soviet leaders.

23. Quoted in a report from the US Embassy in Saigon (Country Team), 7 March 1960, which also mentions the attack of 26 September 1959: *USVNR*, Bk 10, V.B. 3, pp. 1254–75. Cf. also Warner (1964) pp. 159–60.

24. Young (1968) p. 222.

25. *DDQC*, 1977, p. 108, item B.

26. Originally written for the 15th anniversary of the PAVN on 22 December 1959, it was first published in English, as one of a series of articles under the same title, in 1961.

27. Truong Chinh, *March Ahead under the Party's Banner* (Hanoi, 1963). The Third Party Congress ruled that the actual date of the meeting to found the Party had taken place on 3 February 1930.

28. The document in question was captured during Operation 'Crimp' in January 1966, and is quoted in State Department *Working Paper* of 1968. (cf. note 12 above.) For events in Long-An province at this period, see Race (1972) pp. 102, 113.

29. Nguyen Thi Dinh, *No Other Road to Take* (translated as S. E. Asia Program Data Paper, no. 102, Ithaca, N.Y., 1976) pp. 64–5; for the Tay-Ninh guerrilla attack, see Warner (1964) p. 160.

30. See especially the comments in the International Commission's *Tenth Interim Report* (Vietnam), 6 April 1960, and *Eleventh Interim Report*, 18 September 1961 (London: HMSO, 1960 and 1961) Cmnd 1040 and 1551.

NOTES TO CHAPTER 11: THE AMERICAN RESPONSE : FROM AID TO
COUNTERINSURGENCY

1. President's Committee to Study the United States Military Assistance
   Program, *Composite Report*, 2 vols (Washington, D.C., 1959). Established on
   24 November 1958, the Committee made interim reports on 17 March,
   3 June and 20 July, before completing its work on 17 August 1959; the final
   publication also included a series of specialist annexes, some prepared by the
   Committee's own staff and others by outside 'think-tanks'.
2. Six articles by A. M. Colgrove appeared in newspapers of the Scripps–
   Howard chain, starting on 22 July 1959. Hearings began in the House
   Subcommittee on the Far East and the Pacific, from 27 July; and before the
   Senate Subcommittee on State Department Organization on 30 July. A
   detailed account is given by Montgomery (1962) pp. 224–35 and 304–13.
3. NCNA, 15 April 1959: *SWB/FE/3/A3/1*; cf. also *SEATO: Record of Progress
   1958–59* (Bangkok, 1959).
4. See Annexes D and E of the Draper Report, contributed respectively by
   Brigadier-General D. G. Shingler and Colonel R. G. Stilwell. A conference of
   political scientists, organised by RAND in August 1959, also discussed the
   theme; its proceedings were later published as J. J. Johnson (ed.), *The Role
   of the Military in Underdeveloped Countries* (Princeton, N.J. 1962).
5. Jordan (1962) *passim*.
6. *PP* (Gravel), vol. 1, pp. 573–83; vol. 11, pp. 643–9. Cf. Prouty (1973) Chs xvi,
   xix.
7. US State Department, *The Situation in Laos* (Washington, D.C., September
   1959) pp. 22–3; cf. also Prouty (1973) pp. 171–3.
8. NCNA, 25 August 1959, citing sources in Tokyo: *SWB/FE/114/C/4*; cf. also
   P. D. Scott (1972) pp. 11ff.
9. Toye (1968) pp. 132ff.
10. Jordan (1962) p. 10; the figures are for the financial year 1959, ending on
    30 June that year.
11. These moves are briefly indicated in *Vietnam Studies: US Army Special Forces,
    1961–1971* (Washington: Department of the Army, 1973) pp. 4–5; and a paper
    by Lansdale printed in *PP* (Gravel), vol 11, pp. 643–9.
12. This study is mentioned, but not reprinted, in *USVNR*, Bk 2, IV.A.5, pp. 60
    and 83; for the text of the Saigon report of 7 March 1960, see *USVNR*, Bk 10,
    pp. 1254–75.
13. Press release of 5 May 1960, in *USVNR*, Bk 2, IV.A.5, p. 82; and *Eleventh
    Interim Report of the ICSC in Vietnam*, Cmnd 1551.
14. Thomas (1971) pp. 1265–80.
15. Prouty (1973) pp. 400ff. The Draper Reports did not mention the role of CIA;
    but for their emphasis on co-operation between the State and Defence
    Departments, see the report submitted on 3 June 1959, pp. 49–52.
16. For cables exchanged between Durbrow and the State Department together
    with memoranda by Lansdale, in the period September 1960 to January 1961,
    see *USVNR*, Bk 10, V.B.3, pp. 1302–31, and Bk 2, IV.A.5, pp. 66–77; hardly
    any of these documents appear in *PP* (Gravel).
17. *PP* (Gravel), vol. 1, pp. 316–21; and Scigliano (1964) p. 84. The group
    included several ministers and officials of governments before 1954, and two

men who became prime minister in the post-Diem period: Phan Huy Quat and Tran Van Huong.

18. JCS memorandum 232–60, approved 6 June 1960; forwarded by Defence Department Office of International Security Affairs to the Assistant Secretary of State, Far East, on 16 September: mentioned, but not reprinted, in *USVNR*, Bk 2, IV.A.5, p. 61.

## NOTES TO CHAPTER 12: TOWARDS A NEW COLD WAR?

1. This question is discussed in O. Penkovsky, *The Penkovsky Papers* (New York and London, 1965) ch. v; both in the text attributed to Penkovsky and in the commentary. Even if, as has been alleged, the work is an American fake, it was presumably based on carefully analysed intelligence materials not otherwise available. For Khrushchev's speech of 14 January 1960, see RIIA, *Survey of International Affairs 1959–60*, p. 57.

2. NCNA, 5 February 1960: *SWB/FE/253/A3/1–4*.

3. It was noticeable, however, that the tour was covered fully, and Khrushchev himself frequently praised, by *Nhan-Dan* and by Hanoi Radio: *SWB/FE/258/C/7; 259/C/7–8; 264/C/7 passim*. The first reference in *Renmin Ribao*, praising Soviet anti-imperialism, did not come until the tour was over, 6 March 1960: *SWB/FE/278/C/1–2*.

4. For a detailed analysis of Soviet politics in this period, see Tatu (1969).

5. NCNA, 19 April 1960: *SWB/FE/313* and 314/C; reprinted in Hudson *et al.* (1961) pp. 82–112.

6. Tatu (1969) p. 51, citing a speech by L. Ilyichev in October 1961; he is also the source for Soviet leadership changes in early May. For Kuusinen's speech on 22 April, see Hudson *et al.* (1961) pp. 116–22.

7. Translated in Le Duan, *On the Socialist Revolution in Vietnam* (Hanoi, 1965) vol. II, pp. 38–55; this contrast between his views and those of Truong Chinh is evident from a comparison of their many speeches over several decades.

8. Reprinted ibid., vol. I, pp. 9–56; the quotation is on p. 48.

9. Race Document no. 1044, translated in Porter (1979) vol. II, pp. 59–68; cf. also Race (1972) pp. 116–20 (paperback edn).

10. *USVNR*, Bk 10, pp. 1190–5.

11. *Peking Review*, 7 December 1979, p. 15; for the Hanoi 'White Book' reference to 1960, *SWB/FE/6238/A3/12–13*.

12. NCNA, 25 August 1979: *SWB/FE/6208/A3/3*.

13. *Alleged Assassination Plots involving Foreign Leaders* (Report of Select Committee on Intelligence Activities, US Senate: reprinted by W. W. Norton, New York, 1976); for details on Cuba at this period, Thomas (1971) pp. 1279ff.

14. Dake (1973) pp. 85ff.

15. For an account of Sino-Soviet relations before and after Bucharest, see Borisov and Koloskov (1975) pp. 183–5; and Hudson *et al.* (1961) pp. 123ff. For the Soviet decision to withdraw experts in July, see Tatu (1969) p. 103, citing an article in *Renmin Ribao*, 19 July 1963.

16. NCNA, 2 September 1960, partly reproduced in Porter (1979) vol. II, p. 72; for earlier Sino-Vietnamese exchanges and Chinese support, see *Peking Review*, 19 and 26 July 1960.

17. Tran Van Don (1978) p. 70; for other items in this paragraph, see Race Document no. 1049, and *USVNR*, Bk 10, pp. 1298–1301.

18. The full complexity of the events following the coup is suggested by the fact that Toye (1968) pp. 141–9, and Dommen (1971) pp. 140–54, give quite different – and at some points conflicting – accounts of what happened. Neither attempts to relate the situation in Laos to the wider international conflict.

19. Honey (1963) pp. 75ff., citing *Nhan-Dan*, 14 August, and *Pravda*, 16 August 1960. Also on 16 August certain Soviet newspapers published an article pointing out that a country like China could not hope to build socialism without Soviet aid: see Hudson *et al.* (1961) pp. 149–50.

20. *SWB/FE/*381, 382 and 387 give details of the session; for an account of the Third Party Congress, see P. J. Honey in *China Quarterly* (1960) part IV, pp. 66–75.

21. Young (1968) pp. 232ff.; he suggests, on the basis of Zhou Enlai's remarks to Edgar Snow on 30 August 1960, that the Chinese line had already changed irrevocably before 6 September; ibid., pp. 230–1. This is not certain.

22. For the background on Cuba at this period, see Johnson (1965) pp. 45, 54, *passim.*; and Thomas (1971) pp. 1295ff.

23. This is discussed by Dommen (1971) pp. 159–61, and Hilsman (1967).

24. *USVNR*, Bk 10, pp. 1325–6. Durbrow's attempt to put pressure on Diem to reform is noted in Chapter 11 above. He submitted a memorandum to the South Vietnamese president on 14 October 1960, but Diem perhaps knew that he had friends in Washington and could afford to ignore it.

25. They took place from 7 November to 12 December 1960: *SWB/FE/*514/A3/9.

26. *Peking Review*, 4 and 11 October 1960; on the significance of Abbas' visit, cf. Deutscher (1970) pp. 210–14. It was noticeable that no Soviet or East European leaders attended the national day parade in Peking that year, whereas Khrushchev himself had been present in 1959.

27. Borisov and Koloskov (1975) pp. 186–7; the visits were not made public at the time – a reminder that a great deal of Communist diplomacy between Parties is hidden from Western view.

NOTES TO CHAPTER 13: THE NATIONAL LIBERATION FRONT

1. Deutscher (1970) pp. 215–22: article of 7–8 December 1960. For the main texts of the conference, and the period immediately before and after it, see Hudson *et al.* (1961) pp. 157–224. An analysis of the meeting itself, by J. Erickson, appears in RIIA, *Survey of International Affairs 1961*, pp. 173–8. For the VNWP delegation, see *SWB/FE/*480/A2/1.

2. *Peking Review*, 3 February 1961, pp. 9–10; Nguyen Duy Trinh's visits can be followed in *SWB/FE/*508, 546, 555, etc.

3. A report on the meetings and demonstrations appeared in *Peking Review* on 28 April 1961, p. 14; for Ben-Tre province, see Nguyen Thi Dinh, *No Other Road to Take* (translated as S. E. Asia Program, Data Paper, no. 102, Ithaca, N.Y., 1976) p. 76. On Pham Ngoc Thao's continuing affiliation to the Viet-Minh and the NLFSVN, see report by S. Karnow in *International Herald Tribune*, 24 March 1981; he was governor of Ben-Tre from 26 November 1960 until 26 May 1962, but was subsequently killed by supporters of Nguyen Van Thieu in 1965.

4. Hanoi Radio, 19 October 1960: reprinted (from FBIS translation) in Porter (1979) vol. II, pp. 79–82. For the text of the NLFSVN Manifesto and Programme, see Turner (1975) pp. 416–26.
5. G. C. Hickey, *Village in Vietnam* (New Haven, Conn., 1964) pp. 70ff.; the village was that of Khanh-Hau, Long-An province. On the early history of the front and its subsidiary organisations, see Pike (1966) pp. 82–3 *passim*.
6. Pike (1966) pp. 422–3, 426–7.
7. His biography was given in *Nhan-Dan*, 13 May 1978; he is not mentioned by Pike (1966), but the latter has some details on Vo Chi Cong (see p. 434).
8. Hanoi Radio, 15 March 1961: *SWB/FE/593/B/1*. For Nguyen Chi Thanh after 1963, see *Vietnamese Studies*, no. 1 (Hanoi, 1964) and *International Herald Tribune*, 4 December 1967. Hanoi never openly admitted his role in the South even after his death.
9. *SWB/FE/3611/A3/6*.
10. Stanford Research Institute, *Land Reform in Vietnam* (Menlo Park, Calif., 1968) pp. 11, 15 *passim*. On the agreements with France and French landowners, see also Fishel (1961) p. 170.
11. Race (1972) pp. 123–4; information based on South Vietnamese police records.
12. Scigliano (1964) p. 179.
13. For accounts of the abortive coup, see Shaplen (1965) pp. 141–2; Tran Van Don (1978) pp. 79–80; and *USVNR*, Bk 2, p. 44.
14. *USVNR*, Bk 10, pp. 1332–3. The expansion of ARVN evoked protests from the PAVN to the International Commission on 5 December 1960: *SWB/FE/515/A3/4*.
15. For Malaya, see A. Short, *Communist Insurrection in Malaya* (London, 1975) pp. 213, 472 *passim*. For figures in South Vietnam at this period, see *USVNR*, BK 2, p. 89, and Thayer (1977) p. 674. The best comparison of the two cases, in general terms, is R. G. K. Thompson, *Defeating Communist Insurgency* (London, 1966).
16. *Nhan-Dan*, 26 May 1981: original text used. For Pol Pot's version, see his speech of 27 September 1977: *SWB/FE/5629/C2/1–9*.
17. *DDQC*, 1976, p. 52, item F. For the Sino-Cambodian treaty and Sihanouk's visit to Peking, see *Peking Review*, 20 December 1960, pp. 14–17.
18. For these and other diplomatic exchanges on Laos in 1960–1, see *Documents Relating to British Involvement in the Indochina Conflict 1945–1965*, Cmnd 2834 (London: HMSO, 1965) pp. 154ff.
19. Toye (1968) pp. 161ff.; Dommen (1971) pp. 183–4. For a Chinese account of events at this period, see *Peking Review*, 31 March 1961.

NOTES TO CHAPTER 14: KENNEDY'S DILEMMA

1. This point is noted by Schlesinger (1965) Ch. xii, section 3; he says that if Kennedy had sent 10,000 men to Laos in March he would have depleted the strategic reserve entirely. On the missile gap, and the reassessment made later on the basis of satellite photographs of 30 August 1961, see Freedman (1977) p. 73.
2. Schlesinger (1965) Ch. x, based on his own participation in the relevant meetings as a member of the White House staff; cf. also Johnson (1965).

3. Discussed by Hilsman (1967) pp. 127ff. Other useful accounts of the Laos crisis and the Geneva Conference of 1961–2 will be found in Dommen (1971) and Toye (1968). See also *Peking Review*, 31 March 1961.

4. Young (1968) pp. 241–2, 248. Unfortunately his account does not include details of subsequent Warsaw meetings in the early Kennedy period, which may have played an important part in shaping Washington decision-making later in the year.

5. *USVNR*, Bk 11, pp. 62–6; also in Porter (1979) vol. II, pp. 96–9. For Chinese diplomacy during April, see *Peking Review*, 7, 21 and 28 April 1961.

6. On the work of the task-force between then and 6 May, followed by NSAM-52 on 11 May, see *PP* (Gravel), vol. II, pp. 35–55 and 642–3; for additional documents, *USVNR*, Bk 11, pp. 22–56 and 69–87.

7. NSAM-55, 56, 57 all dated 28 June 1961; copies are now deposited in the National Archives, Washington. For a discussion of their significance in relation to the post-Bay of Pigs debate, see Prouty (1973) pp. 114–17 and 402; he draws on his own experience in the Pentagon at the time.

8. For a list of covert actions authorised by NSAM no. 52, 11 May 1961, see *PP* (Gravel), vol. II, pp. 640–2; sabotage and psychological warfare were approved as well as intelligence-gathering; also contingency planning for possible raids against the North by South Vietnamese Rangers.

9. Several American documents on the question of violating the Geneva Agreements, declassified only in 1974–5, are included in Porter (1979) vol. II, pp. 102–12; he also reprints Diem's letter of 9 June 1961, from *USVNR*, Bk 11, pp. 167–73.

10. The best account of the Vienna confrontation is in Schlesinger (1965) ch. xiv. See also Khrushchev (1974) ch. xx.

11. A copy of NSAM no. 41 is deposited in the National Archives, Washington; unfortunately we have none of the supporting memoranda of the kind available (through the *Pentagon Papers*) for Vietnam decision-making. The most useful accounts of the Berlin crisis are those in Slusser (1973), Schlesinger (1965) ch. xv, and RIIA, *Survey of International Affairs 1961*.

12. See, for example, NCNA comments on Harriman's statement at Geneva on 20 June; *SWB/FE/672/C/1*. For an outline of the preparations for the Conference and its early stages, see *Documents Relating to British Involvement in the Indochina Conflict, 1945–1965*, Cmnd 2834 (London: HMSO, 1965) pp. 26ff.

13. *USVNR*, Bk 11, V.B.4, pp. 167–73, 178–244; cf. also Porter (1979) vol. II, pp. 112–16.

14. The details and significance of Pham Van Dong's tour are analysed by P. J. Honey (1961) pp. 42–4; he was originally due to leave for home around 23 July, but stayed in the USSR for three more weeks.

15. Schlesinger (1965) ch. xviii.

16. A detailed analysis of Khrushchev's tactics before and during the Congress, and his conflict with Kozlov, has been made by Slusser (1973).

17. *SWB/FE/793/B/1–2*; *SWB/FE/798/B/1*.

18. The 'fall decisions', culminating in NSAM no. 111 of 22 November 1961, are examined in detail in *PP* (Gravel), vol. II, pp. 73–127.

# Bibliography

## I DOCUMENTARY SOURCES

*United States Documentation*

This is the only area in which official archival materials are so far available, as a result of the publication of the *Pentagon Papers* and the subsequent declassification of confidential and secret government documents under the Freedom of Information Act. The following sources have been used:

(i) *PP* (Gravel) and *USVNR*: the two principal versions of the *Pentagon Papers*:

    (a) *The Pentagon Papers: the Defense Department History of United States Decision-making on Vietnam: Senator Gravel Edition* (Boston, Mass.: Beacon Press, 1971) 4 vols. (So called because it was read into the public record of the Subcommittee on Public Buildings and Grounds by Senator Gravel on 29 June 1971.)

    (b) *United States–Vietnam Relations 1945–1967*, officially published by US Congress, House of Representatives, Armed Services Committee (Oct. 1971) 12 books.

A third version, including a selection of documents and commentaries by staff members, was published by the *New York Times* in one volume (1971).

(ii) *DDQC*: *Declassified Documents Quarterly Catalogue* (Washington, D.C.: Carrollton Press, quarterly from 1975); including also two volumes entitled *Retrospective Collection*. Each volume comprises printed abstracts and an accompanying set of microfilms. Unfortunately, for the period 1955–60 only a relatively small number of documents have so far been declassified.

(iii) Another important type of source material available from United States official sources are captured Communist documents published from time to time by the State Department. For this period the following are especially important:

    (a) *Working Paper on the North Vietnamese Role in the War in South Vietnam* (State Department, May 1968) of which the main text is reprinted in *Vietnam Documents and Research Notes* (Saigon: US Embassy, June 1968), nos 37–8 and also in Falk (1969). The compendium of documentary texts originally put out with this *Working Paper* is very rare, but has been extensively used by Thayer (1977).

(b) *A Threat to the Peace: North Viet-Nam's Effort to Conquer South Viet-Nam* (State Department, December 1961), of which the second part (Appendices) includes a series of documents in facsimile and translation.

Official publications, relevant to specific points, are cited in individual notes where appropriate: for example, the President's Committee to Study the US Military Assistance Program, *Composite Report* (Washington, D.C., 1959) 2 vols (otherwise known as the Draper Report).

*British Sources*

No internal government archives are so far available for research for this period: a thirty-year rule applies to all departments. The following published sources have been used:

(i) HMSO: Her Majesty's Stationery Office (London): as government printer, responsible for publishing documents submitted to Parliament by the Foreign Secretary as Co-chairman of the Geneva Conferences on Indochina, including the *Interim Reports* of the International Commissions of Supervision and Control for the three countries of Indochina. For a useful compendium of diplomatic exchanges, see *Documents Relating to British Involvement in the Indochina Conflict 1945–1965*, Cmnd 2834, submitted to Parliament (December 1965).

(ii) RIIA: Royal Institute of International Affairs (Chatham House): for the period in question (and down to 1963) published annually a *Survey of International Affairs* and also *Documents on International Affairs*; they have no official status but are valuable compendia of information and documentation.

(iii) BBC: British Broadcasting Corporation: see below.

*Monitored Broadcasts*

These represent the most useful way of approaching the mass of source material emanating from Communist media; articles in newspapers and periodicals are frequently also broadcast over the air and therefore appear in full translation or summary in published monitoring. I have relied on the publications of the BBC, Caversham; it is possible to find much of the material also in the corresponding American source compiled by the Federal Broadcasting Information Service (FBIS). The BBC material is published as:

*SWB/FE: Summary of World Broadcasts*, Part v, *Far East*: first series: numbers 1–862, from April 1949 to April 1959; second series: starting from April 1959. References in notes include part numbers, and in some cases also section and page numbers. Volumes for the period 1955–60 were consulted at the British Library London. Note the following abbreviations:
    VNA: Vietnam News Agency (Hanoi, from 1954).
    NCNA: New China News Agency (Peking).
Many items however are from Hanoi and Peking Radio, and were not intended for foreign consumption.

*Communist Periodicals*

These have been consulted in the original in certain cases:

*Nhan-Dan* ('People'): newspaper of the Vietnam Workers' Party, published daily in Hanoi from 1954.
*Peking Review*: published weekly in Peking from 1958 (after 1979, *Beijing Review*).
*People's China*: published twice-monthly in Peking, 1950–8.

In addition, monitored material has included articles (or summaries) translated from:

*Renmin Ribao* ('People's Daily'): newspaper of the Chinese Communist Party, published daily in Peking from 1949.
*Hong-qi* ('Red Flag'): theoretical journal of the CCP, published in Peking from 1958; usually twice-monthly.
*Hoc-Tap* ('Studies'): theoretical journal of Vietnam Workers' Party, published in Hanoi from 1954; monthly.


## II  SECONDARY WORKS AND COLLECTIONS OF DOCUMENTS

This section does not include peripheral works cited from time to time in individual notes.

*Relating to the International Background (including South-East Asia)*

Ambekar, G. V. (1964) *Documents on China's Relations with South and South-East Asia 1949–1962* (Bombay).
Borisov, I. B. and Koloskov, B. T. (1975) *Soviet–Chinese Relations 1945–1970* (Bloomington, Ind.). (Translated from the Russian; originally published in Moscow, 1971.)
Colbert, E. (1977) *Southeast Asia in International Politics 1941–1956* (Ithaca, NY).
Conquest, R. (1961) *Power and Policy in the USSR* (London).
Dake, A. C. A. (1973) *In the Spirit of the Red Banteng* (The Hague).
Deutscher, I. (1970) *Russia, China and the West: A Contemporary Chronicle 1953–1966* (London).
Fejtö, F. (1974) *A History of the People's Democracies: Eastern Europe Since Stalin* (Harmondsworth, Middx.). (French edn, 1969; first translated 1971.)
Fifield, R. H. (1958) *The Diplomacy of Southeast Asia, 1945–1958* (New York).
Fitzgerald, S. (1972) *China and the Overseas Chinese* (Cambridge).
Fleming, D. F. (1961) *The Cold War and its Origins: 1917–1960* 2 vols (New York, London).
Freedman, L. (1977) *US Intelligence and the Soviet Strategic Threat* (London).
Halperin, M. L. (ed.) (1967) *Sino-Soviet Relations and Arms Control* (Cambridge, Mass.).

Hayes, S. P. (ed.) (1971) *The Beginning of American Aid to Southeast Asia: The Griffin Mission of 1950* (Lexington, Mass.).

Hilsman, R. (1967) *To Move a Nation: The Politics of Foreign Policy in the Administration of John F. Kennedy* (New York).

Horne, A. (1977) *A Savage War of Peace: Algeria 1954–1962* (London).

Hudson, G. F., Lowenthal, R. and MacFarquhar, R. (1961) *The Sino-Soviet Dispute* (New York). (Reprinted from *The China Quarterly*, 1961.)

Jain, R. K. (1977) *China and Japan 1949–1976* (London).

Johnson, H. (1965) *The Bay of Pigs: The Invasion of Cuba by Brigade 2506* (London).

Jordan, A. A. (1962) *Foreign Aid and the Defense of Southeast Asia* (New York).

Kalicki, J. H. (1975) *The Pattern of Sino-American Crises* (Cambridge).

Khrushchev, N. S. (1971) *Khrushchev Remembers*, trans. by S. Talbott, vol. I (London).

Khrushchev, N. S. (1974) *Khrushchev Remembers*, trans. by S. Talbott, vol. II (London).

MacFarquhar, R. (1974) *Origins of the Cultural Revolution*, vol. I (London).

Micunovic, V. (1980) *Moscow Diary* (London). (Translated from Yugoslav original of 1978.)

Montgomery, J. D. (1962) *The Politics of Foreign Aid: American Experience in Southeast Asia* (New York).

Moody, P. R. (1973) *The Politics of the Eighth Central Committee of the Communist Party of China* (Hamden, Conn.).

Prouty, L. F. (1973) *The Secret Team: The CIA and its Allies in Control of the United States and the World* (Englewood Cliffs, N.J.).

Ra'anan, U. (1969) *The USSR Arms the Third World: Case Studies in Soviet Foreign Policy* (Cambridge, Mass.).

Rice, E. E. (1974) *Mao's Way* (Berkeley, Calif.).

Scalapino, R. A. and Lee, C. S. (1972) *Communism in Korea* (Berkeley, Calif.) 2 vols.

Schlesinger, A. M. (1965) *A Thousand Days: John F. Kennedy in the White House* (Boston, Mass.).

Schram, S. R. (ed.) (1974) *Mao Tse-tung Unrehearsed: Talks and Letters, 1956–71* (Harmondsworth, Middx.).

Schurmann, F. (1968) *Ideology and Organisation in Communist China*, 2nd edn (Berkeley, Calif.).

Slusser, R. M. (1973) *The Berlin Crisis of 1961: Soviet–American Relations and the Struggle for Power in the Kremlin* (Baltimore; Md.).

Tatu, M. (1969) *Power in the Kremlin: From Khrushchev's Decline to Collective Leadership* (London). (Translated from *Le Pouvoir en URSS*, Paris, 1967.)

Taylor, J. (1976) *China and Southeast Asia: Peking's Relations with Revolutionary Movements*, 2nd edn (New York).

Thomas, H. (1971) *Cuba: the Pursuit of Freedom* (London, New York).

Vasilyev, D. and Lvov, K. (1959) *Soviet Trade and Southeast Asia* (Moscow, in English).

Wilson, D. A. (1967) 'China, Thailand and the Spirit of Bandung', *The China Quarterly*, nos XXX and XXXI.

Yahuda, M. B. (1978) *China's Role in World Affairs* (London).

Young, K. T. (1968) *Negotiating with Chinese Communist, 1953–1967* (New York).

Zagoria, D. S. (1962), *The Sino-Soviet Conflict* (Princeton).

*Relating Specifically to Vietnam, Laos and Cambodia*

Cameron, A. W. (1971) *Viet-Nam Crisis: A Documentary History – I: 1940–1956* (Ithaca, N.Y.).

Dommen, A. J. (1971) *Conflict in Laos: The Politics of Neutrality*, 2nd edn (London).

Donnell, J. C. (1964) 'Politics in South Vietnam: Doctrines of Authority in Conflict', PhD thesis, University of California, Berkeley.

Duncanson, D. J. (1968) *Government and Revolution in Vietnam* (London).

Eckhardt, G. S. (1974) *Command and Control, 1950–1969* (Washington, D.C.: Department of Army).

Falk, R. A. (1969), *The Vietnam War and International Law*, vol. ii (Princeton, N. J.) (for U.S. State Department Working Paper, May 1968: pp. 1183–1205).

Fall, B. B. (1967) *The Two Viet-Nams: A Political and Military Analysis*, 2nd edn (New York).

Fall, B. B. (1969) *Anatomy of a Crisis: The Laotian Crisis of 1960–61* (New York).

Fishel, W. R. (ed.). (1961) *Problems of Freedom: South Vietnam since Independence* (New York and East Lansing, Mich.).

Gelb, L. and Betts, R. K. (1979) *The Irony of Vietnam* (Washington, D.C.).

Gettleman, M. E. (1966) *Vietnam: History, Documents and Opinions on a Major World Crisis* (Harmondsworth, Middx.)

Gittinger, J. P. (1959) 'Communist Land Policy in North Vietnam', *Far Eastern Survey*, vol. xxviii, no. 8.

Honey, P. J. (1961) 'Pham Van Dong's Tour', *The China Quarterly*, no. viii.

Honey, P. J. (1963) *Communism in North Vietnam* (Cambridge, Mass.).

Lancaster, D. (1961) *The Emancipation of French Indochina* (London).

Langer, P. F. and Zasloff, J. J. (1970) *North Vietnam and the Pathet Lao* (Cambridge, Mass.).

Lansdale, E. G. (1972) *In the Midst of Wars: An American's Mission to Southeast Asia* (New York).

Lee, C. J. (1970) *Communist China's Policy Toward Laos: a Case Study 1954–67* (Center for East Asian Studies, Kansas).

McCoy, A. W. (1972) *The Politics of Heroin in Southeast Asia* (New York).

Moise, E. E. (1976) 'Land Reform and Land Reform Errors in North Vietnam', *Pacific Affairs*, vol. xlix.

Nhu Phong (1962) 'Intellectuals, Writers and Artists' (in North Vietnam series), *The China Quarterly*, no. ix.

Norodom Sihanouk and Burchett, W. (1973) *My War with the CIA: Cambodia's Fight for Survival* (London).

'Phetsarath' (1978) *Iron Man of Laos: Prince Phetsarath Ratanavongsa, by '3349'*, Cornell University: S.E. Asia Program, Data Paper, no. 110 (Ithaca, N.Y.).

Pike, D. (1966) *Viet Cong: The Organisation and Techniques of the National Liberation Front of South Vietnam* (Cambridge, Mass.)

Porter, G. (1972) *The Myth of the Bloodbath: North Vietnam's Land Reform Reconsidered* (Ithaca, N.Y.).

Porter, G. (ed.) (1979) *Vietnam: The Definitive Documentation of Human Decisions*, 2 vols (Philadelphia and London).

Race, J. (1972) *War Comes to Long An: Revolutionary Conflict in a Vietnamese Province* (Berkeley, Calif.; references from paperback edn).

Sar Desai, D. R. (1968) *Indian Foreign Policy in Cambodia, Laos and Vietnam, 1947–1964* (Berkeley, Calif.).

Scigliano, R. (1964) *South Vietnam: Nation under Stress* (Boston, Mass.).

Scott, P. D. (1972) *The War Conspiracy: The Secret Road to the Second Indochina War* (New York and Indianapolis).

Shaplen, R. (1965) *The Lost Revolution* (New York).

Smith, R. M. (1965) *Cambodia's Foreign Policy* (Ithaca, N.Y.).

Ta Xuan Linh (1974) 'How Armed Struggle began in Vietnam', *Vietnam Courier*, no. xxii, March 1974.

Ta Xuan Linh (1975) 'Armed Uprisings by Ethnic Minorities along the Truong-son', *Vietnam Courier*, nos xxviii–xxix, September–October 1975.

Thayer, C. A. (1975) 'Southern Vietnamese Revolutionary Organisation and the Vietnam Workers' Party, 1954–74', in Zasloff, J. J. and Brown, M. (eds) *Communism in Indochina* (Lexington, Mass.).

Thayer, C. A. (1977) 'The Origins of the National Front for the Liberation of South Viet-Nam', PhD thesis, Australian National University, Canberra.

Thompson, R. (1967) *Defeating Communist Insurgency: Experiences from Malaya and Vietnam* (London).

Toye, H. (1968) *Laos: Buffer State or Battle Ground* (London).

Tran Van Don (1978) *Our Endless War* (San Rafael).

Turley, W. S. (1972) 'Army Party and Society in the Democratic Republic of Vietnam', PhD thesis, University of Washington, Seattle.

Turner, R. F. (1975) *Vietnamese Communism: its Origins and Development* (Stanford, Calif.).

Vu Can (1968) 'The People's Struggle against the US–Diem Regime from 1954 to 1960', *Vietnamese Studies*, nos 18–19 (1968).

Warner, D. (1964) *The Last Confucian: Vietnam, South-East Asia and the West* (Harmondsworth, Middx.).

Werner, J. S. (1976) 'The Cao Dai: the Politics of a Vietnamese Syncretic Religious Movement', PhD thesis, Cornell University, Ithaca, N.Y.

Zasloff, J. J. (1973) *The Pathet Lao: Leadership and Organisation* (Lexington, Mass.).

# Index